Rails
across
the
Mississippi

Rails across

the Mississippi

A History of the St. Louis Bridge

ROBERT W. JACKSON

University of Illinois Press

Urbana and Chicago

© 2001 by the Board of Trustees
of the University of Illinois
All rights reserved
Manufactured in the United States of America
1 2 3 4 5 C P 5 4 3 2 1

∞ This book is printed on acid-free paper.

Library of Congress Cataloging-in-Publication Data

Jackson, Robert W. (Robert Wendell), 1950–
Rails across the Mississippi : a history of the St. Louis bridge /
Robert W. Jackson.
p.   cm.
ISBN 0-252-02680-2
1. Bridges—Mississippi River.
2. Eads Bridge (Saint Louis, Mo.)
I. Title.
TG25.M6J33   2001
624'.35'0977866—dc21   2001000491

Contents

Illustrations follow pages 60 and 156

Preface

Much has been written about the first bridge across the Mississippi River at St. Louis. It has been the subject of a classic work of engineering literature, *A History of the St. Louis Bridge* (1881), by Calvin M. Woodward; a photographic essay by Quinta Scott and historical appraisal by Howard S. Miller, published together as *The Eads Bridge* (1979, 1999); and several chapters in books about bridges and their builders, including *Engineers of Dreams: Great Bridge Builders and the Spanning of America* (1995), by Henry Petroski. Given the considerable number of existing narratives, it may seem that the full story of how the bridge came to be has already been written.

Woodward, however, was friendly to those men who built the bridge, and he eliminated from his account anything that might sully their reputations. He was particularly protective of the heroic myth attached to the name of that individual most identified with the bridge's creation, chief engineer James B. Eads. Moreover, he provided scant explanation for why the bridge failed as a business venture. Therefore, his work tells only part of the story, and does so from a skewed perspective. Virtually all who have written about the bridge or Eads since Woodward have depended heavily on him for their information, with two exceptions.

Miller, though also relying on Woodward (as we all must), provides fresh insight based on new material. His essay, though relatively short, is the best, most concise, and most comprehensive summary of the bridge's history to date.

The other exception is the work of the modern popular culture scholar John Kouwenhoven, contained in two articles published in 1974, one article published in 1981, and another article published in 1982. Kouwenhoven first became interested in the St. Louis Bridge when working on *Made in America* (1948), currently available under its original subtitle, *The Arts in Modern American Civilization.* He noted that the Chicago architect Louis Sullivan had used the same language to describe the St. Louis Bridge as he used to describe the frescoes in the Sistine Chapel. This intrigued Kouwenhoven, who went to see the bridge for himself. Despite being initially disappointed, he began reading about the structure and soon came to appreciate it as the central figure in an untold story. For nearly four decades he collected data on the bridge in preparation for a book, but he died before that dream could be realized.

My interest in the bridge began with a suggestion by William H. Goetzmann, Jack S. Blanton Sr. Chair in History and American Studies at the University of Texas at Austin. Knowing that no decent biography of James Eads has ever been written, Dr. Goetzmann suggested I explore the possibility of writing such a book. I quickly declined the task, given the scant and widely scattered documentation available about Eads. Like Kouwenhoven, however, I became interested in the more focused story of Eads's best-known work, the bridge that now bears his name.

I have chosen to identify my subject by the name it bore when it was relatively new, the only bridge over the Mississippi River at St. Louis. It is fitting that Miller, Kouwenhoven, Petroski, and others call it the Eads Bridge because people began calling it that even before it was finished. But in consideration of the need to see the bridge as not just the product of one individual's effort, but as a corporate enterprise, I wish to identify it with the name used by Woodward.

Moreover, I have not wished simply to repeat that which had already been said concerning the bridge as an engineered structure. Woodward, Miller, Kouwenhoven, Petroski, and others have done a creditable job of covering that aspect of the bridge, and I have little new information or insight to add to their efforts. My desire has been to communicate that which has not been adequately told or explained about the bridge in past works. Therefore, I have repeated only what is required by fidelity to the general narrative and courtesy to the uninitiated reader.

—⚏—

I would like to acknowledge the contributions and assistance of those who have helped in my effort to tell the story of the St. Louis Bridge. First are Professor William H. Goetzmann and the other scholars who read the dissertation with which this work began: Robert Abzug, Jeffrey Meikle, Robert Mugerauer, and William Stott.

Harold Miller was kind enough to read an early draft of the present work and offer suggestions for its improvement. No one else knows the story of the bridge as well as he, and his insight was invaluable.

I am particularly indebted to William Kessler, Director of Public Affairs; Steve Fusko, Records Manager; and, Mark Mindek, Site Supervisor, United States Steel Corporation, for their assistance in securing access to the Carnegie papers once located at Boyer, Pennsylvania. Their courtesy and cooperation were of great value in my research.

Eric DeLony, Chief, Historic American Engineering Record (HAER), National Park Service, also provided valuable encouragement and support to my efforts. The summers I spent working for Eric as a seasonal historian with HAER, documenting historic bridges in Iowa and Texas, developed an appreciation for these unique contributions to world culture that no other experience could have provided. To whatever extent this book advances the goal of generating new respect for the history of bridge construction in America, the sometimes painful process of writing it will have been worthwhile.

There are several individuals and organizations in St. Louis deserving of my heartfelt thanks, among which are: Martha Clevenger and staff of the Library and Collections Center, Missouri Historical Society; Carole Prietto, University Archivist, University Libraries, Washington University; Jean E. Meeh Gosebrink, Special Collections Librarian, St. Louis Public Library; Charles E. Brown, Head of Reference, and Mark J. Cedeck, Curator, Mercantile Library; John McCarthy, Senior Project Manager, Sverdrup Corporation; and Lawrence A. Morgan, Headmaster, the Thomas Jefferson School.

At the University of Illinois Press I wish to thank Richard Martin, Executive Editor; Theresa L. Sears, Managing Editor; Carol Betts, Associate Editor; and Copenhaver Cumpston, Art Director. Their professionalism was much appreciated.

In Austin, Texas, Michael Arbore demonstrated great skill and patience in preparation of the maps and illustrations, and Kellis Richter lent her considerable organizational skills and emotional support when they were needed most.

I thank all of these individuals most sincerely. Each of them made contributions to the book and are due some credit for its merits, though no blame for its faults.

Rails
across
the
Mississippi

A Creature of Hope

A want has long been felt for a structure of this kind, and, although the subject has been mooted for many years by men who comprehended their own times and saw clearly what the future would produce, yet they treated it as poets and prophets, and it took form as a creature of hope, undefined in time, place and character.

—St. Louis City Engineer Truman J. Homer, 1865

Nearly fifty years before a bridge at St. Louis became a reality, a schoolmaster named Russell from Bluffdale, Illinois, wrote an account of a remarkable "vision of the night" that had come to him "when deep sleep falleth on man."[1] In his dream he was transported three hundred years into the future to find that the sparsely settled banks of the Mississippi River in southern Illinois had become covered in villages. Three great iron bridges spanned the river, and on one of these he rode across into St. Louis. The pride of the city, Chouteau's Pond, had disappeared. Mill Creek was gone as well. The tiny community of the 1820s had become a great city, stretching for miles out to the west, its streets densely packed with people.

The *Missouri Republican* published Russell's vision as a curiosity and as a prophetic testimony of the greatness that awaited the city. It is doubtful, however, that anyone reading the article at the time believed it would take three hundred years for St. Louis to realize its destiny. But visions of a bridge across the river remained little more than dreams for decades to come.

In 1839 the city council authorized Charles Ellet Jr., the first native-born American to receive a formal education in civil engineering, to conduct preliminary surveys and prepare plans for a wagon and pedestrian suspension bridge.[2] But St. Louis's first mayor, William Carr Lane, responded to Ellet's estimate of $737,566 to construct the bridge by saying, "the time is inauspicious for the commencement of an expense involving such an enormous expenditure of money."[3]

Given that St. Louis had a population of only 16,469 in 1840, and no railroads, the subsequent decision of the council to reject Ellet's proposal seemed prudent. A bridge of the length and complexity required would have to generate considerable revenue from tolls to be cost-effective. Even with a much larger population base, the St. Louis area could not generate sufficient wagon traffic to offset the operating cost of a long-span bridge, much less pay back the cost of construction. Only heavy use by railroads promised an adequate return on investment, and many more years would pass before railroads came to St. Louis.

It was not until early in December 1852 that the Pacific Railroad of Missouri commenced operations out of the city. It was still the only western railroad terminating in St. Louis when the Ohio and Mississippi Railroad completed a line into Illinoistown, Illinois (soon to be renamed East St. Louis), in 1854, thus becoming the first eastern line to reach the bank of the river across from St. Louis. But there were several other railroad companies planning the extension of lines into Illinoistown, and it was widely assumed that the North Missouri Railroad and the St. Louis and Iron Mountain Railroad would soon enter St. Louis. Anticipation of the development of these and other railroads led many in the community to believe that the time was near when construction of a bridge across the river would be economically feasible.

Events upstream also indicated that rapid construction of a bridge at St. Louis was a necessity to ensure the city's position as central commercial entrepôt of the Mississippi River Valley. The Chicago and Rock Island Railroad reached the eastern bank of the upper Mississippi River, across from Davenport, Iowa, in February 1854. The officers of the railroad had wisely provided for continuation of their line across the rich farmland of Iowa by buying up a considerable interest in the Mississippi and Missouri Railroad when that company was chartered by the Iowa legislature in 1852. In 1853 they also formed a company for erection of a drawbridge across the river to link the two railroads. Completion of the bridge, already under construction by 1855, would provide for unobstructed shipment of commodities to Chicago from elsewhere in the Middle West.

It was apparent to the railroad promoters of St. Louis that completion of the Rock Island Bridge and the railroads connected by it would result in the diversion of freight traffic away from their city. In response, a number of men associated with the Pacific Railroad of Missouri, along with several men from southern Illinois who judged their interests more closely aligned with St. Louis than with Chicago, formed the St. Louis and Illinois Bridge Company in 1855.[4] The incorporators immediately hired J. W. Bissell, a former assistant to Charles Ellet Jr., as chief engineer and directed him to develop plans for a suspension bridge to unite the tracks of the Ohio and Mississippi Railroad with those of the Pacific Railroad of Missouri.

While Bissell conducted his preliminary studies and the bridge company directors sought funds for construction, traffic began moving over the Rock Island Bridge. On the evening of April 21, 1856, a locomotive pulling ten heavily loaded freight cars crossed into Iowa. The following morning the first passenger train passed over as church bells in Rock Island and Davenport rang out in celebration and crowds along the line cheered.[5]

Within eighteen months, two-thirds of the produce once carried from Davenport to St. Louis by steam-powered riverboats was being shipped to Chicago on steam-powered trains.[6] This fact alone was enough to unite the railroad and steamboat interests of St. Louis in opposition to the bridge.

On the morning of May 6, 1856, a large steamboat on her maiden voyage out of St. Louis, the *Effie Afton,* had just cleared the draw span of the Rock Island Bridge when, caught by the wind and current, it was thrown back against one of the bridge piers. A stove below deck turned over, setting the boat on fire. The flames quickly spread to the wood trusses of the bridge and it also began to burn. As the flames rose higher, the dozen or so boats docked at Davenport and Rock Island and all of the boats steaming on the river opened their whistles in celebration of the bridge's demise. The *Chicago Tribune* later reported that "it sounded like a vast menagerie of elephants and hippopotamuses howling with rage." The noise was so frightful "that all the babies of Davenport went into fits of crying."[7]

There were those up and down the river who claimed that the collision was no accident; that the steamboat interests had intentionally devised a way to put the bridge out of operation. That someone would intentionally destroy a newly constructed and very expensive steamboat simply to prove that the bridge was an obstruction to navigation seems incredible. But the claim reflected the depth of fear and concern felt by those who opposed the bridge. Just days after the event the steamboat *Hamburg* was seen flying a flag that proclaimed, "Mississippi Bridge Destroyed, Let All Rejoice."[8]

Soon after the collision, the owner of the *Effie Afton,* Captain John S. Hurd, sued the bridge company for fifty thousand dollars, the estimated value of the boat, its cargo, and insurance. A delay before the case came to trial allowed the opposing forces to declare their intentions and decide on strategy.

On December 16, 1856, the St. Louis Chamber of Commerce held a meeting at the Merchants Exchange and resolved to support the case against the bridge company. This led to charges by the Chicago newspapers that St. Louis was the real plaintiff, with the *Chicago Daily Press* going so far as to claim that the chamber had raised a half million dollars from cities on the Mississippi and Ohio rivers to aid in prosecuting the lawsuit.[9]

Whatever the amount of money raised, it was clear that many of the business leaders of St. Louis felt that the existence of an upstream bridge placed their essential interests in jeopardy. Some were men so wedded to the steamboat that they were likely to oppose any bridge on the Mississippi River; others, knowing that the era of rail transportation was at hand, merely wished to stall the construction and operation of other bridges until a structure could be erected at St. Louis.

A temporary committee was therefore created to draft resolutions regarding action to be taken against the Rock Island Bridge. This group called for establishment of a permanent committee "to take all necessary steps to cause the proper legal proceedings to be instituted for the removal of said bridge and the obstructions to navigation caused thereby."[10] It was also resolved that another committee, composed mainly of steamboat captains and pilots, be sent to Rock Island to determine the degree of obstruction with the intent of making this information available during the trial.

To no one's surprise, after visiting the site of the collision this group found that the bridge was indeed a great and serious obstacle to navigation. But the members of the group went considerably beyond their charge by stating, "a glance at the map shows that the Mississippi is the natural channel between the far distant basins of the upper Mississippi and Minnesota valleys and the Atlantic Ocean. The advantage, therefore[,] of keeping the great medium of commerce unobstructed, must be obvious to the most casual observer."[11]

Ostensibly the suit, formally known as *Hurd et al. v. Railroad Bridge Company,* questioned whether the accident was caused by faulty handling of the *Effie Afton* or was the result of negligent construction of a serious obstruction to the free navigation of the river. As the trial progressed, however, this basic question was sublimated to the more crucial issue of whether a degree of obstruction might be acceptable in the interest of improved commerce, as represented by the railroad.

The case for the railroad was essentially won due to the arguments of Abraham Lincoln, a young Illinois attorney from Sangamon County who had recently won an important tax case for the Illinois Central Railroad. On September 22, 1857, Lincoln began the defense's summary argument to the jury by saying that he had no prejudice against the steamboat interests or against the people of St. Louis because their feelings were only natural. But, he continued, "there is a travel from east to west whose demands are not less than that of those of the river. It is growing larger and larger, building up new countries with a rapidity never before seen in the history of the world. This current of travel has its rights as well as that of north and south. If the river had not the advantage in priority and legislation, we could enter into free competition with it and we could surpass it." He also appealed to the basic good sense of the jury in arguing that "one man had as good a right to cross a river as another had to sail up or down it."[12]

The Chicago jury, composed of citizens from that city which stood to gain most by railroad expansion at the expense of steamboats, could not reach a unanimous verdict and was discharged. Lincoln and the railroad, therefore, won the first round. But the battle between St. Louis and companies building railroad bridges across the upper Mississippi River would continue, in the courts and halls of Congress, for years to come.

While anticipating further legal challenges to their upstream rival, the incorporators of the St. Louis and Illinois Bridge Company attempted to move forward with their own plans. But they stuck serious obstructions of a different sort.

Bissell's design, finally accepted by the incorporators in 1857, was projected to cost approximately $1.5 million. Even those who were convinced of the need for a bridge regarded this figure as far too great, given that there was still not enough railroad traffic into St. Louis or East St. Louis to justify the projected cost. And there were a number of reasons why this would remain so for many years to come.

The Missouri legislature had been an early leader in state provision of financial assistance to railroad speculators.[13] But unlike Iowa, Missouri had neither the population nor the natural wealth required to support railroads in the prewar period. With so much money available, however, there were fortunes to be made in the mere creation of railroad corporations. The corruption and inefficiency evident in the behavior of both politicians and businessmen during this period eventually resulted in extensive fraud and mismanagement of most of the railroad companies chartered in Missouri. By the close of 1857, the year that a severe financial panic frightened legislators into refusing further funds for new construction, only a few hundred miles of road had actually been put into operation. Both the North Missouri Railroad and the St. Louis and Iron Mountain Railroad failed to make interest payments on their bonds when due on January 1, 1859, and succumbed soon thereafter.

On the other side of the river, the Ohio and Mississippi Railroad was still trying to recover from the effects of an earlier panic, in 1854, when the more severe panic of 1857 hit. Although St. Louis investors tried to effect a settlement that would enable the railroad to meet its financial obligations, the company failed in 1858 and was forced into receivership.

During the Civil War, St. Louis continued to fall further behind Chicago in terms of railroad development. Missouri suffered more destruction of its system of railroads than any other state during the conflict, while Chicago-based railroads actually prospered. Meanwhile, the St. Louis steamboat interests saw their long court battle against the Rock Island Bridge come to naught.

In 1858, James Ward, a St. Louis steamboat captain and member of the Chamber of Commerce committee that had investigated the bridge in 1856, sued to prevent enlargement of the bridge piers. The chamber did its part by paying J. W. Bissell and several of his assistants to gather data for a report to be issued by the Army Corps of Engineers regarding the danger posed by the structure. Although Ward initially won the case when it received its final hearing before the United States District Court for the District of Iowa in 1860, the railroad appealed to the United States Supreme Court and won a split decision by that body in 1863.

To make matters worse, the following year the Albany Bridge Company began erection of another railroad bridge across the Mississippi River between Fulton, Illinois, and Clinton, Iowa. Designed to serve the interests of the Chicago and North Western Railroad, the bridge promised further diversion of trade away from St. Louis. Yet while the bridge was under construction, little real progress toward erection of a competing structure was made in St. Louis.

On February 5, 1864, the Missouri legislature passed an act sponsored by Norman Cutter, a state senator, authorizing incorporation of a new organization with the same name as the dormant entity created in 1855, the St. Louis and Illinois Bridge Company. The language of the Missouri legislation seemed to nullify any previous bridge charters that were in conflict with the Cutter organization. But there were many in St. Louis who believed that the earlier organization, which held charters in Missouri and Illinois, might still have some validity.

It was not until January 1865 that Cutter, the most prominent of the twenty-eight incorporators of the new company, traveled to Springfield, Illinois, to seek introduction of a bill granting the supplementary charter necessary for the bridge company to conduct business in that state.[14] The eleven-month delay in obtaining authorization from the State of Illinois, and the lack of any attempt to develop a specific design, led many to believe that the incorporators had no real intention of building a bridge. It was rumored that they had acted with the speculative intention of eventually selling their charters at a profit, perhaps to entrepreneurs from Chicago.

Suspicion regarding the intentions of the Cutter organization; frustration due to the lack of judicial relief from operation of the Rock Island Bridge; and concern regarding the pending completion of the Clinton Bridge moved the St. Louis Board of Common Council (city council) to meet on Sunday, February 7, 1865. The council appointed a special committee to examine the issues involved in erection of a bridge and recommend action to be taken. It also instructed Truman J. Homer, the city engineer, to make his own report and provide plans and cost estimates.[15]

The pro-railroad faction in the community knew that the war, with its curtailment of St. Louis–based railroad development, was nearing an end. Moreover, they accepted what the steamboat interests could not: swift action toward erection of a bridge for their city was its last, best hope of regaining its rightful trade position. It was therefore with great anticipation that they awaited the response of the city engineer and the special committee.

Homer's report, delivered on February 11, was the most systematic analysis yet conducted concerning the major issues to be examined. After briefly summarizing the history of past efforts, Homer addressed four basic questions: Is a bridge across the Mississippi River at St. Louis really needed? Can such a bridge pay a sufficient revenue upon its cost? What kind of bridge should be built? Where should the bridge be situated? Homer's response to those questions is significant because his basic rationale regarding need, projected revenue, and location was accepted, rightly or wrongly, by those who eventually built the bridge.

In answer to the first question, Homer pointed out that there was considerable commerce across the river, but the three ferries currently used to transport people and freight were inadequate to the task. He also called the cost of transfer via ferry a "tax upon our industry and enterprise."[16] In this, he only reflected the prevailing sentiments of most of the citizens of St. Louis.

Although the transfer of people by ferry was inefficient, expensive, and quite unpleasant for those involved, it did not greatly affect commercial operations in the city. But the necessity of breaking bulk at the river, with associated loss due to spillage and destruction, and the long delays caused by ice accumulation during winter months resulted in high costs for movement of freight. The problem was exacerbated by the arrogant business practices of one of the most powerful organizations in Missouri.[17]

The Wiggins Ferry Company, created in 1820, had a virtual monopoly on commercial transportation between St. Louis and East St. Louis. The two other ferry companies referred to by Homer conducted relatively little business. The considerable power that the Wiggins company exercised over trans-Mississippi commerce was based on a series of actions by the Illinois legislature.

An act passed in 1819 allowed Samuel Wiggins to acquire one mile of waterfront opposite the St. Louis levee, and another act in 1829 stipulated that no competitive service could be established within two miles of the Wiggins ferry. In 1849, the same year that officers of the Pacific Railroad of Missouri first broke ground in St. Louis, Illinoistown was designated as the terminus for all railroads crossing the southern portion of the state. A special act passed in 1853 gave the ferry company the right of perpetual succession, meaning that no other company could ever acquire the right to operate from the Illinois side of the river across from St. Louis.[18]

As eastern railroads began to reach the east bank of the river in the 1850s they found that they had no choice but to do business with the ferry company, which then owned nine hundred acres of land along the waterfront for about two miles north or south of Bloody Island, just across the channel from St. Louis. In addition to providing access to the ferry landings, the ferry company eventually provided warehouses, terminals, elevators, and switching yards for the Ohio and Mississippi Railroad, the Chicago, Alton and St. Louis Railroad, and several smaller lines. The company also had three transfer boats in operation by 1865 dedicated solely to railroad service.[19]

The company's enormous power over the railroads resulted in high rates for shippers and high profits for the men who controlled the company. The dissatisfaction felt by all those who had to submit to this reality was expressed by Illinois farmers who complained in 1865 that the ferry was costing them more than land rent. As one spokesman said, "We will take stock in the Bridge Company, if necessary, anything to free us from that nightmare Ferry, which is not only a terror, but a real vampire, sucking our very lifeblood."[20]

The need and strong desire for a bridge having been noted, Homer also had to show that the structure was economically feasible. Therefore, he had to address the question, What amount of revenue could be directly derived from tolls? In answer he made an estimate of yearly projected income based on charges equal to three-fifths of the revenue then being collected by the three ferry companies. This figure totaled $425,000. In addition, Homer assumed that construction of a bridge would save the people of St. Louis about $1.8 million a year in ferry rates, prevention of coal loss, and other sundry losses due to detention on the waterfront.

Although it was not explicitly stated, Homer's revenue projections were based on virtually doing away with the ferry companies as they existed, since it could hardly be expected that they would survive if a bridge captured a minimum of three-fifths of their revenue. Considering the economic and political power of the men behind those organizations, particularly the Wiggins operation, elimination of the ferries would be no small task.

Clearly, any group of people wishing to build and operate a bridge at St. Louis would have to devise a strategy for dealing with the individuals who controlled the Wiggins company. The options could basically be reduced to two: either beat them or join them. In other words, the bridge company incorporators could attempt to drive the ferry out of business, or they could include among the bridge company investors and directorship men who had an ownership interest in the ferry company, thus negating their opposition by ensuring their continued wealth and power. Simply buying out the ferry company, a tactic that Chicago-based railroads could use to get rid of the smaller companies operating on the upper Mississippi River, was not an option at St. Louis because the cost would be prohibitive.

The first St. Louis and Illinois Bridge Company, chartered in 1855, took the second option by including among its incorporators Andrew Christy, who, along with Mrs. McLane Christy, owned half the stock of the Wiggins Ferry Company and controlled its affairs.[21] The Cutter-led organization, however, did not include anyone having a direct interest in the ferry. Therefore, its plans were in direct opposition to the dominant monopoly in the city. This fact alone may have been a primary reason behind the company's lack of progress toward construction of a bridge. Potential investors, concerned about the cost in time and money of an inevitable battle between the bridge company and the ferry company, probably judged the risk too great.

In his report, however, Homer did not address the obvious implications of opposition to the ferry company. He simply projected revenue as though erection of a bridge would automatically result in a transfer of business from one company to another. Therefore, having arrived at a figure for projected revenue, it remained for him only to suggest a design and estimate what it would cost to build and operate such a structure. In his opinion, a three-span rectangular iron plate tube 1,510 feet long, resting on four piers placed 500 feet apart, would be best. The cost of construction worked out to slightly more than $3.3 million, plus approximately $368,000 estimated for operation and annual interest payment.

Where should the bridge be placed? While admitting that the question was perhaps more difficult than any other connected with the subject, due to potential conflict with individual interests, Homer chose a point directly opposite the high dike across Bloody Island, thus running the eastern approach smack through the heart of the Wiggins operation.

Homer also made brief mention of the possibility that "a grand railway depot might be obtained in the city, that would be convenient to the business centres, but as this is outside of the question under discussion, I will leave it to others for development."[22] Unfortunately for St. Louis, those capitalists who eventually built the bridge would also initially assume that development of proper terminal facilities could be separated from construction of a bridge and "left to others."

While Homer worked on his report, the special committee created by the board, headed by Erastus Wells, called upon Derrick A. January, president of the bridge company chartered in 1855, and learned that the financial crisis of 1857 and the Civil War had prevented the organizers from formally incorporating or making progress toward actual construction. Furthermore, examination of the charters granted by the legislatures of Missouri and Illinois revealed them to be defective in certain respects. Therefore, knowing that the Missouri General Assembly was about to adjourn, Wells and Homer went to Jefferson City, the state capital, to meet with the St. Louis delegation and recommend certain amendments to the 1855 charter. The delegation, however, insisted on making amendments to the Cutter-sponsored charter passed in the last session, and not to the charter approved in 1855.

Having had some success in amending the existing Missouri legislation, including the addition of Homer as an incorporator, and having learned that it was too late to attempt correction of the Illinois charter because the Illinois legislature was about to adjourn, Wells and Homer returned to St. Louis.

Aside from summarizing these efforts, the brief report of the special committee, delivered on February 21, added little to what had already been reported by Homer. It did, however, make a more forceful call for construction of a central freight and passenger depot for all the railroads entering the city. The committee recognized that the erection of a bridge not only rendered such a depot possible, but that the "commercial interests of our people require it, in order to compete, in business facilities, with other cities that are rapidly drawing our trade and commerce from us."[23]

In its conclusion the report touched on the necessity of a bridge across the Mississippi River as a point of junction between the railroad systems of the East and the West, and warned that continued neglect of that need would render the geographical position of the city insufficient for control of Mississippi Valley commerce. Having said this, however, the special committee recommended no specific action other than the formation of a standing committee on "Bridges, Depots, and Steam Railroad Connections."[24]

Although Wells and Homer had been unable to influence amendment of the Illinois charter, a provision was added stating that the eastern abutment of the bridge could not be located more than one hundred feet north or south of the dike that connected Bloody Island with the main Illinois shore.[25] Although it would later be claimed that "it was the openly confessed object of this amendment to kill the enterprise by rendering the acquisition of depot-grounds and the construction of a road through the city fatally expensive," it was, in fact, exactly what Homer had advocated in his report.[26]

The Cutter faction, meanwhile, having secured the necessary legislation from the two states, next sought authority from Congress. This was deemed essential not only to lessen any potential opposition from federal interests, such as the Corps of Engineers, but also to attract investors. The incorporators therefore approached Missouri Senator B. Gratz Brown and asked him to introduce a bill confirming the charters granted by the two states, and granting the bridge company the right to cross a navigable waterway. Brown complied with the request, introducing Senate Bill No. 38 in December 1865.

Soon thereafter a number of other bills were introduced, in both the Senate and House of Representatives, to authorize construction of additional bridges across the Mississippi River and one bridge across the Missouri River at Kansas City. A bill was also introduced calling for the bridge at Clinton to be declared a lawful structure, in terms of federal authority, and a post road.

As this flood of legislation began to flow through the halls of Congress, it became apparent to the steamboat interests of St. Louis that the time had come for passage of a general law regulating the bridging of the Mississippi River. They knew that they would have to give some ground in accommodation of rail-based commerce, but they wanted to make certain that their rights to free navigation of the river were also protected. The St. Louis Merchants Exchange therefore appointed a committee of fifteen members to study the matter and draft a resolution to Congress calling for appropriate restriction of bridge construction.

To ensure successful and expeditious completion of the task, the exchange appointed as chairman of the committee a man well respected in the community for his ability to get things done, a man who had devoted most of his adult life to removing various obstructions from the major western rivers: James B. Eads.

2

Destined to Become

Thomas C. Eads . . . had a son, James, sixteen years old, who came and went; and neither the parents, nor the neighbors nor folks in St. Louis knew that this young man was destined to become one of the world's most famous engineers.

—Charles E. Snyder, "The Eads of Argyle"

.

The legend of James Eads's rise from childhood poverty to eminence as a leading citizen of St. Louis was well known to members of the Merchants Exchange. He was born May 23, 1820, in Lawrenceburg, Indiana, the son of Thomas C. and Ann Buchanan Eads, and christened in honor of his second cousin, an upward-bound Pennsylvania politician who would become the fifteenth president of the United States. The elder Eads was an unsuccessful merchant who moved his family continually west in hopes of greater prosperity, first to Cincinnati when James was only three years old and then to Louisville in 1829. On the trip to Kentucky, the precocious boy so persistently hung about the engine room of the boat bearing them down the Ohio River that the ship's engineer gave him a personal tour, finding him to be an apt pupil in the mechanics of the boat's operation.[1]

When James was thirteen the family moved again, this

time to Missouri. Thomas Eads, having remained behind with the intention of following later with supplies for a shop, was not present when the steamboat bearing his family caught fire as it approached the St. Louis levee. James, his mother, and two older sisters barely managed to escape with the clothes on their backs.

Without the support of her distant husband to rely on, Ann Eads accepted the kindness of some ladies of the oldest French families of the town until she was able to rent a house and take in boarders. James, wishing to help his mother, saw some apples for sale as he walked about the streets one day, and buying as many as he could afford, he peddled them at a profit to passers-by. Soon, however, Barrett Williams, one of Mrs. Eads's boarders, offered James a job as clerk in his dry-goods store. Before long Williams discovered his young employee's aptitude for self-education and allowed James the use of his personal library. Studying at night the scientific books he found there, Eads taught himself much of the mathematics, engineering, and mechanics that would guide his later work.

In 1836 James's oldest sister, Genevieve, died, and his older sister, Eliza Ann, died the next year. It was about this time that his father and mother moved to a place near Davenport, Iowa, leaving James behind in St. Louis. Although he often visited his parents, he was increasingly on his own in the world.

In 1838 Eads became an assistant purser (mud clerk) on the *Knickerbocker,* a Mississippi River steamboat engaged in the iron trade between St. Louis and Galena, Illinois. When the boat struck a snag in the river and went down with all its cargo, Eads again experienced the dangers of the river first hand. The event also suggested a means for acquiring wealth.

Insurance companies paid "wreckers," men who recovered sunken boats, their machinery, and their freight, a large percentage—sometimes half—of the value of recovered cargoes. Any boat sunk for more than five years belonged to anyone who could bring it up. Eads worked out the design of a recovery boat that he believed could do the job more cost-effectively than any other boat on the river. But three years' employment as an assistant purser did not provide him nearly enough savings to build such a craft. He therefore approached two boat builders from St. Louis, Calvin Case and James Nelson, and offered to share the profits of a wrecking business in exchange for their financial backing. The force of his personality, and his ability to present a reasoned, logical proposal, were enough to convince Case and Nelson to accept his offer.

While the first wrecking boat designed by Eads was under construction, he secured a contract to recover lead from a barge that sunk near the rapids at Keane, Iowa. He hired a professional diver from Chicago to execute the underwater work, but that man found the current too strong and refused to complete the job. Displaying the type of initiative that was evident in everything he did, Eads bought a forty-gallon whiskey barrel in Keokuk, knocked the bottom out, placed a seat inside, attached iron weights to one end, hooked it up to the rigging and air lines from his boat, and took the first dive in it himself. Throughout his career as a wrecker he continued to work the bottom of the river, often at great risk to his life and health, thereby demonstrating that he would not ask others to do what he would not do himself.

Soon Eads had a fleet of wrecking boats equipped with rigging and machinery of his own design. When in command of any particular boat he was called "Captain" Eads, and it was for this reason that the title was attached to his name through the remainder of his life.

The partnership with Case and Nelson was extremely successful, but when Eads married Martha Nash Dillon in 1845 he decided to find a way of making a living that would not keep him away from home. After much study of the opportunities available, and with financial support from Case and Nelson, he opened the St. Louis Glass Works Company at the corner of Monroe Street and Broadway. It was the first glass factory west of the Mississippi River. The business was not a success, however, and after three years he sold the company, took another loan from his partners, and returned to the wrecking business.

As is so often the case with individuals destined for greatness, fate intervened at a crucial point in Eads's life to aid his financial recovery. In 1849 a fire began on the steamer *White Cloud,* spread to twenty-three other boats tied up along the levee, and then leapt to the tons of freight and other material that cluttered the shoreline. The woefully inadequate fire-fighting capabilities of the city were soon apparent as the fire jumped to buildings in the business district. The wind-whipped flames advanced throughout the night, block after block, until checked by the expediency of blowing up structures (and one firefighter) in the path of the fire.[2]

Approximately six hundred thousand dollars worth of steamboats and their cargoes was sunk. But the event, which represented tragedy to some, meant opportunity for Eads. He secured lucrative contracts for the bulk of the recovery work and profited handsomely from the great calamity. The loan from his partners was easily repaid.

After Calvin Case's death in a railroad bridge collapse in 1855, Eads began working on a scheme to organize a new company with the purpose of clearing the Mississippi, Missouri, Arkansas, Red, and Ohio Rivers of snags and obstructions. He planned to obtain congressional legislation that would fund an exclusive contract between the federal government and his new firm, the Western River Wrecking and Improvement Company, to conduct the initial clearing and to keep the channels open for a certain number of years thereafter. With the help of some politically powerful friends, Eads had a bill for that purpose introduced in Congress in 1856, but the opposition of Secretary of War Jefferson Davis, among others, doomed the proposal.

Eads did manage, however, to secure the necessary financial backing of several marine insurance companies. Additional investment was obtained from wealthy speculators willing to accept high risk in return for potentially great rewards. In 1857 Eads also succeeded in acquiring a liberal charter from the Missouri legislature that provided the wrecking company with an initial capital of $250,000.

However, when his health began to fail in 1857 Eads retired from the wrecking business. The following year the last attempt to secure congressional legislation for the wrecking scheme failed and the business began to take a turn for the worse. But Eads was able to retire with a small fortune because he disposed of his stock in the company when it was still thought to be a profitable investment—when all that was known of its value was from the representations of interested parties.

From 1857 to 1861 Eads lived in semi-retirement with his second wife, Eunice, his two daughters from his first marriage, and three stepdaughters.[3] He occasionally indulged in a trip to Europe, but for the first time in his life he did not have responsibilities on the river to take him away from home and was thus able to participate in the social life of the community. The rather large Eads home at 1613 South Compton Avenue was often filled with guests, and Eads enjoyed entertaining.

Despite his occasional ill health and small build (he was about five feet, nine inches in height, and wiry), he had a robust constitution that matched his expansive personality. Although many found him pompous and self-important, others found him charming and gracious in his manner and speech. He always maintained an impeccable personal appearance that made him appear anything other than a man who had once performed physical work for a living.

When the Civil War began, Eads was summoned to Washington, D.C., to advise President Lincoln on the best methods of utilizing the western rivers for attack and defense. His long experience on every branch of the great network of those rivers provided him some claim as an expert on their nature. Eads proposed a fleet of armor-plated, steam-powered gunboats, and when bids were solicited he submitted one for the construction of seven 600-ton vessels, ready for armament in sixty-five days. Before the war was over he built a total of fourteen armored gun-

boats—ships that played a decisive role in the Union victory over the Confedera-
cy in the river war.

At the time of his appointment as chairman of the special committee, Eads was
an investor in several banks, a streetcar company, and a few real estate develop-
ments. His main interest, however, was the design of new types of naval ordnance,
and that task consumed most of his energies. But he also retained a continuing
concern with the existence of obstructions to free navigation of the western rivers, and he was involved in several business enterprises, including railroads, that
might be affected by passage of the pending legislation. He therefore accepted the
post and attacked his duties with characteristic fervor.

On April 18, 1866, the Eads-led committee unanimously reported a number of
restrictions to be placed in any congressional legislation by the Missouri delegation. Number four called for a ban on drawbridges, and number five for a ban on
suspension bridges. No reason was given for these prohibitions, probably because
the case against these types was well known. Steamboat operators had already had
plenty of bad experience with drawbridges, which were notoriously difficult structures to pass through. And long-span suspension bridges, though often proposed
by certain bridge designers such as Charles Ellet Jr. and John Roebling, generally
could not stand the stresses caused by railroad operations. Even when used pure-
ly as wagon bridges they tended to fall down with alarming frequency.

All of the other restrictions were primarily intended for application to so-called
"high" truss bridges. One would require that all bridges across the Mississippi have
a clear height of fifty feet over the main channel between the lower part of the
bridge and the high-water mark, measured in the center of the greatest span. Another provision required any bridges built below the mouth of the Missouri River
(meaning St. Louis) to have one clear span of 600 feet, or two spans of 450 feet each,
in the clear of abutments. The committee also suggested that the same restrictions
apply to bridges over the Missouri River, with the exception that two spans of 300
feet should be required.[4]

The debate that ensued in Congress over the various proposed bills reveals the
strong desire of both the Senate and the House of Representatives to accommodate the needs of rail transport without creating undue obstructions to water navigation. Fulfillment of this desire required Congress to engage in fairly precise
determinants of appropriate bridge design.

After long consideration, it was agreed to combine all of the various bridge
proposals into one bill, Senate Bill No. 236. This comprehensive piece of legisla-

tion, approved by both houses of Congress and signed into law by President Andrew Johnson on July 25, 1866, authorized the construction of bridges across the Mississippi River at Winona, Minnesota; Prairie du Chien, Wisconsin; Dubuque, Iowa; Burlington, Iowa; Quincy, Illinois; Hannibal, Missouri; and St. Louis. A special clause also authorized a bridge across the Missouri River at Kansas City. The bridge at Clinton was considered separately and finally declared a post road on February 21, 1867.

The bill included the requirements demanded by the Eads committee with the exception that any bridge built at St. Louis would be required to have one span of 500 feet in the clear, or two spans of 350 feet in the clear of abutments. The provisions suggested by the St. Louis Chamber of Commerce were not, however, made generally applicable to the other bridges authorized by that legislation.

B. Gratz Brown would later claim that "so great was the antagonism from rival commercial routes" it was only when these limitations were included "that hostility could be so allayed as to permit the passage of the bill. It was upon the tacit assumption by its opponents of its utter impracticability that antagonism gave way. In fact the utterance was then and there boldly made that the genius did not exist in the country capable of erecting such a structure."[5]

For his part, Eads would later state that in recommending such unusually long spans the committee was acting on his assurance that truss spans of such length were not practicable, and that only arch spans could met these requirements. This opinion was extremely bold given that Eads was not a trained engineer and had no experience with bridge design. But at the time he could be confident in suggesting design standards that he assumed others would have to meet. After all, no one in the world was building railroad bridges with arches of such lengths, and, certainly, no one at the time dreamed that anyone would ever try to do so on the Mississippi or Missouri Rivers.

On February 19, 1866, shortly before formation of the Eads-led subcommittee of the Merchants Exchange, the incorporators of the (second) St. Louis and Illinois Bridge Company met at Jefferson City and formally accepted the state charters, elected a board, and appointed officers.

Because the necessary capital did not exist at that time to fund the project, either in St. Louis or New York, the bridge company directors began to look overseas. European banking and investment houses, particularly those in London, had long been the source of capital for expansion of railroads into the American West, and since the primary justification for the bridge was its function as part of a railway network, it made sense to approach the English. None of the capitalists contacted, however, would consent to back the bridge unless certain amendments to the Illinois charter were first obtained.[6]

It was about this time that a bridge builder from Chicago, Lucius B. Boomer, approached Cutter with the intention of securing the contract for construction. The Boomer name was known in St. Louis, partly due to establishment of a St. Louis branch office of an earlier Boomer bridge company in 1852. It was the first large bridge-building company located in the city. Under the direction of younger brother George B. Boomer, the firm immediately began to prosper. But a Boomer-built bridge erected over the Gasconade River for the Pacific Railroad of Missouri collapsed in 1855, killing forty-three and injuring another seventy. Many of the dead and injured were prominent citizens of St. Louis, including Eads's business partner Calvin Case. In addition to his association with that disaster, Boomer was known as the builder of the much-hated Rock Island Bridge, although his company only erected the superstructure and was not responsible for the poor design and construction of the substructure. The St. Louis office, however, did not survive the death of George Boomer during the Civil War and had long been closed by the time Lucius Boomer approached Norman Cutter.

Boomer quickly found out that the St. Louis and Illinois Bridge Company could not award the construction contract to any firm until changes were made to the Illinois charter and financing secured. He therefore pledged to do what he could in Springfield, Illinois, to help obtain the necessary amendments.

Those amendments included stipulations that the bridge company have an exclusive right for twenty-five years to bridge the Mississippi River at St. Louis; that construction must begin within two years and be completed in five; that the clause limiting the location of the eastern abutment to within one hundred feet of Dyke Avenue must be repealed; and, that a majority of the stockholders of the bridge company must be residents of St. Louis. In exchange for his role in securing these amendments, Boomer was promised the contract to build the bridge.

A meeting of the bridge company incorporators was called for December 18, 1866, at the St. Louis office of Judge John M. Krum. The officers read the charters, ratified the agreement between Cutter and Boomer, appointed a committee to open books and solicit subscriptions to the capital stock, and discussed the need for certain additional amendments to the Illinois charter. A committee was then appointed to meet in Springfield with Boomer and his legal counsel, Judge Corydon Beckwith.[7] Beckwith, a former justice of the Illinois Supreme Court, was well versed in the politics of railroad bridges over the Mississippi River. He had served as counsel for Captain Hurd in the *Effie Afton* case.

News of the meeting between the Cutter group and Boomer soon began to spread through the halls of the Merchants Exchange. Some members believed that the St. Louis and Illinois Bridge Company was about to sell its charter to people from Chicago, people who did not have the best interests of St. Louis in mind. A meeting was therefore held at the exchange on January 17, 1867, at which James Eads was appointed chairman. Upon taking the chair, Eads stated that he believed the people of St. Louis were pretty well convinced of the necessity of a bridge, and that the energy and activity of "our Northern competitors" in extending their communications with the West admonished the people of St. Louis "to do something."[8] The first step he recommended was to ascertain the status of the legislation already passed, and he asked if there was anyone present who could provide any information on the subject.

At this point Truman Homer stepped forward to summarize the plans of the Cutter group and mentioned that the bridge company was preparing a pamphlet in order to provide information to potential investors.[9] After a discussion of the existing legislation, William Taussig, a St. Louis physician turned financier, rose to suggest that a committee of seven be appointed by Eads for the purpose of conferring with the incorporators to determine how plans toward construction could be speeded up. The proposal was accepted, and a committee that included Taussig was charged with the responsibility of seeking the facts of the situation and reporting back to the exchange at the next regular meeting.

About the same time, the bill to amend the Illinois charter of the Cutter group was introduced in the Illinois House of Representatives and it easily passed. Because the bill also seemed to be acceptable to the Senate, Cutter and Krum decided to leave the matter in the hands of Judge Beckwith and return to St. Louis. What happened next is unclear, but the ramifications were considerable. At some point, Boomer and Beckwith had a bill introduced in the Senate to repeal the charter of the St. Louis and Illinois Bridge Company, and they also had a bill introduced to incorporate a new organization, the Illinois and St. Louis Bridge Company.

While the Senate considered this legislation, another meeting was held at the St. Louis Merchants Exchange. At half past twelve o'clock on Saturday, February 16, 1867, the exchange was called to order and Eads took the floor. He first asked Taussig to make a report, but Taussig could do little more than read an evasive letter from Judge Krum in which he claimed ignorance of any impropriety and refuted rumors that his organization planned to sell out to people from Chicago.

After Taussig finished reading the letter there was considerable debate about the danger of the charter falling into the hands of men representing the interests of either Chicago or the Wiggins Ferry Company. To guard against this possibility a committee was dispatched to Springfield the next day.

Thanks to the efforts of this committee the bill to repeal the St. Louis and Illinois Bridge Company charter never passed, but the new charter approving the Illinois and St. Louis Bridge Company was approved February 21. This charter included some of the provisions that the Cutter group sought to place in the charter of its own company, such as an exclusive right for twenty-five years to build from the Illinois shore opposite St. Louis. But it also stated that the company could build its bridge "at any point or place on the Mississippi River opposite to the city of St. Louis."[10] This meant that the eastern approach to the bridge would not necessarily have to cut through the heart of the Wiggins Ferry Company operation.

Section 7 of the act provided that "any railroad company, town, city or county, shall have power to take and subscribe for and to purchase and hold stock of said company."[11] This provision ensured that the railroads then terminating in East St. Louis and St. Louis could fully participate in the ownership and operation of the bridge, and therefore would have no reason to continue their reliance on the ferry company.

Section 8 of the act further stated that the bridge company "may consolidate its property and franchisees with the property and franchises of any bridge company authorized by the laws of Missouri to construct a bridge so as to connect with the one herein authorized."[12] This provision allowed the company to unite with the Cutter corporation, or any other bridge corporation, chartered by the Missouri legislature.

The incorporators of the Illinois and St. Louis Bridge Company included nineteen men from Illinois, including Lucius Boomer. Three of these men, Joseph Gillespie, John M. Palmer, and Gustavus A. Koerner, were incorporators of the first St. Louis and Illinois Bridge Company, organized in 1855. But Cutter and Krum, the leaders of the second organization, were not included. On February 19, 1867, just three days after the meeting at the exchange, the Illinois and St. Louis Bridge Company (of Missouri) formally organized, and three days later the Articles of Association of that company were filed with the Missouri secretary of state. Thus, the company organizers were authorized to conduct business in both states.

When news of the events in Springfield reached St. Louis, many of the town's citizens immediately assumed that Boomer and Beckwith had duped their supposed partners from Missouri. But the two men may not have acted all that unscrupulously. The legislators from southern Illinois, whose interests were more close-ly associated with St. Louis than with Chicago, defended their action by claiming to be under the impression that the friends of the two charters were substantially the same. In fact, the inclusion of men from Illinois in the scheme made sense only from a political standpoint.[13]

The introduction of R. P. Tansey as an incorporator and officer was particular-ly wise. Tansey was a competitor of the St. Louis Transfer Company, a firm first incorporated in 1857 as the Valentine Freight Express Company to transfer freight and passengers between St. Louis and East St. Louis on board the boats of the Wig-gins Ferry Company. In 1859 this company was taken over by officers of the Ohio and Mississippi Railroad and renamed the Ohio and Mississippi Transfer Compa-ny. In 1860 its name was changed to the St. Louis Transfer Company.

Although the Wiggins Ferry Company owned a monopoly on the ferry business and controlled all the land in East St. Louis used by the eastern railroads for han-dling freight and passengers in Illinois, the St. Louis Transfer Company, through agreement with the Wiggins Ferry Company, owned a monopoly on the handling of freight and passengers on the other side of the river.

In 1864 the firm of Mitchell, Miltenberger, and Tansey established the East St. Louis Transfer Company and began competing with the St. Louis Transfer Com-pany. These two firms would later merge, but in 1867 Tansey began making plans to purchase the Madison County Ferry Company, which operated between St. Louis and Venice, Illinois. Located just outside the area controlled by the Wiggins company, Venice was a small town that was then being contemplated as a termi-nus for railroads not yet terminating in East St. Louis. Thus, as a competitor to the interests of the Wiggins Ferry, Tansey was a potentially valuable ally of anyone attempting to put the Wiggins company out of business.

None of this, however, was likely apparent to James Eads, who was so convinced that the interests of St. Louis were imperiled by the action of Boomer and Beckwith that he didn't wait for news from Springfield to take control of the matter. One day after the meeting at the Merchants Exchange on February 16, Eads asked several members of the St. Louis and Illinois Bridge Company, along with a number of his closest friends and business associates, to come to his office in the Southern Ho-tel. In language that belied the historic nature of the event, Taussig would later describe the purpose of the meeting as "the propriety of building a railway and highway bridge across the river at St. Louis on plans as they had been preliminar-ily prepared by Mr. Eads."[14]

Historical accounts of the building of the St. Louis Bridge have tended to claim that Eads was picked as chief engineer of the bridge company by the business leaders of St. Louis because of his extensive and unique knowledge of the bottom of the Mississippi River, and because of his reputation as a man who could push projects through to completion. This explanation provides scant justification for entrusting such a massive project to a man who was not recognized as an engineer and had neither designed nor built a single bridge.

In truth, Eads wasn't selected by any group of men. Instead, he decided to take over the St. Louis and Illinois Bridge Company, selected men he would invite to participate in the venture (many of the original incorporators would be forced out), and showed them plans of the type of bridge that he intended to build. The fact that the men selected by Eads were willing to go along with him says something about their confidence in his drive, determination, organizational abilities, and capacity for handling complex construction problems. Undoubtedly they recognized in Eads a man who probably knew as much about the nature of the Mississippi River as any man alive. But these were not their primary reasons for entrusting him with their investment. The most important factor in measuring the potential success of the bridge-building effort was the ability of the bridge company to secure funding, and Eads's perceived skill as a capitalist was much admired by the businessmen who participated in his plan.[15]

Emerson W. Gould, captain of the *Knickerbocker* during Eads's tenure as mudclerk, said several years after Eads's death that the St. Louis Bridge was a monument to his public spirit, to his genius, and above all, to his financial ability. "Whatever credit is due him as an engineer, or for his mechanical and inventive genius, all sink into insignificance when compared to his ability as a *financier.*"[16]

This statement is remarkable given that Gould was an investor in the Western River Wrecking and Improvement Company. As late as 1889 Gould could still claim that "the result of this investment is still fresh in the recollection of many of Capt. Eads' contemporaries, as it was the means of wrecking some of them and in time was itself wrecked."[17] Gould, it seems, thought Eads a genius at finance because he knew when to take profit from a failing enterprise and get out with that profit intact.

Eads's unique position in regard to the bridge company is probably best summed up by a letter written to Eads on May 5, 1869, by W. Milnor Roberts, an engineer hired as a temporary replacement for Eads during an extended illness. Roberts wrote, "The Chief Engineer of this particular bridge, is somewhat peculiarly situated; he is different in position from Chief Engineers in general, not merely from being the *pro-*

jector as well as the designer of the work, but because he is one of the largest owners, and one who has induced the subscriptions, and who is, justly, looked up to by all the stockholders, and held by them specially responsible."[18]

Perhaps the fact that Eads had no experience in bridge building did not unduly alarm the other participants in the bridge-building project because he was smart enough to announce at the second meeting of the investment group, held at the Planter's House on March 23, that he intended to acquire the services of able and experienced assistants. Therefore, a formal motion to elect Eads as chief engineer of the bridge company was readily approved.

Shortly after the meeting, Eads sought out a German-born civil engineer named Henry Flad to serve as first assistant engineer. A graduate of the University of Munich, Flad gained his first professional experience as a hydraulic engineer working for the Bavarian government on river improvement projects along the Rhine. During the revolution of 1848 he served the Parliamentary army as captain of engineers, but escaped to the United States in 1849 by way of France after the defeat of Parliamentary forces. His first employment in America was on the western end of the Erie Railroad, and he later worked between Cincinnati and St. Louis on the Ohio and Missouri Railroad. In 1854 he moved to Missouri and worked as resident engineer on the St. Louis and Iron Mountain Railroad, then constructing a line between St. Louis and the iron mines of Pilot Knob. He also made surveys for several other roads in Missouri.

Flad later found employment in the St. Louis area designing the water works of Compton Hill and Bissell's Point. On March 13, 1867, just days before the bridge company elected its board of directors, Flad was named to a new Board of Waterworks Commissioners, a position he retained for eight years. Because Flad's duties as commissioner would not take all of his time, he accepted Eads's offer of employment on the bridge project and immediately began work.[19]

On May 1, 1867, the stockholders of the bridge company met at the company's new offices on Pine Street between Third and Fourth Streets, just upstairs from the quarters of the National Bank of the State of Missouri. Eads took control of the meeting and made most of the motions. The group elected a board of directors, which included Eads, Taussig, Josiah Fogg, Charles K. Dickson, Barton Bates, and Thomas A. Scott of the Pennsylvania Railroad. Close examination of the prior relationships among these men reveals much about their business practices and helps explain the later fortunes of the bridge company.

The election of Dickson as president ensured that Eads would retain a high degree of control over the decision-making process within the company due to their association in several St. Louis banks, and to the complete confidence that Dickson had in Eads's judgment concerning finance.

Dickson first came to St. Louis in 1837 and soon thereafter formed a partnership with John J. Murdock. The two men established the auction and commission house of Murdock and Dickson, dealers in dry goods, notions, and clothing. In the early 1850s Eads became involved in several real estate speculations with Murdock and Dickson, including the new Stoddard Addition west of Jefferson Avenue. The firm may also have been involved when Eads laid out several "Eads Additions" in South St. Louis about the same time. Dickson also became one of the largest private investors and one of five directors, along with Emerson W. Gould, in the wrecking company set up by Eads. The offices of the company were located on the north side of Pine Street just east of Main Street in a building owned by Dickson and partially occupied by Murdock and Dickson.[20]

On March 15, 1866, the Missouri legislature passed an act authorizing Governor Thomas C. Fletcher to appoint an agent for the sale of the state's interest in the Bank of the State of Missouri and authorizing the receipt of state bonds as payment for the stock.[21] Fletcher appointed Josiah Fogg, already an associate of Eads, as agent for the sale.[22]

Eads quickly assembled a seven-member syndicate for purchase of the stock that included Dickson and several other men who served with Eads as directors of the Third National Bank. When Fogg opened the bids there were only two submitted: one from Robert A. Barnes, president of the bank; the other from Eads. The market value of the stock at this point had depreciated to about $65 a share of the par value of $100 per share. As one student of the affair later claimed, "Owing to some alleged irregularity in regard to the proposals, the bid of Eads was accepted, although it was said that Barnes was ready to pay more for the stock than Eads offered for it."[23]

The pool formed by Eads borrowed state bonds from various parties to exchange for the stock of the bank, with the largest amount borrowed from the Bank of Commerce of New York City. These bonds were borrowed for a period long enough to enable the Eads syndicate to acquire control of the bank, convert it to a national association, and elect themselves directors.

On September 26, 1866, the Eads syndicate applied to the New York bank for a loan of $1,000,000 to the Bank of the State of Missouri, and the New York bank's board of directors unanimously approved that loan. The loan was not payable, however, until the Eads syndicate actually took control of the bank. The Bank of the State of Missouri was converted into the National Bank of the State of Missouri on October 30, 1866, with the seven members of the Eads syndicate as directors. In December, the loan was officially contracted for in the name of the national bank, with the directors as sureties for the bank.

Charles H. Russell, president of the Bank of Commerce of New York City and its largest stockholder, arranged the deal. Russell had previous dealings with Eads's close friend William McPherson and was undoubtedly influenced by that relationship. When he retired from the bank in June 1868, Eads sent him a warm letter of thanks for his assistance.[24]

Even though the Eads-negotiated loan was made to the National Bank of the State of Missouri, the bank never had full use of it. The syndicate, acting as directors of the bank, loaned themselves the money as individuals. For example, on December 29, shortly after the loan from the Bank of Commerce of New York City came through, Eads made out and signed a bank draft to "myself" for $47,452.50.[25] This practice was followed on numerous other occasions through the next few years.

The syndicate paid the 3 percent interest on the loan from dividends on its million dollars' worth of stock. Funds of the bank that were not lent to the individual syndicate members were later loaned to the bridge company and the associated tunnel company, and to the railroads in which syndicate members were involved.

Barton Bates, also elected to the bridge company board of directors on May 1, 1867, was the eldest son of Abraham Lincoln's attorney general, Edward Bates. It was Edward Bates who called Eads to Washington in 1861 to tell President Lincoln about his plan for construction of a fleet of ironclad warships in order to keep the western rivers open to commerce. Barton Bates, Dickson, Eads, and Henry T. Blow incorporated the Granby Mining and Smelting Company in April 1866, and it was this incorporation that eventually led to Eads's involvement in railroads.

Blow was president of the Collier White Lead and Oil Company until he resigned to run for Congress in 1861. Even after he resigned he remained the principal stockholder of the company, which consumed a large amount of lead ore. For several years prior to the war, Blow's brother Peter mined and smelted lead in Washington County. Just prior to the outbreak of hostilities, Peter Blow became associated with Ferdinand Kennett in the Blow and Kennett Mining Company, which obtained a lease from the Pacific Railroad to begin mining operations in Newton County on the future site of the town of Granby. The railroad had acquired the property as part of its land grant from the Missouri legislature. The company also had large holdings in Joplin and Oronogo in Jasper County. Henry had an interest in this company, and when Kennett died the Blow brothers bought his share of the business. After the war, the brothers sought out investors to help finance an expansion of the mining operation, at which time Eads, Dickson, and Bates became involved.

The material obtained from these mines was first transported in wagons, over bad roads, to a point on the Mississippi River for shipment to St. Louis. Completion of the Southwest Branch of the Missouri Pacific Railroad to Rolla created a railhead to which the ore could be transported, but this still involved a 160-mile wagon haul. The difficulty of this transportation could have been eased significantly by rapid completion of the railroad, but progress was slow under the leadership of John C. Frémont. There were calls from agricultural interests in the area for the state to take control of the railroad, but it was rumored that Governor Fletcher was associated with the Granby Mining and Smelting Company, which ultimately gained more from private ownership of the railroad than it would from state control.[26]

On July 27, 1866, the Southwest Branch of the Missouri Pacific was re-chartered as the Atlantic and Pacific Railroad, with James Eads as one of the primary incorporators from Missouri. Another incorporator was Fletcher, who had appointed Josiah Fogg as agent for sale of the Bank of the State of Missouri earlier in the year, and who oversaw the sale of the bank to the Eads syndicate.

Two of the Atlantic and Pacific Railroad incorporators from outside of Missouri, J. Edgar Thomson and Thomas A. Scott, were officers of the Pennsylvania Railroad, which controlled the St. Louis, Vandalia and Terre Haute Railroad Company, a branch line projected to enter East St. Louis. A bridge over the Mississippi River would give the Pennsylvania Railroad a connection with the Atlantic and Pacific Railroad, thus advancing Thomson and Scott's plans for a transcontinental railroad empire. This partly explains why Scott was one of the men elected as a director of the bridge company on May 1. As a director he could represent the interests of his mentor, Thomson, who never served on the board but became an investor in the bridge company through Scott's agency.

Thomson and Scott's participation in the project was of crucial importance because they brought to the enterprise two elements that none of the local entrepreneurs could—connection to a regionally powerful eastern trunk line with transcontinental ambitions, and connection to sources of European capital.

Long-span railroad bridges across the major western rivers were built with more than just stone, wood, and metal. They were built with borrowed money. The bridge at St. Louis was expected to cost four or five times what any bridge on the upper Mississippi had or would cost and thus represented a much greater financial risk to those having the necessary capital to construct it. That risk was significantly lowered when Thomson and Scott committed to the scheme because they were known on the national (and international) level for the same qualities that Eads was known for in St. Louis. They were men who knew how to get things done and had a record of success in finance and construction. And like Eads, they had the power to make or break the project.

Other People's Money

It should not be considered unprofessional for an engineer to be a capitalist, and, when he takes his proper place as promoter and organizer and shares in the profits of engineering enterprise, he will no longer be taunted with the saying, that "an engineer is only good to spend other people's money."

—Onward Bates, President, American Society of Civil Engineers, 1909

At the time they decided to participate in the St. Louis Bridge project, J. Edgar Thomson and Thomas A. Scott were major players in a drama of economic and technological development being acted out on a stage that stretched across the continent and beyond. Thomson, president of the Pennsylvania Railroad Company, and Scott, vice president, were part of a loose and ever changing association of Philadelphia-based entrepreneurs who had a variety of business interests related to extension of the country's transportation and communication network.

Thomson, born in 1808 to Pennsylvanian Quaker parents, developed an interest in mechanics at an early age due to the influence of his father, and he followed the elder Thomson into the surveyor's trade. Like many young men of his age with technical expertise and energy, he quickly rose through the ranks from rod man on a railroad survey crew to assistant engineer, working primarily on railroads connected to Philadelphia.

His abilities brought him to the attention of some Georgia railroad promoters, who hired him in 1834 as chief engineer of the Georgia Railroad and Banking Company in 1834. This position developed not only his skills as an engineer, but also his knowledge of corporate administration. His salary was more than sufficient to provide him a surplus after attending to basic needs, and he soon discovered the rewards of capital investment by acquiring stocks, bonds, and real estate.

Thomson returned to Pennsylvania in 1847 to accept the position of chief engineer for the Pennsylvania Railroad. He was soon promoted to general superintendent, and he became president of the corporation in 1852. His early years as president were marked by great engineering achievements that allowed the railroad to cross the barrier of the Alleghenies, such as the Allegheny Mountain Tunnel and the great Horseshoe Curve. But Thomson proved to be even better at playing the game of corporate politics and at finding creative ways to fund the company's westward expansion.

Although he had great ambitions for himself and his company, Thomson differed from many railroad executives of his age in that he was careful in acceptance of risk. Every move was well thought out, and every decision was made after due deliberation. He was unlike many other entrepreneurs in another respect; he was a man of his word, a man who could be trusted to stand by his commitments.

Undoubtedly one of the greatest business leaders of the nineteenth century, Thomson became personally involved in coal, iron, and oil companies, many real estate ventures, a variety of manufacturing and construction concerns, and, on a smaller scale, in insurance, lumber, and various mineral extraction firms.

His experience as chief engineer of the Georgia Railroad probably kindled a lifelong interest in southern railroads that influenced his later speculations in transcontinental railroad development. But it was Jay Gould's attempt to win a tactical victory in the race to create a transcontinental railway network by purchasing the Pennsylvania's western connections in 1867 that led Thomson to concentrate on a line that would pass through St. Louis.[1]

Although the acknowledged head of the Pennsylvania interests, Thomson left much of the planning for transcontinental railroad development to his protégé, Thomas Scott.

Scott, another self-made Pennsylvanian, was a twenty-seven-year-old freight forwarding agent for Leech and Company in 1850 when he came to the attention of Herman Haupt, superintendent of transportation for the Pennsylvania Railroad.

It was through Haupt's influence that Scott was appointed as the railroad's station agent at Hollidaysburg, Pennsylvania. His drive, ambition, and aptitude led to his advancement to the post of company vice president by 1860.

Having survived several business disasters before his association with the railroad, Scott learned at an early age that failure could be overcome with great measures of hard work and a dollop of luck. He therefore was more risk-prone than Thomson. He was also more likely to engage in shady business practices to ensure that those risks paid off. With his good looks, confident bearing, and a charming personality, Scott made the perfect front man for the taciturn Thomson in execution of the widely scattered schemes of the Pennsylvania investment group.[2]

Thomson and Scott had expectations regarding the benefits of a bridge at St. Louis long before Eads emerged as a potential business partner. They intended to follow the pattern established by those Chicago-based railroads that had bridged or were planning to bridge the upper Mississippi by associating themselves with politically powerful and financially successful local businessmen with whom they could form a profitable alliance. But unlike the situation in smaller towns on the upper Mississippi, there was more than one group of powerful men in St. Louis with whom an alliance could be formed. The success of their plans depended on selecting the right group with whom to do business. Their participation in the Eads-led corporation, at this point, stemmed from their prior association with Eads in the Atlantic and Pacific Railroad and could be subject to change based on the performance of the organization.

Eads and his associates, for their part, were certainly aware that they needed the advice and assistance of entrepreneurs who were better versed in the intricacies of railroad finance and operation than they were. The bridge, after all, would not be worth the cost of construction unless it was properly connected to a national rail network entering St. Louis from the east and west, and most of the men who composed the Eads organization were still relative neophytes concerning railroad development. Moreover, the bridge would be financed in much the same manner as a railroad, and that implied that funds would have to be obtained from London via banking houses in New York or Boston. The long-established connections of the Philadelphia interests to these sources of financing were of vital importance.

Thomson and Scott probably made their first contributions to the joint enterprise prior to Scott's election as director on May 1 by putting Eads in touch with Andrew Carnegie, Scott's protégé and a key member of the Pennsylvania interests.

As Harold Livesay, a biographer of Carnegie, has observed, Carnegie and Scott had much in common. They both came from very modest backgrounds and lacked parental leadership as children. Both had "a restless desire to succeed, an ability to master detail, a charismatic personality, and a determination to acquire through self-education the culture and urbanity that circumstances had denied them."[3] In this respect they shared much with their new business partner, James Eads.

Carnegie was an important contributor to the bridge-company enterprise due to his position as vice president of and partner in the Keystone Bridge Company, one of two main types of companies involved in production of long-span railroad bridges following the Civil War.

The St. Louis and Illinois Bridge Company was an example of the first type, the bridge-financing corporation. These organizations were formed for the purpose of bringing together capital, real estate, labor, and political power to create a functional, engineered structure of utility to railroad companies. They secured financing from Europe via New York and Boston, contracted out the work of construction to specialized bridge-building companies, and then maintained and operated the completed structure as a toll bridge, charging railroads for its use. In those situations where the bridge was built as both a railway and highway, or "combination," bridge, tolls were also collected for wagon, animal, and pedestrian traffic.

Keystone represented the other type of bridge company, the specialized bridge-building firm. The men who served as owner-managers of these companies often tended to be professional engineers who first learned the art and science of bridge design and construction by working as salaried employees of railroad companies. During and after the Civil War, from about 1860 to 1870, some bridge engineers began to leave the railroads and form their own companies, contracting to build bridges either directly for the railroads, or for semi-independent bridge-financing firms of the type identified above. They often specialized in the manufacture and erection of a certain type of bridge that was the patent design of the engineer who formed the company.

The genesis of the Keystone Bridge Company may be traced back to 1856, when Carnegie, a twenty-one-year-old Scottish immigrant then serving as an assistant to Scott, witnessed the fabrication of a small iron bridge at the Pennsylvania Railroad facility in Altoona. Carnegie was impressed by the bridge and with John Piper, chief mechanic in charge of the bridge's fabrication, and the two men struck up a close friendship. In 1862 Carnegie suggested that Piper and the general bridge supervisor Aaron Shiffler form an independent company for the erection of iron railroad bridges. This was accomplished in February 1862 with Carnegie, Thomson, Scott, Piper, Shiffler, and Jacob Linville (the designer of the little bridge Carnegie saw at Altoona) as partners.

Linville was still an employee of the Pennsylvania Railroad in July 1862 when Congress authorized the Hollidays Cove Railroad, a company first organized by Thomson and Scott in 1860 for construction of a line from the Pennsylvania border to Steubenville, Ohio, to erect a railroad bridge across the Ohio River. The Steubenville Bridge, which featured a main channel span 320 feet long, was designed by Linville and built by the Piper and Shiffler Bridge Company. Generally regarded as the first long-span railroad bridge in the United States, the structure was completed in 1864 and then leased, along with the railroad, to George W. McCook, a Thomson associate. McCook immediately assigned the lease to Thomson as trustee for the bondholder. The Steubenville and Indiana Railroad Company and the Pittsburgh and Steubenville Railroad Company, subsidiaries of the Pennsylvania Railroad that were connected to the Hollidays Cove Railroad at its western and eastern ends, paid tolls to the Hollidays Cove Railroad for the right to cross the bridge. Thomson and Scott thus profited from their interest in both the company that financed and owned the bridge (Hollidays Cove Railroad) and the company that built the bridge (Piper and Shiffler Bridge Company) in a way that would have been impossible had the company they served as employees (Pennsylvania Railroad) built the structure.[4]

In creating independent companies to finance and construct the railroad and bridge, Thomson and Scott established a model of entrepreneurial behavior that they would later attempt to replicate, as much as possible, as the nation's railroad network moved further west. Clearly, they intended to place the generation of personal wealth somewhat ahead of their fiduciary responsibility as officers of the Pennsylvania Railroad.

The experience of building the Steubenville Bridge convinced Carnegie that a significant expansion of the firm's capabilities would be necessary in order to construct the other long-span bridges that would eventually be required by railroads crossing the Ohio, Mississippi, and Missouri Rivers. He therefore reorganized the company in 1865 with an initial capital of $300,000 and with Linville as president, Piper as general manager, Shiffler as assistant general manager, and Walter Katté as chief engineer. Scott served as a silent partner, subscribing to half of Carnegie's $80,000 stock investment. Thomson took about a 5 percent interest but held the stock in his wife's name. The infusion of new capital allowed for enlargement and improvement of the original bridge works, and the firm, now named Keystone in honor of Carnegie's adopted state, prepared for the opportunities ahead.[5]

Carnegie also held a majority interest in the Union Iron Mills, a company formed in 1865 from the remnants of earlier endeavors in order to provide a reliable source of material for the bridges built by Keystone. Piper and Linville were also partners in this business.

The bridge at St. Louis, due to the complexity of bridging the river at that location and the importance of the city as a center of commerce, promised to be the most profitable and reputation-enhancing of all the bridges authorized by Congress to span the Mississippi and Missouri Rivers. It was therefore very important to the Philadelphia interests that Keystone win the contract for superstructure erection.[6]

The involvement of Keystone was so crucial to the success and profitability of the scheme that Scott undoubtedly urged Eads to work with Keystone's officers on the design of the bridge before acceding to serve on the board of directors of the St. Louis and Illinois Bridge Company. Eads agreed to this consultation and traveled to Philadelphia in late April or early May of 1867 to show Linville some rough sketches of his design.

Shortly after Scott's May 1 election, steps were taken to strengthen the company by the addition of financiers from outside St. Louis. On June 5, 1867, Robert L. Kennedy and Henry F. Vail, bankers connected with the Bank of Commerce of New York City, were added to the list of bridge company stockholders. Kennedy became president of the bank one year later when Russell retired. By the end of October two more New Yorkers, Edwin D. Morgan and John A. Ubsdell, had purchased stock.[7]

Morgan, a United States senator first elected in 1863, was also a former Hartford, Connecticut, merchant and city council member (1832), a former New York state senator (1850–53), and onetime governor of New York (1859–63). In 1842 he founded E. D. Morgan and Company, a private banking house based in New York City that became respected and prosperous. He also had extensive railroad experience, serving as president of the Hudson River Railroad from 1851 to 1855 and sitting on the board of several other roads, including the Michigan Southern and Northern Indiana Railroad.[8]

Ubsdell, senior partner of the New York dry-goods house of Ubsdell, Peirson, and Company, married Eads's stepdaughter Genevieve in 1858 or 1859, approximately ten years after opening a St. Louis branch of the New York firm. He was also a member of the Eads-led syndicate that purchased the stock of the State Bank of Missouri in 1866.[9]

Thomas D. Gaylord of Cincinnati also became a subscriber at this time, as did four associates of Eads from St. Louis: John J. Roe, Gerald B. Allen, John Knapp, and

William M. McPherson. Each of the men who became investors from June through October subscribed to 200 shares, or $20,000 each.[10]

Roe, Allen, Knapp, and McPherson came into positions of prominence in the St. Louis community before the Civil War and represented the postwar business leadership of the city. United by bonds of social position, common business interest, and faith in Eads's ability to increase their wealth, they gladly accepted Eads's offer to participate in the enterprise.

John Roe, one of Eads's closest friends, was elected a director of the Southern Bank of St. Louis on April 6, 1857, and subsequently became a director of the National Bank of the State of Missouri when the Eads syndicate took over the State Bank in 1866. It was also in 1866 that Roe became, along with Eads and Dickson, an incorporator of the Tower Grove and Lafayette Railway Company, a streetcar line.

Gerald Allen, destined to become third president of the bridge company, moved to St. Louis in 1837 and became a building contractor. In 1855 he established his own business, the Fulton Iron Works, with Oliver D. Filley as his principal partner. In 1861 the company made some of the machinery for the gunboats being constructed by Eads at the Carondelet shipyards, and in 1864 it manufactured the armor and turrets for Eads's river monitor *Kickapoo*.[11]

John Knapp was not an intimate of Eads, but he was brought into the bridge scheme due to his ability to influence public perceptions of the enterprise. In 1852, he purchased an interest in the *Missouri Republican*. His older brother, George, later became a co-owner of the newspaper and was among the incorporators of the Atlantic and Pacific Railroad.[12]

On September 30, 1867, an agreement was made whereby John and George Knapp received fifty shares of bridge company stock in exchange for agreeing "to receive and publish for its [the company's] benefit, such statistics, facts and communications as its projectors might deem of advantage to the enterprise during its construction."[13] The payment was not actually made until May 27, 1869, but Eads later wrote a letter in which he stated that John Knapp's service to the bridge company, "independent of your friendly (and voluntary) editorials," would have been worth twenty thousand dollars.[14]

William M. McPherson, a lawyer, was an influential member of the St. Louis business community and one of Eads's most trusted business partners. He was elected to the first board of directors of the St. Louis and Iron Mountain Railroad, and in 1856 he succeeded James H. Lucas as president of the Pacific Railroad Company, holding that office for almost two years. In 1859 McPherson became an incorporator, along with William T. Sherman, Derrick A. January (president of the first St. Louis and Illinois Bridge Company), Robert Barnes, James H. Lucas, and five other gentlemen of the St. Louis Railroad Company (another streetcar line). McPherson also served two terms as a prosecuting attorney in St. Louis and one term in the state legislature, and managed to amass a considerable holding in St. Louis real estate.[15] Before the Civil War he built a block of buildings located on Washington Street between Fifth and Fourth Streets, known as the Verandah Row, with Barton Bates. It would later be claimed that McPherson and Bates made a considerable amount of money by selling this property to the bridge company.

During the summer of 1867, the bridge company vice president, James Blackman, and the secretary, Joseph Cabot, resigned their positions and were replaced by Barton Bates and John A. Dillon, son of Eliza Eads Dillon and therefore Eads's cousin and the half-brother of Eads's first wife, Martha Dillon. Dillon was also owner of the *St. Louis Post*. The participation of Dillon, Knapp, and William McKee (principal owner of the *St. Louis Democrat*) in the bridge enterprise virtually guaranteed that the activities of the Eads-led bridge company would be given favorable coverage in the three most influential St. Louis newspapers.

On July 15 the directors held a meeting and formed an Executive and Financial Committee of four with William Taussig acting as chairman. Taussig was authorized to open negotiations with banking firms in Europe for purposes of securing construction financing, but in order for such financing to be obtained a general plan of the bridge first had to be approved by the board. Eads therefore presented a preliminary design that was sufficiently complete to allow publication, with the details to be determined at a later date. The board approved the plans and authorized Eads to begin active operations as soon as he deemed it practical to do so.

There were, however, obstacles in the path of the company that would prove as difficult to overcome as the barrier of the river itself. Other entrepreneurs, in pursuit of their own dreams and visions, were claiming the right to build the first bridge at St. Louis and competing for financial backing. As the Eads group was soon to learn, opposition from these competitors would first have to be eliminated in order for their plans to be realized.

4

Mongrel Structures

We would advise against the bridge being made other than a railroad bridge—the pecuniary results arising from the accommodation of wagon traffic are not by any means commensurate with the disadvantages under which these mongrel structures, adapted to both railroad and common road purposes, always labor.

—Benjamin H. Latrobe, Consulting Engineer; C. Shaler Smith, Civil Engineer, 1867

The Boomer-led Illinois and St. Louis Bridge Company certainly represented the greatest obstacle to the efforts of the Eads-led organization, but it was not the only threat.

On February 25, 1867, Congress passed an act authorizing the Mississippi Submerged Tubular Bridge Company, a corporation organized under the laws of the State of Missouri, to build an iron bridge between St. Louis and East St. Louis. The act stipulated that the bridge be sunk below the bed of the river, and that the tolls charged by the company be no more than those charged by the Wiggins Ferry Company. The impracticality of such a proposal doomed the company, and it soon faded from public view. But another group formed about the same time with a plan that had real potential for drawing political, financial, and popular support away from both Boomer and Eads.

The exclusive right possessed by the Illinois and St. Louis Bridge Company to build from the Illinois shore opposite the city of St. Louis was confined to St. Clair County, Illinois, the northern boundary of which was about two and one-half miles north of Dyke Avenue in East St. Louis. Therefore, anyone wishing to erect a bridge from any point in Illinois outside the bounds of that county had no legal impediment to doing so.

On March 6, 1867, the Illinois legislature authorized the Alton and St. Charles County Bridge Company to erect a railroad-only toll bridge from any point in Madison County, located just north of St. Clair County, to any point in Missouri "opposite thereunto." Among the incorporators and investors were Levi Davis, Henry C. Moore, John J. Mitchell, William Shepard, and Levi L. Ashbrook.[1]

Davis was a director of the St. Louis, Alton and Terre Haute Railroad, whose superintendent was Henry Moore.[2] Moore was also chief engineer and superintendent of the Pacific Railroad of Missouri. He took that position when his predecessor was fired for not accepting a bribe to participate in a scheme to cheat the railroad.[3]

Following a meeting in 1866 with Daniel Garrison, vice president of the Pacific Railroad, Thomas Scott and two of his associates created the St. Louis and Pacific Fast Freight Express Company (the White Line). Garrison then persuaded the railroad's board of directors to approve a contract allowing the White Line to run its cars on Pacific Railroad trains, carrying first- and second-class freight at third- and fourth-class rates. The White Line collected $120 a car for shipments to Kansas City and paid the railroad $56 a car. Six of the Pacific Railroad's directors, including Garrison, were allowed to buy shares in the White Line at half of par value in exchange for going along with the fraudulent arrangement. When the superintendent refused a gift of fifty shares of stock to ensure his silence and participation, he was fired. Moore then took the job and the shares.[4]

John J. Mitchell created the Alton and St. Louis Railroad in 1861 to connect East St. Louis (Illinoistown) with the Chicago and Alton Railroad.[5] His major interest, however, was the East St. Louis Transfer Company, created by Mitchell, Miltenberger, and Tansey in 1864 to compete with the St. Louis Transfer Company. This company transported passengers and freight across the river to and from the depot of the Chicago and Alton Railroad and was sometimes called the Chicago and Alton Transfer System.[6]

Like Mitchell and Moore, William Shepard also had an interest in railroad speculation as a director of the St. Louis, Jacksonville and Chicago Railroad.[7] Levi L.

Ashbrook, a pork packer and cattle merchant from St. Louis, also played a significant role as president of the Madison Ferry Company.[8]

Several important St. Louis businessmen, including Isaac H. Sturgeon, president
of the North Missouri Railroad, were allied with this group in seeking the charter
necessary to do business in the state of Missouri. In anticipation of receiving that
charter, Sturgeon hired two respected engineers from Baltimore, Benjamin Henry
Latrobe II and C. Shaler Smith, to suggest a specific location and design for a bridge.
While awaiting the results of the engineer's report, Sturgeon and his associates
began to speak against the plans of both the Boomer and Eads organizations.

Although the interests of the Alton and St. Charles Bridge Company were in
direct opposition to those of Boomer, three of its incorporators, Moore, Davis, and
Shepard, were incorporators of the Illinois and St. Louis Bridge Company as re-
chartered by Boomer in Illinois. Shepard was also, along with Mitchell and Zephe-
niah Job, an incorporator of the Illinois and St. Louis Bridge Company formed by
Boomer in Missouri. The exact motivations of these men are unclear. They may
have participated in the Boomer organizations just in case his plan prevailed, or
they may have hoped to profit by sale of the rights granted to the corporations
formed by Boomer if such a sale could be made. Whatever their intentions, Boomer
must have been dismayed to find that some of his partners had plans of their own.

But with confidence in the exclusive rights granted his Illinois corporation, and
in consideration of a clause in the charter of that organization requiring the company to spend at least fifty thousand dollars during 1867 in the construction of a
bridge, Boomer had already made arrangements to organize a competent engineering staff. In March he hired a man named Anderson as chief engineer, Simeon S.
Post as consulting engineer, and an able corps of assistant engineers. Within a few
weeks Anderson, former chief engineer of U.S. military roads and former general
superintendent of the Union Pacific Railway, Eastern Division, had established his
office in a small building at the corner of Seventh and Pine Streets.[9] This placed
him about one block south of the Benoist mansion, where Eads, with Henry Flad's
assistance, first sketched out the plan of his bridge.[10]

At this point there was still a great deal of design work to be performed by the
engineers for the competing companies, but the general type of bridge to be utilized by each had already been determined. Boomer intended to use the iron Post
truss, a type patented in 1863 that enjoyed a brief period of popularity after the
Civil War for use in long-span railway bridges. Boomer had acquired the right to
market the Post truss shortly after it was first used at Washingtonville, New York,
on a branch of the Erie Railroad.

Latrobe and Smith, who made their report to Sturgeon on April 4, stated that "any good iron truss, such as the Linville, Fink, Post, or Trellis" could be used, but they recommended the Fink as "most economical for these long spans."[11] In both cases, the type selected reflected fairly conservative, rational judgments in line with current practices of the engineering profession. But Eads, the only man among the engineers with no experience in railroad or bridge engineering, had rejected the iron truss in favor of a radical design that shattered engineering precedent.

At the meeting held in his office on February 17, Eads announced his intention to build an arch bridge composed of three spans. The main channel span would have to be no less than five hundred feet in order to comply with the authorizing act of Congress, thus making it the longest arch span in the world. The other spans would be almost as long, thus reducing the number of obstructing piers placed in the river to only two. Moreover, the arches would be made of steel, a material thought unsuitable for long-span bridges by virtually every engineer in America and Europe due to its high cost, the difficulties of its fabrication, and the belief that it became brittle in cold weather.

In late April or early May 1867, at the urging of Scott and Carnegie, Eads traveled to Philadelphia to show Jacob Linville some rough sketches of his design. Linville was one of the most prominent and respected bridge engineers in the country, and Scott had prevailed upon the bridge company board of directors to hire him as a consulting engineer.

Linville's reputation began when he designed and built a bridge in 1861 over the Schuylkill River on the Delaware extension of the Pennsylvania Railroad. This bridge featured the first use of wide forged eye-bars and posts formed of wrought-iron sections. Linville's eye-bar design soon became one of the distinctive features of American bridge construction.[12]

His stature was further enhanced with erection of the Steubenville Bridge, which required the creation of special tools, machinery, testing apparatus, and appliances of erection due to its unusual dimensions, length, and proportions. This included invention of a 500-ton-capacity machine designed in 1863 by William Sellers of Philadelphia that allowed the testing of full-sized structural members to the point of failure.[13] The design of the bridge, the testing program adopted for fabrication of its main structural members, and the methodology employed in its erection marked a new era in the development of industrial technology.

This explains why Carnegie had asked Eads to show his plans to "the one man in the United States who knew the subject best—our Mr. Linville."[14] But after a preliminary examination, Linville went to Carnegie "in great concern," saying,

"The bridge if built upon these plans will not stand up; it will not carry its own weight."[15] He was so concerned about his association with such a radical design that he informed Carnegie, "I cannot consent to imperil my reputation by appearing to encourage or approve of its adoption. I deem it entirely unsafe and impracticable, as well as in fault in the qualities of durability."[16] Carnegie responded by saying, "Well, Captain Eads will come to see you and in talking over matters explain this to him gently, get it into proper shape, lead him into the straight path and say nothing to others."[17]

On June 3, Eads sent Linville further rough sketches of his proposed design. These tracings had no dimensions of parts on them and exhibited no completed system of bracing, either horizontal, vertical, or transverse. Nothing, in fact, was illustrated except a method of bracing between the four arched ribs, and the struts and tension rods located between the arches and the top member, the position, number, and size of which had not been determined nor the counter-bracing shown.[18] Most important, perhaps, was the absence of a wind truss.

Despite having been asked by Carnegie to exert his influence on Eads, Linville responded to these preliminary sketches by proposing a truss bridge of his own design. His plan was to build three truss spans on pontoons at a sheltered site, float them into position between the bridge piers, and then raise them onto their seats by use of hydraulic jacks. This proposal led the bridge company board of directors to terminate Linville's association as consulting engineer on July 13.[19]

Shortly thereafter, by the third week of July, Eads had solidified his overall plan enough to release it for public examination. The *St. Louis Democrat* published the first description of the structure and the particulars of the project on July 21.[20] Projected to cost $5 million and to take from three to four years to construct, the bridge would be composed of three ribbed arches of cast steel, the central span being 515 feet long and the side spans being 497 feet each. Each arch would be composed of two members, seven feet apart, held in place by a system of diagonal steel braces.

The two river piers would be tremendous masses of masonry, sunk all the way to bedrock. The largest pier would be about 200 feet from top to bottom, 110 feet long, and 55 feet wide at the base tapering to 40 feet at the top. The second pier, located closer to the Missouri side of the river where bedrock was not as deep, would be about 170 feet from top to bottom.

The upper wagon and pedestrian deck would carry a double line of rails so streetcars could pass going either way. A lower rail deck would also carry a double line of tracks to accommodate both narrow gauge and standard gauge cars, thus allowing trains from either the east or west to use the bridge. The tracks, carried over Main

Street on the St. Louis side by a series of masonry arches, at a height sufficient to avoid any interference with street traffic, would enter a tunnel under Washington Avenue. At Ninth Street the tunnel would curve to the south and continue under Eleventh Street from Olive Street to Clark Avenue, and then emerge into the open near the site of a planned union depot.[21]

Correspondence between Eads and Linville, and the drawings that survive from early 1867, provide evidence that Eads's preliminary design of the bridge differed in several important respects from what was actually built. For example, the steel arches, the most unique and notable feature of the bridge, were first designed to be rectangular in section instead of tubular, and braced instead of ribbed. In fact, many changes were made in the design before and after construction commenced in response to design flaws discovered during construction and in response to limitations of the fabrication capabilities of the iron and steel industry. But the most disturbing aspect of the design in Linville's initial estimation may have been its fundamental structural elements and not the absence of detailed information.

The arch bridge, particularly when constructed of masonry, was one of the oldest types in existence and had exerted a powerful influence on European designers, who often preferred the arch to the truss form due to its superior appearance.[22] Eads chose as his model the Koblenz railroad bridge across the Rhine River, completed in 1864, primarily due to its attractiveness. But, as he wrote to Linville, he also believed that the arch form would offer "beauty with economy."[23] American railroad bridge designers, however, who were generally less concerned with aesthetics, had found the truss form to offer greater simplicity and economy in the conditions encountered in the United States.[24] Therefore, the metal arch had been used for only a small number of short-span bridges in this country.

The only such bridge of any importance was the so-called water-pipe bridge constructed over Rock Creek in Washington, D.C., by Montgomery C. Meigs in 1858. Although Eads may have had this structure in mind when he later decided to make the arch members of his bridge tubular instead of rectangular, the Meigs bridge was built using cast iron. Eads, however, intended to construct the arches and some supporting structural components of his bridge from cast steel.

Steel, an alloy of iron and carbon modified by small amounts of phosphorus, sulfur, silicon, manganese, chromium, or other substances, had properties that generally made it stronger than iron for a given unit of weight. It had first been used in bridge construction for the eye-bar chains of the 300-foot suspension span erected across the Danube Canal near Vienna, Austria, in 1828. But the difficulties involved in its manufacture made it both extremely expensive and unreliable, and its use for bridges in America was virtually abandoned after 1828.[25]

Eads may have become acquainted with the potential of steel due to his association with members of the Naval Ordnance Bureau both during and after the Civil War. These men would have had knowledge of the experimental use of steel in ordnance manufacturing during the 1860s and could have passed that knowledge on to Eads while he was engaged in development of his gun-carriage design.[26] By the time he made his decision he may also have seen a January 1866 publication of the Dutch government detailing plans to use steel for the deck of the Kuilenberg railroad bridge. Over a year later, Eads would cite this bridge as precedent for the construction of spans in excess of five hundred feet. But the negative performance of steel in this and other Dutch bridges led to the total abandonment of that material in Holland by 1879.[27] American engineers, concerned with both the safety of steel and its high cost compared to iron, were less adventurous than the Dutch and shunned its use.

Therefore, it should not be surprising that Linville's response to Eads's preliminary design was far less favorable than Eads might have hoped for. After all, he was asked to pass judgment on the very rough plans of a man who had absolutely no experience in bridge design and was not even considered to be an engineer until he appointed himself to that position. Linville knew, as later events would prove, that the American steel industry was not capable in 1867 of manufacturing the necessary components of a bridge such as that proposed by Eads. Although Eads may well have suggested that such components could be produced in Europe if unavailable in the United States, this could hardly have bolstered Linville's confidence in the use of this material.

Many years later Carnegie indicated in his autobiography that establishment of a relationship between the two men sufficient to make Eads's basic design feasible "was successfully accomplished."[28] But increasingly after his dismissal as consulting engineer, Linville chose to deal with Eads through intermediaries whenever possible and his contribution to the final design was probably negligible.

Unconcerned by Linville's opposition, and confident of the Eads design, the St. Louis and Illinois Bridge Company began to move forward with the project. On Wednesday, July 31, the company sent James S. Thomas, mayor of St. Louis, a letter asking permission from the city to occupy the levee between Washington Avenue and Green Street with stone and other material to be used in construction of the west bridge abutment. A few days later, Eads announced that all the necessary financial and other arrangements had been completed, and that as soon as the level of the river fell a few feet, perhaps in another ten days, work would commence construction of a cofferdam for the west abutment.[29]

In truth, however, the financing for the bridge had not yet been arranged and the Eads company was far from ready to begin construction of the bridge. Preliminary work on the west abutment was really somewhat of a bluff, intended to present the illusion of progress to the community and potential investors in hopes of weakening the challenge presented by Eads's chief opponent, Lucius Boomer.[30]

Eads did, however, make an excellent addition to his engineering staff on August 19, 1867, by hiring Charles Pfeifer as assistant engineer. Pfeifer had come to the United States from Stuttgart early in 1867, with an excellent education in engineering and mathematics and the intention of settling among the large German community in St. Louis. His thesis on the theory of arch-bridge design had won a prize in his native country, and his expertise in that area may have encouraged him to approach the bridge company for a job. He immediately began working very closely with Flad on the mathematical computations upon which later detailed drawings were based.[31]

While Eads attempted to begin work on the west abutment, Boomer took decisive steps to rid himself of the Eads incubus by assembling in St. Louis a convention of the country's most respected bridge, railroad, and hydraulic engineers. His intention was to convince the people of St. Louis, and potential financial backers from outside the city, that he had the more workable design in terms of both engineering and financial feasibility. If successful, such an attempt would preclude the necessity of engaging in a costly and time-consuming legal battle with the Eads group over who held the dominant charter.

Eads began work on the west abutment cofferdam on August 20, and the next day the convention called by Boomer met in Parlor No. 6 of the Southern Hotel. After Anderson called the meeting to order, William McAlpine was elected president of the convention. In his opening remarks to those assembled he said, "although we have been convened at the request of one of the rival companies, yet we are to consider all of the questions bearing on this subject, without reference to any particular plan or company."[32] In an attempt at impartiality, he made certain that both Eads and Flad were invited to attend the convention, though both elected not to do so.

The presence of Boomer's staff and business partners, his attendance at all the business meetings of the group, and the nearly sixty-three thousand dollars in expenses incurred by him in hosting the convention encouraged some to claim that the sole intent of the meeting was to discredit the Eads plan while recommending that of Boomer. The primary mission of the convention, however, was to pass judgment on the two general options dictated by Congress in the enabling legislation passed in 1866. The bridge at St. Louis could be constructed with either one span of 500 feet in the clear over the main river channel, or with two spans, each of a minimum width of 350 feet in the clear.[33]

Whether or not the convention acted with impartiality became a matter for debate soon after the proceedings closed, but the manner in which the engineers examined the multitude of issues involved certainly gives the appearance of a genuine attempt at fairness. A number of committees were established, each staffed by those engineers considered to be most knowledgeable concerning the topic covered by the individual committee. Topics addressed were the regimen of the river and the character of its bottom; foundations and piers; superstructure and approaches; river commerce and its navigation; and commerce crossing the bridge.

On August 27, McAlpine accepted the committee reports from the various chairmen, and on the thirty-first he submitted to the convention a draft of a general report that consisted of a preface, a résumé of the several reports, and the full reports of the committees as amended. It was then resolved that all the members present sign the report, and that each member not present (several had left early) be sent a copy and requested to sign and return it.

The report stated that whereas a bridge with a 500-foot main span would be considerably more expensive than a bridge with two main spans of 350 feet, and whereas there was no bridge of such length in existence that had stood long enough to provide a reliable example, the committee members recommended adopting "the minimum spans allowed by the law as more economical, less hazardous in construction and maintenance, and affording ample accommodation to the commerce of the river and the port of St. Louis."[34]

One of the most prominent engineers involved, Octave Chanute, later commented on these points, stating that "it was understood that a rival company [the St. Louis and Illinois Bridge Company] proposed to adopt the 500-foot span, while the plans of superstructure which were submitted to the convention [by the Boomer-led company] were for beam-trusses, the construction of which, as well as the methods proposed for putting in the foundations, we found to be practical and efficient."[35] Although it was generally agreed that spans of 500 feet could be built, they would be very costly, and a mistake in plan, material, or workmanship would be far more disastrous than in shorter spans. Thus, shorter spans were recommended.

The best summation of the prevailing attitude at the time was later provided by W. W. Evans, an engineer from New York, who said, "Captain Eads is a bold man to design an arched bridge with spans of 500 feet, and will deserve credit for his boldness and nerve if successful, but I doubt if he will deserve or receive much credit for spending two or three times the amount the circumstances called for."[36]

The issue regarding proper span length could not, however, be separated from considerations regarding the proper depth of pier foundations. Generally speaking, the deeper one had to sink the piers in order to keep the current of the river from washing out their foundations, the more it would cost in terms of time and money. Past a certain level of cost, the savings derived from short spans would be offset by the increased cost of additional piers, relative to the fewer number of piers required for longer spans. One of the long acknowledged difficulties of building a bridge at St. Louis was that the river was much deeper and the current much stronger at that location than on the upper Mississippi, thus making the task of sinking piers more challenging.

It was well known by engineers at this time that the bottom of the Mississippi River did not lie at a fixed point. The water passing over the river bottom contained a large amount of suspended materials, such as soil, rocks, portions of trees or other vegetation, and in winter, ice. These materials, in combination with the velocity of the water flow, tended to dig out or "scour" the bottom of the river. Under certain conditions, such as an increase in the suspended material caused by heavy runoff upstream or a decrease in the flow rate, materials could be deposited on the river bottom, thus raising its level. At other times, conditions might cause the bottom to be gouged out and carried away, thus lowering the bottom level. The relevant question to be answered in the case of bridge foundations was, How far down was the limit of the river's ability to scour the bottom? This was a vitally important question because if the support structure of the bridge did not extend below this limit, the foundations of the bridge would be undermined and the whole works could be washed downstream.

The Committee on the Regimen of the River and the Character of Its Bottom, using information obtained from soundings of the river for a distance of twenty miles both above and below St. Louis, made during the low-water period of 1860–61, determined that even under "peculiar circumstances, such as a bridge pier might present, the scouring influence might extend to forty feet in depth."[37] With this information before them and with an extra five feet added to the estimate for the sake of safety, the Committee on Foundations and Piers determined that forty-five feet was a safe scour limit.

Eads, however, believed that he knew better. Soundings conducted under his supervision in July 1867 indicated that the bottom of the river had been cut out eighteen feet lower than when soundings in the same location had been conducted in April. For reasons never fully explained, this convinced Eads that in times of flood the bottom could be cut out to two or three times the depth shown by his soundings, and perhaps even to the underlying bedrock located from fifteen (near the Missouri side) to one hundred feet (near the Illinois side) below the sand. He therefore determined that the foundations of the piers of the bridge would have to rest on bedrock.[38]

When Eads made his first official report as chief engineer to the president and directors of the bridge company in 1868, a report intended as much as anything to justify decisions he had already made and to quell the fears of potential investors concerning the propriety of those decisions, he provided support for his decision regarding the depth of pier foundations. He related that while examining the bottom of the river below Cairo during the flood of 1851, at a depth of sixty-five feet below the surface of the water, he found the bed of the river, "for at least three feet in depth," a moving mass so unstable that he could feel the sand rushing past his hands, "driven by a current apparently as rapid as that at the surface." He continued his story, saying, "I could discover the sand in motion at least two feet below the surface of the bottom, and moving with a velocity diminishing in proportion to the depth at which I thrust my hand into it."[39]

According to Eads, the river's ability to scour out its bottom increased with the velocity of its flow. His point in telling the story of his experience near Cairo was supposedly to indicate that the river's capacity to scour out the bottom at St. Louis, where it was more constrained in its channel and thus prone to flow faster in times of flood, was much greater. But what did this story actually prove?

Although Eads seems to contradict himself regarding how far below the "bottom" the material was in motion, he does state that the movement diminished in velocity "in proportion to the depth at which I thrust my hand into it," meaning that the scour of the current decreased noticeably within a few feet of the surface of the bottom on which he stood. This does not seem to be a great deal of scour and certainly doesn't prove that the river could remove nearly one hundred feet of deposit near the Illinois shore.

But Eads had other "proof" of his position to offer. He also noted that the wreck of the steamboat *America,* after being submerged for twenty years at a point one hundred miles below the mouth of the Ohio River, during which time an island was formed over it and a farm established, was uncovered during a flood in 1856 at a depth of forty feet below the low-water mark. Once again, it may be said that what occurs on other parts of the river is a poor indication of what may occur at St. Louis, but even if such information were relevant, it would only tend to confirm the scour limit estimate of the committee.

Another claim later used by Eads to support his position was that a scour probably sufficient to lay bare the rock at mid-channel occurs not just during periods of flood or high water, but also during periods of low water in the winter when a sheet of ice from ten to fifteen inches thick is formed. On two occasions Eads had cut a channel in the ice in an attempt to remove valuable wrecking boats from ice gorges (accumulations of ice in large masses at narrow points of the river) to places of safety. He was successful only in one case, finding that after the surface ice was cut away and removed to the side, the quantity of submerged ice that continually arose seemed inexhaustible.

It was Eads's assumption that the accumulated submerged ice, held in place by the surface ice, caused the water to "back up" ten or twenty feet above its former level in the wide-open stretches of river north of St. Louis. "The great height attained by the 'backing up' of the water above the gorge increases the currents that are sweeping below the ice to a degree probably greatly exceeding that of the floods," and, further, "these currents . . . would prove too great to be resisted by any ordinary rip-rap (or loose stone) usually used to protect foundations not resting on the rock."[40] However, by Eads's own calculations the scour would have to remove approximately eighty feet of sand at mid-channel to expose bedrock.

It was later claimed that Eads's findings regarding the possibility of currents scouring away the hard-packed sand of the river bottom were "verified during construction when chunks of coal and unpetrified bones and sticks were found deep in this layer, and the bedrock had been worn smooth by alluvial action."[41] But the Committee on the Regimen of the River and the Character of Its Bottom had also addressed this possibility in 1867. Despite finding that the depth of rock under the riverbed was such that it was difficult to conceive of how the scouring effects of the currents could ever reach so low, committee members admitted that "it is manifest that the deep bed of the river has been excavated out of the rock by the action of currents of water"; and, they asked, "if the forces which produced this be still active, may the river not again scour to an equal depth?" In answer, they determined that even though it was more than possible that remains of timber might be found to a depth of forty or fifty feet below the river bottom, it was unlikely that the forces that once scoured the bed of the river down to bedrock, and once deposited material deep into the sand, were still active. "The tendency of the river has been to cover the bed-work [*sic*] deeper and deeper, . . . and the deep scouring of a former period is not possible to occur again."[42]

In their final analysis, the engineers attending the convention left the final method of founding the piers of a bridge at St. Louis to those who would be directly responsible for its erection, due to their understanding that conditions discovered during construction might require an alteration of plans. We can never know how Boomer's engineers might have reacted to conditions as they encountered them during construction. The "final" plans, made public at the end of the year (1867), called for the first four piers extending from East St. Louis to be driven from forty-seven feet to sixty feet below the low-water line of 1863. Piers five and six, supporting the main channel span, would be driven to bedrock.[43]

What is certain is that Eads's early decision to take the piers of his bridge all the way to bedrock ensured the structure's permanence, while also promising high costs for substructure construction.

5

Fighting for It Still

Do not neglect to build the bridge across the Mississippi at this point;
nothing is more important at this moment. At the much less important
points, Quincy, Keokuk, Burlington, Davenport, Clinton, &c., bridges have
been, or are being built with all possible speed, and here we are fighting
for it still.

—Letter from "One of your young merchants" to the *Missouri
Republican,* December 18, 1867

Despite the thoroughness of the report produced by
the convention of engineers, its effect was not
what Boomer had wished for. The Eads organization was not knocked out of the competition, and
the capitalists of New York and Europe continued to with-
hold funding until a clear victor emerged from the battle.
But both Eads and Boomer realized that an appearance of
progress toward construction was necessary in order to prevent further damage to the credibility of their projects.
Therefore, as summer yielded to autumn, crews of the Illinois and St. Louis Bridge Company moved forward with
plans for construction in Illinois, while across the river, the
St. Louis and Illinois Bridge Company continued work on
the west abutment, using money provided by the bridge
company stockholders.

As the *Missouri Republican* reported on September 30, "work on the bridge at Washington Avenue is being prosecuted by the chief engineer of the company, Capt. Eads, with the same degree of energy that marked his operations when creating the iron-clad navy of the Mississippi."[1] In reality, Eads was so involved in arranging financing for the bridge and attending to his other business interests that he was seldom seen at the construction site. The work was instead carried out under the supervision of assistant engineer Benjamin R. Singleton.

A double row of piles was already in place to support a portion of a framework that, when erected, would measure about 100 feet by 90 feet and stand 50 or 60 feet above the surface of the river. The remainder of the framework would rest on the levee. This framework was designed to support eight travelers (a system of movable pulleys and swing arms) and other machinery required to move the huge blocks of stone forming the foundation of the abutment. The unusually large travelers, all specially designed by Eads, would lift the stones from barges anchored outside a large cofferdam built around the base of the pier and then lower them into position within the cofferdam as guided by the masons. Each traveler could be operated by one man, and each was powered by a twenty-horsepower steam engine. But there were a number of difficulties that had to be solved in construction of the cofferdam before the travelers and other equipment could even be erected.

The cofferdam was an elliptical curb of plate iron open at the top and bottom, braced on the inside with heavy angle irons. The sides of the cofferdam were formed of two courses of sheet piling, six feet apart, which were filled in-between with clay. It was imperative that the cofferdam be watertight in order for the masons to execute their duties without interruption.

A large crew of about 125 carpenters and laborers conducted the work of constructing the traveler framework and cofferdam. Singleton drove the crew hard in order to complete a substantial amount of the work before onset of the worst winter weather. It was anticipated at the start of the project that within eight or nine days the cofferdam would be far enough along that a wrecking boat could be brought up from Carondelet and its powerful pumps could begin the job of removing water from inside the cofferdam.

While crews labored at the foot of Washington Avenue, the contractor for the masonry of the bridge, James Andrews of Pittsburgh (recommended for the job by Scott), commenced operations at the stone quarries near Grafton, Illinois, just below the confluence of the Mississippi and Illinois Rivers. Limestone from these quarries initially provided most of the structure for the abutments and piers, which were going to be dressed out with granite above water.

The process of excavating the area within the confines of the cofferdam was proving to be much more difficult than expected, however, and the project was well behind schedule. The difficulty arose partly from continued, uncontrolled flooding of the cofferdam, and partly from the nature of the material embedded in the sand at that location. The site of the abutment had been a part of the steamboat wharf for over sixty years. As such it received every kind of useless material thrown overboard from the various steamers lying over it during that time. As Eads later informed the directors of the bridge company, old sheet iron that had enveloped steamboat furnaces, worn-out grate bars, fire bricks, parts of smokestacks, stone, coal cinders and clinker, "and every manner of things entering into the construction of a Mississippi steamer, seemed to have found a resting-place at this spot, and constituted a deposit averaging 12 feet in depth over the rock."[2]

There was a greater problem than the presence of loose debris, however. Considerable difficulties were encountered in cutting through and removing the wrecks of several steamers and barges that had sunk at the site, including some not removed by Eads after the Great Fire of 1849. The cofferdam constructed to enclose the area had to be driven down through the thick hulks of these wrecks, some of which had bottom planking of oak three to four inches thick. As Eads reported, "To drive the sheet piling down through these hulks, an oak beam, six by ten inches square, armed with a huge steel chisel, was first driven down as far as a steam piledriver could force it. It was then withdrawn and a sheet-pile, five by ten inches square, was driven down in its place."[3]

But despite the difficulty and delay of excavating and pumping out the area enclosed by the dam, by November 25 the job was substantially complete and the last of the excavating and lifting machinery erected. At about the same time the first of approximately fifty barge loads of stone to be transported to the site before the river froze were unloaded on the levee.[4]

On the other side of the river, the Illinois and St. Louis Bridge Company had also been at work, albeit without making much progress. A considerable amount of material had been delivered, and excavations begun, but the work was progressing slowly. East St. Louis police had made matters difficult by twice arresting Boomer's workmen, claiming that they had not secured the proper authority to occupy the riverbank.

With crews representing the Eads and Boomer organizations busily at work during the autumn of 1867, and representatives of the Alton and St. Charles County Bridge Company actively promoting their own plan, the outcome of the struggle to build the first bridge at St. Louis was much in doubt. But the Philadelphia interests bolstered Eads in his battle by making their support unequivocal. On October 29, 1867, Carnegie wrote Eads that he had just returned from a meeting with Thomson and Scott in Philadelphia, and he had no hesitation in stating two points. First was that Eads had the proper location, and second was that Eads and his associates "were *the* men of St. Louis to whom the Penn R. R. should adhere. I think you can safely rest in the opinion that these points are admitted by our Philad [*sic*] friends." Carnegie also wrote, "I can assure you that Messrs. Thomson & Scott recognize in you the person in St. Louis, of all others, they would like to operate with."[5]

Despite the commitment of the Philadelphia interests, however, it was becoming evident toward the end of the year that financial backing would not be forthcoming until all but one of the competing groups were forced to abandon their plans.

In an attempt to resolve what seemed to be an impasse, and in response to concerns being expressed on the streets of St. Louis and in the halls of the Merchants Exchange regarding control of the Illinois and St. Louis Bridge Company by men from Chicago, Boomer resigned his position as president and director of the company on November 25, 1867. Corydon Beckwith, the second-most suspect of all the members of the company's board of directors due to his questionable activities in securing passage of the Illinois charter, also resigned his position on that day. The places formerly held on the board by these two men were filled by J. R. Stanford and Daniel Gillespie, both of Illinois.[6]

Gillespie was one of the incorporators of the Alton and St. Charles County Bridge Company. Apparently, the men behind this organization had not completely abandoned their intentions to build a railroad-only bridge upriver across from Alton. The following month they succeeded, along with a few St. Louis partners, in forming the St. Louis and Madison County Bridge Company, the shadow organization necessary to do business in Missouri. But they never received the support of either the railroads or the public (who desired a combination bridge so that wagon and pedestrian traffic could be accommodated), and with so many of their investors also committed to the Boomer plan, they soon abandoned their efforts.

The directorship of the Illinois and St. Louis Bridge Company also began to better reflect the interests of St. Louis on November 25 by the election of St. Louis businessmen Daniel R. Garrison, Charles P. Chouteau, and James Harrison to the board.

Garrison, who was immediately elected president of the bridge company in place of Boomer, first came to St. Louis in 1835. He was hired as construction superintendent of the Pacific Railroad of Missouri in the late 1850s, and during the Civil War he became vice president and general manager of the company. He had played a crucial role in persuading the directors of the railroad to accept the contract that permitted Scott's White Line to rob the Pacific of potential revenue.[7] He had also been, along with Thomson, Scott, and Eads, an incorporator of the Atlantic and Pacific Railroad.[8]

Harrison was one of the directors of the Pacific Railroad who profited by turning a blind eye to Garrison's malfeasance. And in March 1868, less than four months after becoming a director of the bridge company, he and Chouteau became two of the incorporators of the newly created South Pacific Railroad Company (the old Southwest Pacific Railroad), having made a late bid in order that they might be bribed.[9]

For several weeks after the organizational shakeup, the two bridge companies fought a public-relations battle in the pages of the St. Louis newspapers. But the Eads group was clearly winning the battle for the hearts and minds of the St. Louis business establishment. No one, it seemed, could accept that Boomer, who still held a majority of stock in the Illinois and St. Louis Bridge Company, might have anything but evil intentions in regard to erection of a bridge at the doorstep of Chicago's greatest rival. Therefore, on January 6, 1868, the St. Louis Board of Trade adopted a resolution calling for the appointment of a ten-member committee to urge upon Congress the passage of additional legislation specifically authorizing the Eads-led company to build the bridge.

Having failed to convince St. Louis of its honorable intentions, the Boomer company responded by filing a writ of *quo warranto,* requiring representatives of the Eads company to appear before the St. Clair County Court in Illinois and prove the validity of their charter. Knowing that he had little chance of success in an Illinois court, Eads now placed all his hopes in the uncertain possibility of securing new legislation from Congress.

But through the intervention of friends they had in common, most particularly William A. Pile, a Missouri congressman, a late January meeting was set up in Washington, D.C., between Eads and Harrison. In fairly short order an agreement was reached whereby the two companies would consolidate, as allowed by the enabling legislation of both states and Congress. This may well have been what Boomer originally intended a year earlier when he induced Krum and Cutter to leave Springfield, and then had a bill introduced authorizing the organization of the Illinois and St. Louis Bridge Company with him as the head.

Harrison and Eads returned to St. Louis together to submit the agreement to their respective companies.[10] There were many fine points still to be negotiated, and it wasn't until March 5, 1868, that both parties signed the agreement. An act authorizing the consolidation was presented to the General Assembly of Missouri and approved March 19. As required by this act the Articles of Consolidation were redrawn and signed by the directors of both companies. This second document is dated April 4, 1868.[11]

The terms of the agreement dictated that the consolidated company would thereafter be known as the Illinois and St. Louis Bridge Company, and that all the corporate powers, franchises, and property belonging to either party were to be transferred to the consolidated company. The first board of directors of the consolidated company would be Dickson, Taussig, Allen, McPherson, Bates, and John Lionberger, all from the Eads company; and Garrison, Harrison, William Morrison, Beckwith, Tansey, and Robert M. Renick from the Boomer company. The new directorship would decide details regarding the type of bridge to be built, and anyone who did not agree with the decision would have his shares bought out by the company.

It seemed that both sides were evenly represented. But Eads, whose skill at chess was so great that he could play several distant opponents at once, keeping all the games in his head, proved to have the better endgame. He won election as chief engineer and his plans were approved. Most of the former members of the Boomer organization therefore decided to sell out. Despite having had the stronger legal position, Boomer was out maneuvered. After being reimbursed for his expenses to date, he left town.

With Boomer no longer a contender, there seemed to be no reason for the Eads faction to press forward with their plans to ask Congress for additional authority to construct the bridge. But for some reason—perhaps to ward off future attempts by competitors—the directors of the consolidated company continued to request specific authorization for the new company.

By act of Congress approved July 20, 1868, the consolidation of the two companies was sanctioned and the privileges conveyed by the legislation approved July 25, 1866, were granted the new company, with one addition. The steamboat interests made certain that the new act required one span of at least five hundred feet clear between the piers. Now there was no choice in regard to length of the main channel span. Eads, both in his actions as head of the committee appointed by the St. Louis Chamber of Commerce in 1866, and by his pursuit of new legislation in 1868, had saddled his company with a requirement that no other bridge company in the country had to meet. Nonetheless, the company could now proceed with the business at hand.

The consolidation had encouraged Eads to request from the Missouri legislature a law granting the citizens of St. Louis the right to vote on a proposition for the city to guarantee $4 million in bonds for the bridge company. Despite opposition from the ferry companies and friends of the defunct Boomer organization, the law was passed on March 24. The subsequent election resulted in a decisive victory for the bridge company, but after due deliberation the board of directors wisely dropped the plan.[12]

The fact that men susceptible to bribery and prone to chicanery were in control of the city government was acceptable to the bridge company as long as those men saw things the company's way. But their loyalty, and their longevity in office, was far from certain. It therefore seemed prudent to the board members to find private sources of financing, rather than surrender any measure of control to men they could not trust.

The prospects seemed bright for obtaining that funding because Boomer, the most serious threat to the Eads group, had been chased out of town. As for the backers of the Alton and St. Charles County Bridge Company, they had managed during the previous December to obtain a Missouri charter for a complementary organization, the St. Louis and Madison County Bridge Company. But that was their last hurrah. The community did not support a railroad-only bridge, and there had been insufficient interest in the plan from the railroads. This group no longer represented a viable alternative to the Illinois and St. Louis Bridge Company.

With opposition neutralized, at least for the time being, there were three distinct things that had to occur for the consolidated bridge company to succeed as a profit-making venture. If any one of the three did not come about, the bridge would be a failure. First, the company had to construct, expeditiously and economically, not only the bridge but also the tunnel that would link the bridge to western railroads. Without the tunnel, the bridge was virtually useless. Second, passenger and freight terminal facilities, along with a system of tracks connecting the bridge to these facilities, would have to be constructed. If these facilities and tracks were not built by the railroads, then they would have to be built by those men who were behind the bridge company. And third, the railroads terminating in St. Louis and East St. Louis had to commit to use of the bridge and tunnel when completed.

In terms of the first task, Eads had already made some progress in construction of the west abutment. Despite delays caused by flooding of the cofferdam and the difficulty of cutting through numerous wrecks and other material, the first stone of the foundation was laid on bedrock fifty-five feet below the high-water mark on February 25, 1868. Approximately 1,040 cubic yards of stone were laid by March 15, but at this point the seasonal rising of the river, coupled with the failure of the company to increase stock subscriptions, brought active work to a halt.

In an effort to allay the fears and doubts of potential investors, Eads published a comprehensive report of his plans on June 1, 1868, justifying in detail his decisions and forcefully addressing doubts that had arisen in the minds of many. Although the report generally exhibited Eads's remarkable capacity for presenting his ideas in a way that seemed rational and irrefutable, it fell short in several respects.

First, Eads offered a very reasoned argument for placement of the bridge at the foot of Washington Avenue. Of course, he wasn't about to admit that the original authorizing legislation had stipulated that location as a way of killing the project. Having already begun construction at that point, he had no choice but to defend it as the best of all possible places to build a bridge.

He stated, as though it were a positive thing, that a bridge at Washington Avenue would nearly equally divide the wharf, thus making it "unnecessary" for the steamboats traveling on the upper rivers to pass under the bridge. And those boats engaged in trade on the Ohio River or other lower rivers would seldom be required to pass above it.

This was particularly fortuitous, given Eads's stunning acknowledgment of a fact that had long been recognized by opponents of the bridge. He admitted, "It is idle to talk of bridging the river, and planting piers in its channel, without obstructing navigation. No matter how wide the spans may be, every pier that is placed in the river is an obstruction, calculated to create danger, and cause anxiety to those who navigate it."[13]

In this one small part of the report, the man who had led the efforts of the Merchants Exchange in 1866 to impose tough requirements for Mississippi River bridges, in order that they not obstruct navigation, was now admitting that he was going to build an obstruction that would divide the river in two.

Another part of the report touched on the depot issue. It had long been assumed by just about everyone who had contemplated a bridge at St. Louis that a union depot, available to all railroads entering St. Louis and serving both freight and passenger traffic, would have to be constructed as a corollary to erection of a bridge. But in Eads's report he claimed that two depots had to be built: one for freight in East St. Louis where land was cheaper; the other for passengers at the terminus of the tunnel in the drained bed of Chouteau's Pond. "Of course," he continued, "the establishment of these two union depots for freight and passengers will not prevent the several roads from having such other depots as they may find useful."[14]

The difficulties of such a chaotic system apparently didn't occur to Eads. He also failed to grasp that since the bridge company did not intend to build these union depots, and the railroads could maintain whatever individual depots they wished and thus avoid the cost of constructing the union depots, there was little likelihood that such depots would be built.

Another statement in Eads's report that should have indicated future problems is contained in the section on anticipated revenue, where he compounded the mistake made by Truman Homer nearly two and one-half years earlier. Homer made his estimate of annual revenue by simply calculating toll charges at a conservative three-fifths of the fare then collected by the ferries.[15] Obviously, if you attempt to take away three-fifths of a company's revenue, and that company is one of the wealthiest and most politically connected in the city, then you are likely to have a nasty fight on your hands.

But Eads went Homer one better. He simply counted up *all* the railroad freight and tonnage forwarded to and from St. Louis in the previous year, added all the other potential toll-paying traffic crossing the bridge, from rail and foot passengers to pleasure carriages, and assumed that it would all end up in the coffers of the bridge company.[16] No doubt he was smart enough to realize that the Wiggins Ferry Company and the various transfer companies might take exception to his seduction of their business. What he did not guess was that the erection of a bridge would not necessarily constitute a fatal blow to these companies; that they might be able to respond in some manner that allowed them to stay in business and compete with the bridge for traffic.

Shortly after the bridge company published the report, Eads went to New York in an attempt to secure financial backing for the project. While there, as he later wrote his friend Gideon Welles on June 29, "I contracted a severe cold which has so fastened itself on my lungs that my Dr. advises me to go abroad for a few months or a year, and I have nearly made up my mind to do so. If I go I shall depart about the last of July."[17]

At this point, Eads was able to spend no more three hours a day in his office, and he could only do a little writing. The many years spent working on and under the muddy waters of the Mississippi River, combined with the stress of battling Boomer while also attempting to arrange financing for the bridge, had finally caught up with him.

His doctor, like many men of intellect in America at that time, believed that the old world was somehow more healthy than the new. This notion, which went back at least as far as the writings of the French naturalist Georges Louis Leclerc, comte de Buffon (1707–88), often led those who could afford the expense to go to Europe in hopes of improving their health.

Despite his responsibilities to the bridge project and a number of other business ventures in which he was involved, Eads decided to resign as chief engineer of the bridge company and quit the project within a few days of writing Welles. Although the board of directors refused to accept Eads's resignation, it acknowledged his need for a leave of absence and allowed him to appoint an associate engineer to run things until he could return. In an attempt to find a replacement, Eads wrote to Octave Chanute and asked him to take over the project. But Chanute was busy with the Kansas City Bridge and wrote Eads that he could not accept additional responsibilities.

Probably at the urging of Thomson and Scott, Eads next contacted W. Milnor Roberts, an engineer known for his survey of the Cumberland Railroad in the early 1830s and for numerous other internal improvement projects in Pennsylvania.[18] Roberts agreed to take over as chief engineer, even though he was then engaged in work that would keep him from moving to St. Louis until October.

On July 22, 1868, Eads departed New York for Liverpool, not knowing when he could return. As Henry Flad observed, with the originator and guiding light of the project gone, "all the life of the company seemed to go out."[19] Flad measured a baseline on the eastern shore of the river and made the necessary triangulations for accurate placement of the river piers, but little else was accomplished. On September 1, the company discharged all employees, except for Flad, assistant engineer Pfeifer, and two other men.

When Roberts arrived in October he suggested to Flad that an estimate be made of the cost to raise the west abutment to a height of twelve feet above low water. The figure arrived at was $40,000. James Andrews agreed to perform the job for an immediate payment of $25,000. Some of the bridge company directors, wishing to see the abutment constructed high enough to prevent damage from ice during the coming winter, managed to raise the money and work resumed on October 28.[20]

The delay caused by Eads's departure must have been of considerable concern to the Philadelphia interests, but they could do little regarding the situation in St. Louis until Eads regained his health, if ever, and returned to work. The bridge at St. Louis, however, was just one of many in which they had an interest, and long before departure of the chief engineer steps had been taken to pursue other opportunities.

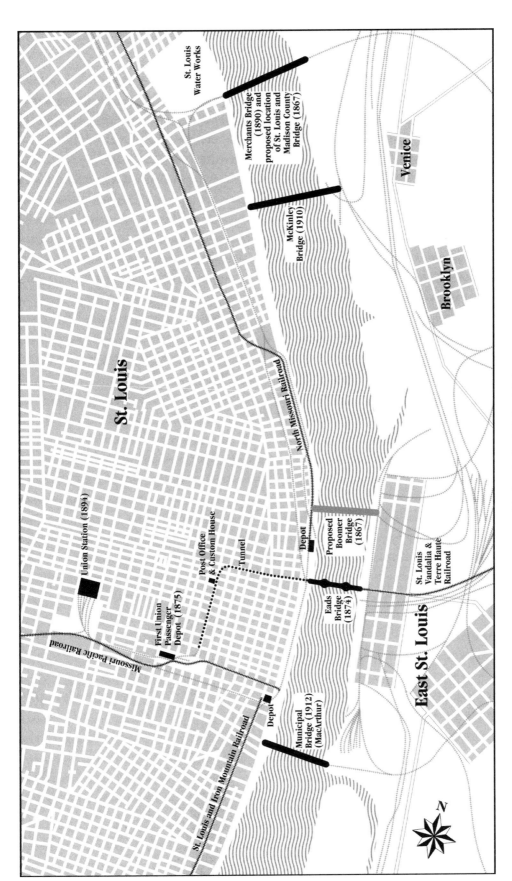

Map of St. Louis, by Michael Arbore

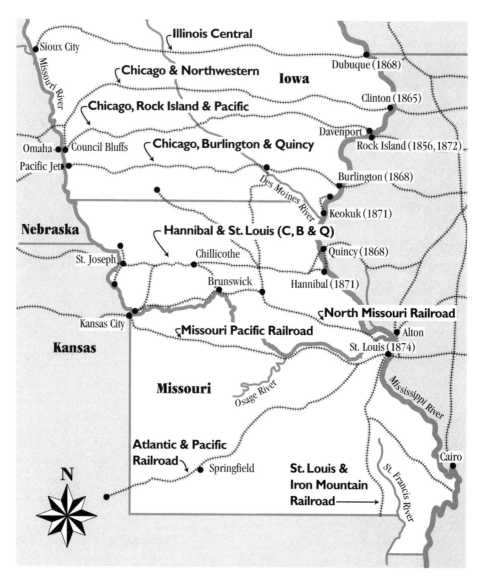

Railroads and bridges, ca. 1870s. Dates in parentheses indicate when Mississippi River was bridged. Map by Michael Arbore.

James B. Eads (C. M. Woodward, *A History of the St. Louis
Bridge* [St. Louis: G. I. Jones,
1881]. Unless noted otherwise, all illustrations are
from this source.)

William Taussig (William
Hyde and Howard L. Con-
rad, eds., *Encyclopedia of the
History of St. Louis,* 4 vols.
[New York: Southern History
Company, 1899].)

Andrew Carnegie (Carnegie Library of Pittsburgh)

J. Edgar Thomson (John Edgar Thomson Foundation)

Thomas A. Scott (From *Addresses delivered at the Unveiling of the Portrait of Colonel Thomas Alexander Scott,* Library and Archives Division, Historical Society of Western Pennsylvania, Pittsburgh, Pa.; used with permission.)

Lucius B. Boomer (Chicago Historical Society, ICHi 28455)

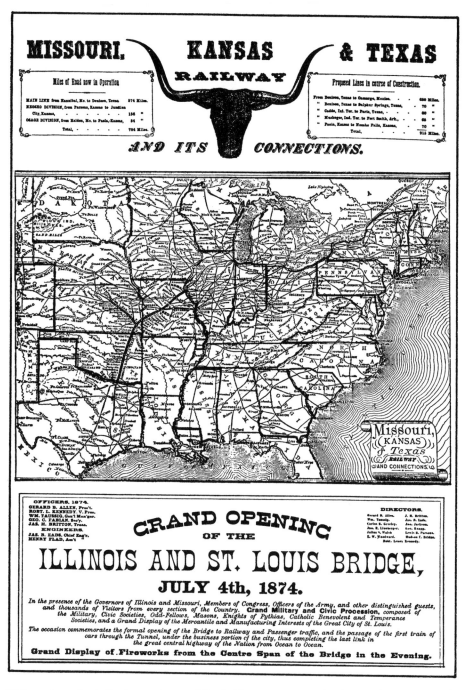

This poster reflects the importance of the bridge as a gateway in the southwestern trade corridor. (From V. V. Masterson, *The Katy Railroad and the Last Frontier* [Norman: University of Oklahoma Press, 1952; used with permission.)

6

The Center of the World

We are in the center of the world; with one hand stretched out on Europe, the other on Asia, we will control the interchange of their commerce, and the business will pass this way. St. Louis will be the great central depot between New York and San Francisco.

—Committee on River and Its Navigation, Convention of Engineers, 1867

The banks of the major western rivers defined lines of commerce during the steamboat era. That is why the geographic location of St. Louis had long conferred upon that city a position of strategic importance in regard to the trade of the Middle West, a position some accepted almost as a divine right. Engineers began to change all that, first by the construction of canals, and later by the construction of railroads and bridges. Technology would create new corridors of trade in the latter part of the nineteenth century, and St. Louis, if it hesitated in embracing new technology, was likely to become just one among many points on the map. Men like Thomson, Scott, and Carnegie understood this reality and made plans accordingly.

Three of the new bridges approved by Congress for erection across the Mississippi River, and one across the Missouri River, were already under construction when Eads left for Europe. Keystone was one of thirteen bridge companies that bid on the superstructure contract for the Chicago, Burlington and Quincy Railroad Bridge at Quincy, Illinois, on March 1, 1867. It lost the contract for that bridge, and for a very similar Chicago, Burlington and Quincy Railroad Bridge then being built about eighty miles north of Quincy at Burlington, Iowa, to the Detroit Bridge and Iron Works. Keystone had been successful, however, in beating out four contenders on October 30, 1867, for the contract to erect the superstructure of the bridge at Kansas City.

Two of the six congressionally authorized Mississippi River bridges not yet under construction were not likely to be erected anytime in the near future. These were the bridges at Winona, Minnesota, and Prairie du Chien, Wisconsin.[1] But the corporations behind creation of the remaining four, located at Dubuque, Iowa; Hannibal, Missouri; Keokuk, Iowa; and St. Louis, could all be expected to let contracts in 1868, with Dubuque being the first of that group. In addition, the two poorly built, mainly wood-truss Rock Island and Clinton bridges would probably have to be rebuilt in the near future using iron trusses.

Early in January 1868, Carnegie traveled to Dubuque, Iowa, with Keystone Bridge Company engineer Walter Katté. He made the mid-winter journey because he believed that his personal attention was crucial to the success of Keystone's efforts to win the construction contract for the Dubuque Bridge.[2]

Erecting the trusses of the structure, which Carnegie later characterized as "the most important railway bridge that had been built up to that time," would help establish Keystone as the leading builder of long-span iron railroad bridges across the major Western rivers. The company would then be in an excellent position to obtain contracts for the Mississippi River bridges for which contracts had not been let, as well as contracts for the numerous bridges across lesser waterways that would have to be built with further expansion of the nation's rail network.

But the construction contracts for these bridges represented only the tip of the financial iceberg that lay beneath the surface of the Keystone operation. Carnegie, along with his partners Thomson and Scott, also expected to profit from the sale of iron provided by the Union Iron Mills to the Keystone Bridge Company; from the sale of iron rails to the railroads using those bridges; from ownership of stock in many of those railroads; from ownership of stock in the construction companies that built the railroads; and from commissions on the sale of bonds used to finance both the bridge companies and the railroads.[3]

After arriving at the terminus of the Illinois Central Railroad line in Dunleith, Illinois, Carnegie and Katté crossed the frozen Mississippi in a sleigh drawn by four horses. Upon arriving in Dubuque, they found that the Dunleith and Dubuque Bridge Company had already decided to award the construction contract to the low bidder, Lucius B. Boomer. But Carnegie was not about to let such an important opportunity slip through his hands. He went to work on the bridge company directors, finding them to be "delightfully ignorant of the merits of cast- and wrought-iron. We had always made the upper chord of the bridge of the latter, while our rivals' were made of cast iron. This furnished my text."[4]

Picturing for these men the result of a steamboat striking against a bridge made entirely of cast iron, as opposed to one of cast and wrought-iron, he claimed that, "in the case of the wrought-iron chord it would probably only bend; in the case of the cast-iron it would certainly break and down would come the bridge." At this moment Platt Smith, a man known for his hardheaded practical approach to the problems of building the Iowa railroads that would benefit from existence of the bridge, reinforced Carnegie's argument. He told the board that on a recent cold night he had run his buggy against a cast-iron lamppost, which shattered into pieces.[5] Seizing the moment, Carnegie exclaimed, "Ah, gentlemen, there is the point. A little more money and you could have had the indestructible wrought-iron and your bridge would stand against any steamboat. We never have built and we never will build a cheap bridge. Ours don't fall."

In this, Carnegie was quite correct. Linville had designed a type of truss that proved to be far superior, both in terms of design and materials, to the patented Post truss used by Boomer. Linville-designed bridges remained standing throughout their projected economic life, and sometimes beyond, while many others did not.

The directors, however, proved to be just as shrewd as Carnegie. After a pause, the president of the bridge company, Congressman William Boyd Allison, asked if Carnegie would excuse the board for a few moments. Soon they recalled him and offered the contract, provided that Keystone take it for the lower price bid by Boomer. In so doing, they were being a bit disingenuous.

Boomer's company was somewhat unusual at this time in that it had the capability of erecting both the substructure (piers and foundations) and the superstructure of long-span railway bridges. Most competing bridge-building companies, such as Keystone, erected only the superstructures, leaving substructure construction to firms that specialized in that type of work. Apparently Boomer had learned from the example of the Rock Island Bridge and no longer wished to rest the superstructures built by his company on the poorly constructed foundations built by others. Therefore, the directors of the Dunleith and Dubuque Bridge Company were not comparing similar proposals. Nonetheless, Carnegie agreed to their conditions and when the bids were formally opened on January 13, Keystone was awarded the contract for the superstructure. The substructure contract went to Reynolds, Saulpaugh and Company, and Boomer was thus shut out once again.

Flush with his success in securing the Dubuque contract, Carnegie returned to Pittsburgh and composed a letter to the president and directors of the Keystone Bridge Company. Dated January 25, 1868, the letter begged his associates to consider that "the success of Iron Bridging has attracted the attention of several parties who are anxious for an opportunity to embark on it. Among those may be mentioned Reeves, Jones, Boomer & c—all of whom are trying to secure an important work upon which to found [a] reputation." Should Keystone be unable to compete with these companies due to a lack of plant capacity, they would be given an opportunity that could result only in permanent damage to the fortunes of Keystone. As Carnegie noted, "There is only one way of defeating these parties & that is to place ourselves in position to bid for & construct the Iron Bridging already concluded upon & certain to be built by somebody."[6]

Carnegie continued, stating that the cost of creating reserve machine and blacksmith shop capacity, beyond that required for the work then under contract, would be the most valuable investment the company could make. Citing numerous bridge contracts likely to come up for bids in the near future, including those for the Union Pacific Railroad Bridge at Omaha and the replacement bridge at Rock Island, he warned that unless action was taken promptly the firm would be unable to bid on these jobs. "I for one am not willing any longer to shoulder the responsibility of neglecting to act in this matter," he wrote.[7]

Without meaning to criticize those who were then managing the company (meaning Linville, Piper, Shiffler, and his own brother Thomas, who was treasurer of the company), Carnegie insisted that their views regarding the future of "iron bridging" were far too narrow. "They fail to see that it is only in its infancy in this country." He therefore urged an expansion of plant facilities by construction of a larger blacksmith shop, the purchase of new machinery for the machine shop, the acquisition of land across the Allegheny River for a new foundry and additional fitting shops, and a change in plant personnel. He also decided to send Katté to Chicago to open up a western branch office of Keystone on Dearborn Street, virtually on Boomer's doorstep.[8]

While the officers of Keystone began formulating plans in response to Carnegie's proposal, Reynolds, Saulpaugh and Company began construction of the Dubuque Bridge foundations. Work progressed so rapidly that by March 1868 Keystone was ready to begin erection of the superstructure. In the same month, Keystone began erecting the first span of the bridge at Kansas City. It was Carnegie's intention that the design of the Dubuque, Kansas City, Keokuk, and Hannibal bridges; the materials they were made from; and the business arrangements made for associated enterprises, such as railroads, depots, and construction companies, be as similar as possible in the interest of efficiency and maximization of profit.

Whether or not the same principle could be applied in relation to the St. Louis Bridge remained to be seen. Carnegie could win the contract for superstructure construction at that location, and all the associated contracts and commissions that went with it, only if the Eads faction succeeded in securing financing. But with Eads out of the country, matters in St. Louis were moving at a snail's pace. Carnegie had no choice, therefore, but to concentrate on other opportunities.

On October 1, 1868, Carnegie wrote Linville a letter concerning the status of the Kansas City and Dubuque jobs that also revealed his concern about the state of affairs in St. Louis. "St. Louis Br. & other matters are up & we don't stand exactly where we should with these." He added, "I trust you have Rock Island Br. matters in credible shape."[9]

Congress had determined that the old Rock Island Bridge was a serious and unnecessary obstruction to navigation. Therefore, on June 27, 1866, it authorized the reestablishment of an arsenal on Rock Island and approved the preliminary steps necessary for construction of a new bridge under the supervision of the Ordnance Corps, with the cost to be split (though not necessarily on an equal basis) between the federal government and the Chicago, Rock Island and Pacific Railroad.

After a long delay, the government and the railroad finally signed an agreement early in September 1868, and on September 10 the chief of ordnance requested authority to begin construction and to employ a competent civil engineer to aid in the work. Carnegie showed his usual initiative by sending a letter on October 28 to General T. J. Rodman, commanding officer of the Rock Island Arsenal, recommending Linville for the job of consultant. Mentioning that Linville had just been appointed to design a railroad and wagon bridge across the Ohio River at Cincinnati, Ohio, Carnegie called him "the most eminent engineer in the profession."[10]

Carnegie was anxious to secure a contract for the new Rock Island Bridge as another foothold for his participation in Iowa railroads. The Philadelphia interests already had a variety of other long-standing business involvements in the Davenport area, including Thomas Scott's participation as incorporator of the Davenport City Railway in 1867.

On the day after Carnegie sent his letter to General Rodman, he also sent a personal letter to Thomson suggesting that Thomson have Linville look at plans and specifications and prepare an estimate for bid. Thomson should then deduct an amount from these figures that reflected the full cost of transporting construction material, assuming that the railroads would agree to carry such material free or at cost. "Ascertaining what the actual cost to us would be," he wrote, "we could then make the Bridge parties a proposition to furnish the superstructure taking their Stock."[11]

This suggestion reflects an approach that became increasingly popular with Carnegie, Scott, and Thomson, whereby they acquired a personal financial interest in a promising corporate enterprise in exchange for the labor, materials, and technological and managerial expertise supplied by companies, such as Keystone, that they controlled. This practice helps explain why Carnegie said late in his life that the Keystone Bridge Company, although never as profitable as some of his other enterprises, had "always been my pet as being the parent of all the other works."[12]

Despite all his efforts, as the end of the year approached it became clear that there was little chance of Keystone's winning the contract for construction of the new Rock Island Bridge. But Carnegie could rejoice in having snatched one other prize away from his competitors.

On December 10, 1868, the Keokuk and Hamilton Bridge Company finalized an agreement with Keystone that called for construction of a combination railroad and wagon bridge of eleven spans, including a pivot span with two openings each 160 feet in the clear. The total length would be slightly in excess of 2,000 feet. All of the trusses were to be of the Linville and Piper patent wrought-iron design, and the entire bridge was to be completed and ready for use on January 1, 1870. The contract price was $800,000, exclusive of land damages, and "the Materials, workmanship and general plan [are] to be similar to the Bridge erected at Dubuque and guaranteed first class in every respect."[13] In addition, Keystone was to act as general contractor, meaning that it would hire the subcontractor for the foundation work.

Eighteen days after Keystone won the Keokuk contract, the first train passed over the newly completed Dubuque Bridge. Finished one month ahead of schedule, the approximately 1,760-foot-long bridge cost slightly more than $800,000, not counting the cost of approaches. Keystone had used the knowledge gained in erecting the superstructure of the Dubuque Bridge to estimate the bid price of the slightly longer but similar Keokuk Bridge.

Thomson wrote the prospectus of the Keokuk and Hamilton Bridge Company shortly after the company signed the contract with Keystone. Thomson, Scott, and Carnegie took stock and bonds in the bridge company as payment for the Keystone contract, and by December 17 Thomson had already disposed of about half of the bonds at a profit.[14] Carnegie, for his part, using the contract between the Dunleith and Dubuque Bridge Company and the connecting railroads as his guide, wrote a contract between the Keokuk and Hamilton Bridge Company and the railroads planning to use the bridge.[15] The three partners probably assumed that the methodology employed in this case would work equally well in St. Louis, once the bridge there was actually under construction.

Despite continued ill health, Eads tried to do what he could to move the project along by briefly returning to New York in December. He found that publication of his report to the president and directors of the bridge company had been well received by the capitalists of that city. But after about a month of making the rounds of railroad and banking offices with those officers of the bridge company who went there to assist him, his poor physical condition forced him to return to England.[16]

About the same time that Eads again left the country, on January 18, 1869, the St. Louis foundry of Chouteau, Harrison, and Valle received an order to begin immediately the shipment of the first truss spans for the Union Pacific Railroad Bridge at Omaha, Nebraska.[17] The bridge was the largest planned for erection across the Missouri River, and Carnegie had hoped to win the construction contract for Keystone. But the order had been placed by the man Carnegie beat out in Dubuque, Lucius Boomer. The eleven-span Omaha Bridge would mark the greatest utilization of the iron Post truss in any railroad bridge ever constructed, and the greatest employment of Boomer's special method of concrete and iron pier construction.

Carnegie had little time to worry about having lost the Omaha contract. On January 19, 1869, the day after Boomer placed his order, a new contract was signed between the Keokuk and Hamilton Bridge Company and the Toledo, Peoria and Warsaw Railway Company; the Des Moines Valley Railroad Company; and the Columbus, Chicago and Indiana Central Railway Company, stipulating the terms, conditions, and rate schedules under which the bridge would accommodate the traffic of the various railroads.

After the original contract had been drawn up, but before it was executed, the Indiana Central Company entered into an indenture with the Pennsylvania Railroad and its subsidiary, the Pittsburgh, Cincinnati and St. Louis Railway Company, by which it leased its franchises and road to the latter company for ninety-nine years. The thirteenth and the sixteenth articles of the lease manifest that one of the main purposes of the agreement was to establish a continuous line for quick transportation from Pennsylvania to the West, and to procure freight and passengers at each end of the line. They also contained special provisions calling for action by the Pennsylvania Railroad Company to promote that object. The Pennsylvania guaranteed the performance of all the covenants of the Pittsburgh railroad as lessee. Thomson took this action without any formal approval of the directors or stockholders of the Pennsylvania Railroad Company.[18]

Thomson made various changes to the bridge company prospectus in January and February before the bridge company stockholders were ready to sign the bridge use contract on February 6, 1869. Three days later, the bridge company president, H. T. Reid, directed Carnegie to begin work on the bridge. On February 16, the Pittsburgh, Cincinnati and St. Louis Railway Company formally joined in the bridge use agreement. A second amendment, adjusting the financial arrangements and dealing with the takeover of the ferry company operating at Keokuk, would be added on November 25, 1871.[19]

The manner in which the Keokuk Bridge fit into Thomson, Scott, and Carnegie's dreams of a transcontinental railroad empire is revealed by Thomson's "Annual Report to the Stockholders of the Pennsylvania Railroad," dated February 10, 1869. Thomson noted that the rapid progress made by the Union and Central Pacific Companies indicated the completion of a railway across the continent during the ensuing summer. Following its completion, the Pennsylvania Railroad and its immediate western connections would "present the shortest line to and from the great cities of the Atlantic seaboard, either by way of Chicago, St. Louis, or by an intermediate route in progress from Keokuk west, connecting with the Union Pacific Road near Ft. Kearny." That advantage would secure to the railroad "at least a fair and reasonable share of the large traffic that will be carried between the Atlantic and Pacific States."[20]

The implications of this document for future success of the bridge at St. Louis may not have been obvious but were profound. Thomson was essentially saying that it should matter little to the stockholders of the Pennsylvania Railroad whether transcontinental connections across the Mississippi River were provided by a bridge at St. Louis or elsewhere, since the railroad (thanks to Thomson, Scott, and Carnegie) had interests in several different bridges. The railroad would profit regardless of the route taken, and so would Thomson, Scott, and Carnegie since they stood to gain financially merely by construction of the connections.

In the year prior to release of this report, however, the Philadelphia interests still had hopes that the bridge at St. Louis would soon be built, despite the problems caused by Eads's ill health.

The directors of the Illinois and St. Louis Bridge Company, for their part, were attempting to move the project forward. Whatever salubrious effect Eads's brief visit to the country may have had on the spirits of his friends, his rapid return to Europe fostered a growing realization by the board that it was not prudent to let the situation simmer until Eads could resume his duties. As McPherson wrote Eads in New York on January 12, 1869, "we must get the bridge going this year or I fear St. Louis will dry up with the Bridges north of us spanning the river every few miles."[21]

Taussig therefore drew up a prospectus and McPherson created a financial plan that was adopted in order for the piers to be built to a point above low water, without which the bonds of the company were probably unnegotiable. The capital stock of the company was to be increased to $4 million, and subscriptions were to increase to $3 million, 40 percent of which was to be in cash as required. It was assumed that this would yield $1.2 million in available funds for construction of the bridge foundations. It was also assumed that this would be enough to negotiate $4 million in 7 percent, first mortgage gold bonds. Sold at a 10 percent discount, these bonds would provide $3.6 million, which, when combined with the $1.2 million from subscriptions, would be enough to complete the bridge. The directors believed that about two-fifths of the subscriptions could be raised in St. Louis, and the rest could be raised in New York.

In February 1869, McPherson and Amos Cotting, of the New York firm of Jameson, Smith and Cotting, were able to sell $1.8 million in subscriptions in New York, and upon his return to St. Louis McPherson sold the remaining $1.2 million in just two days. The subscription books were then closed. With this injection of funds, the directors resolved on March 22 to push construction of the bridge ahead.[22]

The reaction of the Philadelphia interests to the availability of funds may be judged by a memorandum prepared by Carnegie for Thomson and Scott. The officers of Keystone had informed Carnegie that they would agree to manufacture, raise, and paint the bridge at 10 percent above their cost. Carnegie then proposed, "Suppose we [meaning Carnegie, Thomson, and Scott] offer to furnish superstructure for Twenty per cent above cost and contract with Keystone Co at ten."[23] In other words, Carnegie, Thomson, and Scott would charge the Illinois and St. Louis Bridge Company what it cost the Keystone Company to manufacture, erect, and finish the bridge, plus 20 percent. They would then pay Keystone that company's cost plus 10 percent, keeping the remainder as their fee for arranging the contract.

This portion of the memo again illustrates why Keystone was of such great importance to Carnegie, Scott, and Thomson. Because Carnegie was the majority shareholder in the Union Iron Mills, he received the majority of profit on the sale of iron to Keystone. Thomson also owned shares in the company, and Scott probably had a silent interest. Then, as shareholders in Keystone, the three men received part of the profit from any contracts awarded to that company. And by serving as agents for the Keystone contract, Carnegie, Thomson, and Scott also profited by remitting back to Keystone less than what they charged for the work performed.

The next part of the memo reveals other aspects of the deal contemplated by Carnegie. He noted that the bridge company had already issued $3 million in stock, against which it intended to call in 40 percent as a cash payment from the stockholders. Its charter gave it the right to issue another $1 million in stock. Forty percent of the additional issue would equal approximately $400,000 in cash. The bridge company could pay Carnegie and his associates by issuing them $1 million in stock, worth $400,000 in cash. Since this is about equal to what Carnegie estimated that he, Scott, and Thomson could expect in profit from the Keystone contract, the stock would end up costing them virtually nothing.[24] Comparison of this document with that prepared for the Keokuk Bridge reveals how consistent were the schemes of the three men from Philadelphia.

In the letter that McPherson wrote to Eads on January 12, right before Eads returned to Europe, McPherson revealed his suspicions concerning the plans of Carnegie and his associates. He informed Eads that the bridge company board of directors had "a free discussion of matters" and had determined to raise the necessary funds in St. Louis and New York. If successful, "we could then sell our bonds without their [Carnegie and associates] endorsement and make the money for our stockholders. If we take all the risk there is no reason that they shall have all the cream." McPherson also made it clear to Eads that he preferred "the Pennsylvania parties for partners on any equitable basis to anybody else as they are people I like to work with, but I confess that I think they want to cut it a little fat."[25]

This caution regarding the intentions of Carnegie, Scott, and Thomson partially explains why negotiations between the two parties lagged during 1869. The absence of Eads was also a factor, even though the board did its best to arrange financing to sink the piers without waiting for his return.

Unbeknownst to the directors, however, Eads had acquired new information from European engineers that would cause him to revise extensively his plans for sinking the piers. Adoption of the revisions would undo much of the design work performed by the assistant engineers in Eads's absence and would significantly increase both the costs of the bridge and the time it took to build it. And time was the enemy of the enterprise.

7

The Great Bugbear

It was determined to prepare for sinking both river piers at once by the use of compressed air. The one to be begun first was the East Pier, the larger and deeper of the two. Mr. Eads justified this step on the ground that the great bugbear to all parties who might wish to take the first mortgage bonds was this East Pier, which involved engineering difficulties not yet successfully met.

—C. M. Woodward, *A History of the St. Louis Bridge,* 1881

While in Europe, Eads traveled to France to speak with some engineers about the possibility of obtaining steel from foundries in that country. Before returning to England he was invited to observe the use of pneumatic caissons in construction of subaqueous piers for a bridge across the Allier River in Vichy. The process had long been used in France, where the word *caisson* referred to a *caisse de plongeur,* or "diving box." The resident engineer at Vichy, a man named Audernt, had been constructing foundations by use of the plenum pneumatic method for fourteen years and had sunk approximately forty piers by that process.[1]

In England a pneumatic caisson had been used as early as 1851 to sink a bridge foundation for piers in the Medway River at Rochester.[2] In 1858, Isambard Kingdom Brunel used a fairly large pneumatic caisson, subdivided into compartments, to sink founda-tions for the Royal Albert Bridge across the Tamar River at Saltash, in southeast-ern England. Taken down eighty to ninety feet below the surface of the water, with great difficulty and risk, the caisson had been successfully employed.

The board of civil engineers convened by Boomer in 1867 was knowledgeable concerning European use of inverted pneumatic caissons and had recommended their use as one option for sinking the piers of a bridge at St. Louis while rejecting the use of cofferdams as unduly expensive and hazardous.[3] Eads, however, intend-ed to use cofferdams, also called open or direct caissons, in founding the river piers of the St. Louis Bridge.

In England Eads spoke with several bridge engineers regarding the use of steel for superstructures and the use of inverted pneumatic caissons for sinking piers. An engineer named Brereton, who had worked on the Royal Albert Bridge under Brunel, was particularly helpful.[4] By the time Eads returned to St. Louis in April 1869, he had determined to abandon the use of cofferdams and to use pneumatic caissons instead.

The assistant engineers of the bridge company quickly set to work making new drawings, preparing new estimates of cost, and remodeling the floating machin-ery to be used in sinking the piers. Since March a barge had been anchored over the site of the east pier and measurements had been taken to determine just how far down bedrock could be found. The measurements confirmed previous esti-mates that the east pier would have to descend more than 120 feet below the city directrix, the curbstone on the wharf between Market and Walnut Streets that marked the high-water mark of 1826.[5] Given the size of the piers and the depth to which they would have to be sunk, caissons of an unprecedented size and strength would be required.

As Eads explained in a letter to an old friend, Rear Admiral John A. Dahlgren, written on July 18, 1869, the sinking of these two massive masonry piers, "of greater magnitude than any others of which I have knowledge," would require the use of the largest caissons ever constructed. The air chamber inside the caissons would be about nine feet high and divided into three compartments, each connected by a permanent opening. The caissons would be composed of oak timbers, with riv-eted plate iron covering the entire outer surface. When properly caulked, each caisson would be air- and watertight. Pumps would force compressed air into the chambers at a pressure great enough to keep water out. The deeper the caisson descended underneath the surface, the greater the pressure of water trying to force its way into the air chamber, and thus the greater the air pressure required within the chamber to keep water from seeping in. Air locks to admit workmen and materials into the air chambers would be placed *in* the air chamber, not on top of large iron access tubes extending up through the pier, as practiced in Europe. Eads was rather proud of this innovation because it meant that the lock would not have to be continually repositioned on top of the circular access shaft to which it was attached as the caisson descended and the shaft lengthened.

A type of sand pump invented by Eads would remove the sand underneath the open-bottomed caissons. Use of this pump was one factor in Eads's remarkable success as a wrecker, due to its ability to clear large amounts of sand in a relatively short period of time. He described this machine as being "somewhat like that in Giffard's injector," with water being used instead of steam. It was composed mainly of a simple pipe with a three-inch bore and a bell muzzle at the lower end. A stream of water is forced by an engine down to the bottom of the pump where it is discharged by an angular jet into the pump in an upward motion. This creates suction. As sand, gravel, and small stones are sucked up, the cutting edge of the caisson, covered with a sheet of iron three inches thick and extending two feet below the oak dividing walls of the chamber, descends further into the sand. As the caisson descends, masonry is laid on top of the roof, which is braced with thirteen plate-iron girders, each five feet high, spaced five and one-half inches apart. The further down the caisson descends, the more masonry is laid, with the walls of the semi-hollow pier always kept higher than the level of the surrounding water. When bedrock is reached, the air chamber and access shafts of the pier would be filled with cement and sealed off, and the caisson would thus become the base of the pier.[6]

Carnegie's thoughts concerning the change in plans are unknown, but he was certainly more interested in that part of the bridge his company would erect (the superstructure), and in details of the business deal, than he was in the design of the foundations. He wrote his brother Thomas on April 27, saying, "Capt. Eads & party talk well, they will offer our party a part in the enterprise & give us the Superstructure for our Subscription &c.—I hope we can get Messrs. Thomson & Scott to arrange matters in this way—I am to meet their man here today."[7]

On June 18, Carnegie wrote to Eads, letting him know that drawings of the bridge were being returned by Adams Express after having been thoroughly examined by Keystone engineers. What Keystone needed in order to proceed were specifications and estimates of weights in order to estimate the cost of erection.[8] On the following day Carnegie sent a letter and copies of Eads's drawings to Linville and suggested that if the information already received from Eads was not enough to make a bid, then Katté and either Piper or Shiffler should meet Eads in St. Louis.

Carnegie was clearly most concerned at this point about the lack of progress on contract negotiations. As he wrote Linville on June 19, he had decided it was time to meet Eads personally "and get the inside track on this enterprise, even if I fail in my effort to get a bond and stock arrangement for myself and friends."[9] He knew that the feasibility of Eads's design was in doubt, but he felt that Eads was amenable to suggestions from practical men like Piper and Shiffler and was disposed to do anything reasonable concerning detailed design and construction issues.

Carnegie therefore dispatched a letter to Piper on the same day that he wrote to Linville, forcefully suggesting that Piper travel to St. Louis to meet Eads in person. To help spur the reluctant Piper into action he also wrote Shiffler on June 22 and asked him to force Piper to make the trip. But instead of Keystone personnel visiting St. Louis, the bridge company officers traveled to Pittsburgh and met with Carnegie on July 11. Afterward Carnegie assumed that the negotiations were in satisfactory shape, even though Keystone still didn't have a proper set of plans.[10]

Eads, for his part, was busy preparing for the sinking of the two river piers. Whereas progress in St. Louis seemed stalled from Carnegie's perspective in Pittsburgh, the return of the chief engineer had rejuvenated the project and the offices of the Illinois and St. Louis Bridge Company were charged with the energy created by the chief engineer's daring new plan.

The trip to Europe must have rejuvenated Eads as well because he personally explored the east pier site in a diving bell prior to the beginning of construction. On at least one occasion he even took his stepdaughter Josephine down to the river bottom with him.[11]

In order to inspire potential financial backers and make up for lost time, the bridge company decided in May that it would be necessary to sink both river piers almost simultaneously, even though Eads informed the directors that this would cost at least $150,000 more than he had originally estimated to bring the masonry ten feet above the low-water mark by fall. This increase was due to the necessity of duplicating nearly all of the floating machinery, engines, barges, travelers, derricks, and other equipment and for the employment of additional personnel.

Eads intended to commence sinking the larger east pier first, sometime toward the end of August. This pier would go down through twenty feet of water and eighty feet of sand and cover an area on the rock 82 feet by 60 feet. The smaller west pier, beginning about a month after the east pier, would go down through 20 feet of water and 50 feet of sand and occupy a base 82 feet by 48 feet.

One of the first tasks to be accomplished was the selection of a contractor for construction of the caissons. As usual, Eads chose to work with someone from his circle of business associates. On May 17 the construction committee, composed of Allen, Lionberger, John Copelin, and Eads, passed a resolution to employ William Nelson to "put up" the first caisson and to "cut apart and work in all the material that can be used from the gun boat Milwaukee in said Caisson."[12]

The *Milwaukee,* the remains of which had been purchased from a wrecking company during the winter, was one of four vessels designed and built by Eads for use on the lower Mississippi River and the Gulf of Mexico during the Civil War, and one of two such boats using steam-operated gun turrets designed by Eads.[13] The turrets were the first of their kind ever constructed and could fire every forty-five seconds.[14] But despite the efficiency of its armament, the *Milwaukee* was sent to the bottom of Mobile Bay by a Confederate mine on March 27, 1865, while supporting Admiral David Farragut's assault.[15]

On subsequent days additional contract proposals by Nelson for labor and materials needed for the caissons and the east abutment cofferdam were approved. Iron plates that could not be salvaged by Nelson were to be obtained from Gaylord, Son and Company, a firm owned by a bridge investor. A number of other contracts were soon let for materials or services necessary for the work, such as boats and barges, hydraulic jacks, timber and finished lumber, rivets, hydraulic brick, pumps, cement, and transportation of materials from New Orleans.

On August 12 two large steam pile drivers began driving piles into the sandy bottom of the river to form breakwaters about two hundred feet above the site of the piers. These V-shaped structures were designed to protect the work site from rafts, floating debris, and ice, if the work should be delayed past November.

While the work of driving the piles proceeded, the executive committee, composed of Dickson, McPherson, James Britton, and Taussig, continued its efforts to secure financing for the project. McPherson was instructed to consult with Morris K. Jessup, the New York financier and stockholder in the bridge company who recently had become a stockholder in the St. Louis, Chillicothe and Omaha Railroad Company. Taussig was assigned to prepare a schedule for issuance of bonds to be submitted at the next committee meeting.

As part of the effort to prepare for bond sales, Eads made his second official report to the president and directors of the bridge company on September 1, 1869. Much shorter than his first report, this document outlined the work completed to date, plans for the piers, equipment purchased or constructed, the design of the caissons and the method by which they would be sunk, expenditures to date, experiments that had been performed on cast steel, and various other sundry matters.

At this point Eads had been in charge of the bridge project for more than two and one-half years. Yet there was little evidence of the bridge company's efforts other than a rusty cofferdam that hid the paltry five feet of west abutment masonry then rising above the line of low water; the foundations of two piers of the western approach, which were constructed only to the level of the wharf; and the ever increasing, jumbled piles of masonry and equipment for construction of the river piers strewn about the levee. Although at least one thousand men had been constantly employed since the middle of June in preparations for sinking the two river piers, it was difficult for anyone standing on the levee to see what they were actually accomplishing.

Eads's report, containing detailed explanations for the numerous delays, along with his provision of information concerning activities that were taking place outside the purview of the idle onlooker, temporarily generated new enthusiasm among the citizens of St. Louis. As summer gave way to autumn, however, it became clear that pier construction was falling well behind schedule.

Eads believed in July that by November he would have both caissons sunk nearly to bedrock. But the failure of Gaylord, Son and Company to deliver sheet iron for the caissons and the slowness of Norway Iron Manufacturing Company in providing rivets had delayed work at the shipyards. It wasn't until shortly before noon on October 18 that the tugboat *Fisher* began to slowly tow the east pier caisson up from Carondelet and maneuver it into position over the pier site. A temporary false bottom attached to the 437-ton inverted hexagonal box allowed it to float into place. With iron outer walls extending ten feet above the roof of the air chamber forming a sort of cofferdam, it was a strange sight to observers on shore as it bucked against the current on its way up river, its bottom immersed approximately three and one-half feet below the surface of the water.[16]

At the east pier site, eight guide-piles—each three and one-half feet in diameter and eighty feet long—were framed together. The bottom twelve feet of each guide-pile was an open-ended hollow tube. For a few feet above this, the tube, except for a central hole approximately one foot in diameter, was filled with iron to give it weight. The remainder of the pile was formed of timbers, strapped and bolted together. A sand pump was inserted through the center of each guide-pile to suck out sand and gravel until each pile had been driven about twenty feet into the riverbed. The tops of the guide-piles extended almost thirty feet above the surface of the water.

Ten large suspension screws, each about twenty feet long and supported by the braced piles, were to be attached to the bottom of the caisson once it was in position. They were not intended to support any part of the weight of the pier when the masonry was evenly distributed, but only to regulate the rate of descent of the caisson and help keep it level on its way to the rock, 120 feet below the city directrix. This method of lowering caissons had been used first in construction of the Kehl Bridge, erected across the Rhine between Alsace and Baden in 1858, and had been employed in Europe several times since.[17] Now it would be adapted for use in a new environment, on a project the scale of which was beyond the experience of any European engineer.

As soon as the caisson was secured within the guide-piles, two pontoon barges containing machinery and supporting the derricks needed for construction of the piers were anchored along the east and west sides just outside of the guide-piles. They provided a working platform for engineers, riveters, and carpenters who spent the next week attaching the caisson to the suspension screws, connecting various air and water hoses, pumping out the air chamber, and repairing leaks. As soon as the majority of the leaks were caulked, a tugboat drew out the temporary wood bottom of the caisson in sections. Then, two more guide-piles were sunk on the downstream side of the caisson to complete the enclosure.[18]

It was bitterly cold on the morning of October 25. A strong wind whistled through the network of wire ropes at the pier site and lashed the river into frothy whitecaps. Despite the harsh weather, Eads and a small party of bridge company officials and friends motored out to the site about 11:00 A.M. to watch as the first stones were laid on the roof of the caisson.[19] Several of the party, including Mrs. Eads and two other ladies, made use of the opportunity to go down, as far as they could, into the air chamber. After first passing through the air lock they descended along scaffolding to a point just above the surface of the water. As a reporter for the *Missouri Republican* described the novel experience for his readers, "Such a visit is full of interest, wonder and astonishment, as it is there one gets the nearest conception of the grandeur and magnitude of the mechanism necessary to the undertaking."[20]

Shortly before noon, after everyone who wished to visit the air chamber had done so, the gangways were cleared and every man ordered to his post. The limestone blocks, having already been dressed on shore, matched, and numbered, were brought up next to the caisson on barges. They were quickly picked up by the travelers, placed into position, and lowered into a bed of Louisville cement. It took only a few minutes to lay twelve huge stones, six on each side, each one weighing about three and a half tons. A small ceremony was held, after which the chilled visitors gladly returned to the shore. From that point on, the work of laying masonry continued around the clock, with the area illuminated at night by calcium lights located at each end of the work site.

As the caisson descended, additional plates were added to the iron wall extending above the roof of the caisson so that the top of this iron envelope was always five to seven feet above the surface of the water. Timber braces were used to stiffen the envelope and prevent its collapse due to increased pressure from the surrounding water. Two engines, one at the north end of the caisson and one at the south end, continually pumped air into the inner chamber to compensate for air lost through small leaks or through the occasional tilting of the caisson. Regulating the number of revolutions at which each pump ran controlled the amount of air pumped.

On November 17, 1869, the caisson reached the sandy bed of the river, at a depth of approximately thirty-four feet. Soundings indicated that the current was scouring out the sand at the bow, and because it was necessary to level the caisson as much as possible before excavation of the bottom could begin, it was decided to quickly lower the caisson as far as possible to check the scour. The initial sinking was accomplished by turning the nuts on the suspension screws three inches and then turning off the pumps, thus allowing the caisson to lose buoyancy and sink three inches; restarting the pumps and running them at their former rate for a period of time as the nuts were turned another three inches; and then turning the pumps off again to allow more settling. This procedure was repeated until the caisson had been lowered twenty-nine inches in forty-five minutes. The pier was now about thirty-four feet below the surface of the water, and the difficult task of excavating sand and sinking the pier to bedrock, over sixty feet further down, could commence.

There were seven air locks in the east caisson, each a vertical cylinder made of one-half-inch-thick plates of iron. The central lock, positioned entirely within the air chamber, was six feet in diameter and six feet in height. Approximately five people could comfortably fit within the lock at one time. The remaining locks, located partly within and partly above the air chamber, were five feet in diameter and from ten feet to twelve feet high. Each lock had two tight-fitting doors, one opening into the air chamber and the other opening into the access shaft above it. The central lock was used for passage of workmen, and the others were mainly used for the admission of concrete or equipment and the removal of material, such as logs, that could not be excavated by the sand pumps.

The design of the west pier caisson, launched on January 3, 1870, was similar to that of the east pier caisson, although it was smaller, being eighty-three feet long and forty-eight feet wide. Its ironwork was a bit lighter, and it had only five air locks instead of seven. In most other respects, what was true concerning operations and conditions in the east caisson was true for the west caisson as well.

To enter the air chamber of either caisson, workmen descended the candlelighted spiral stairway that ran down the interior of the access shaft, and passed through the upper door. Once inside the lock, the door was closed with a loud clang behind them and a valve opened to admit compressed air from the chamber into the lock. When the air pressure in the lock equaled that in the chamber, the lower door fell open and the workmen climbed down an iron ladder to the sandy floor of the chamber. The process of exiting was very similar. The workmen entered the lock through the lower door, closed and secured it behind them, turned a valve to let the air within the lock escape, and once the air pressure within the lock equaled the ambient pressure in the shaft, the upper door was opened and the workmen could then ascend the stairs.[21]

As simple as this procedure sounds, passage into and out of the air chamber was attended by such novel sensations that only the most experienced workers eventually found it to be routine. The first thing one noticed upon initiation of the process was the screeching of the air as it passed through the valve, then its warmth, humidity, and smell. Compression of the air pumped into the caisson caused a rise in its temperature, and regardless of conditions on the surface it was always warm and humid inside the chamber. The stink of half-naked men working in close quarters, mixed with the odor generated by candles and lamps, was almost intolerable to casual visitors. Some found breathing difficult.

If compressed air from the chamber was let into the lock too rapidly, or after its pressure had increased when the caisson was at lower levels, a severe pain in the ears or head often accompanied the process. Sometimes swallowing could lessen this discomfort, and Eads ordered a pail of water and a cup placed in the lock. But occasionally a visitor would become terror-stricken or incapacitated by pain and the process would have to be immediately reversed. Many an otherwise brave man was humbled to find that he could not endure the passage while seemingly delicate ladies could.

When compressed air in the lock was allowed to escape during the process of returning to the surface, so much vital heat was lost due to expansion that those in transition involuntarily shuddered. Visitors who survived the process, relieved to have it behind them, began spreading stories about the horrors of the experience. Since the objectionable aspects of the process became greater with increased depth of the caisson, it became progressively more difficult to find workers who would stay on the job for any length of time.

Once inside the chamber, the feeling of having descended into the underworld was compounded by the flickering light produced by lamps and candles that illuminated the dank interior. Various types of lanterns were tried, but none with much success. They all burned with a very dull flame and emitted such copious amounts of smoke that water sprays were utilized to reduce the amount of floating carbon in the air. Oil was found to be such a dangerous fuel in a compressed-air environment that its use was banned entirely. The clothing of two men caught fire as a result of contact with a hand-lamp or candle and it was almost impossible to extinguish the flames. As the depth of the caisson increased it became progressively more difficult to blow out candles. At one point, Eads blew out a candle thirteen times in about half a minute, and each time the flame returned to the wick.

The increased air pressure produced other strange effects. Burly workmen began to speak in high-pitched, nasal tones and found that they could not whistle. One visitor took a flask of brandy with him and passed it around to his friends inside the chamber. When he returned to the surface the tightly capped flask exploded in his pocket.

Water constantly dripped from the roof of the chamber as the men used shovels, wheelbarrows, and water jets from hand-held hoses to move sand, gravel, and small rocks underneath one of the seven sand pumps. The discharge pipes of the pumps had been increased from three inches to five inches in diameter in order to more efficiently excavate the large amount of material, so much material that it accumulated outside of the caisson until a mound of it could be seen above the surface of the water.

The force of suction created by pressure differential between the chamber and the outside was demonstrated when the jet of a pump was out of order in the east caisson and the water turned off. The suction pipe was uncoupled, leaving an open pipe about three feet above the sandy floor of the chamber. The men inside the chamber had erroneously assumed that the pipe had been capped on top, but they soon discovered their mistake when air began rushing out with great violence. The foreman then on duty quickly whipped off his hat and placed it over the mouth of the pipe, only to see it go whooshing through to the surface. That having failed, he folded his coat and stopped the leak by jamming the coat in the pipe until it could be capped.

Logs and pieces of wood too large to pass through the discharge pipes were taken out through one of the air locks. All stones, pieces of coal, and fragments of brick too large for the pumps were laid on shelves, to be used later in filling the chamber. Although this portion of the work proceeded without great difficulty, there were delays due to interruptions in the provision of masonry or the difficulty of constructing and bracing the iron cofferdam that arose around the top of the caisson, or due to the weather. As Eads feared, the process of sinking the east pier had continued past the time when ice began flowing in the river and there were several occasions during the winter when crews at the work site were isolated from the shore because tugs could not break through the ice.

By December 11 the ice was running so thick in the river that the *Hewitt,* the tender used to transport men and materials to the pier, could not be run at night. On December 23 conditions were such that no boat could reach the site. Superintendent William K. McComas therefore wrote messages regarding progress of the work on placards that Eads could read from shore with the aid of a telescope. Although a boat was able to reach the pier about noon of the following day, on January 7 the crews were once again ice-bound, as they would be on several other occasions during the winter.

Although icing of the river was an irritant, work was not held up. McComas had enough foresight to lay in supplies sufficient to sustain the crews during periods of isolation from the shore. The greatest problem to afflict the workers during the first few months of 1870 had nothing to do with the weather, and it was something that foresight alone could not have solved.

8

The Grecian Bend

Ordinarily the effect of working in the chamber is not at all serious
and has been a matter of jesting allusion among the men engaged in
the chamber, who style the muscular contraction of the back, which
sometimes ensues, "the Grecian bend."

—*Missouri Republican,* March 25, 1870

After the east pier caisson had sunk beyond about forty feet into the sand, Superintendent McComas began to notice an increasing incapacitation among some of his crew. Coming to the surface at the end of their shift, several workers began experiencing an occasional muscular paralysis of the lower limbs, at first unaccompanied by pain. As the depth of the caisson increased beyond sixty feet many men began experiencing paralysis in the upper body, often with terrible pain in the joints, back, stomach, and head. Because this affliction usually passed after a few hours, or at the most, days, it was not at first thought to be serious. In fact, it was considered good sport when a new man was in the air lock at the beginning or end of a shift to increase or release the air pressure as rapidly as possible, thus causing no small amount of terror and discomfort to those unaccustomed to the experience.

Workmen experiencing pain in the joints or cramps of

the abdomen often walked about slightly bent over. This posture resembled an affected walk, called the "Grecian bend," taken up by fashionable ladies of the time who wished to display their bustles. This name was jokingly applied to those afflicted men who walked about in a similar posture. Although they didn't know it at the time, the workers were suffering from decompression sickness, later called "caisson disease" and now known to scuba divers as simply "the bends."

Gases such as nitrogen will enter into a liquid, such as blood, in proportion to the partial pressure of the gas. A doubling of the pressure also doubles the amount of nitrogen that can be dissolved in the blood and tissues of the body. If the pressure is tripled, blood and tissues will hold three times the amount of nitrogen. This dissolved nitrogen is harmless as long as it stays dissolved. But if the pressure is decreased too rapidly, the dissolved nitrogen can come out of solution and form tiny bubbles in the blood and tissues of the body.[1] This is what happened to the men who worked in the caisson. At the end of their shift they were anxious to go home or to one of the area bars, and so they passed through the air lock and ascended the stairs as quickly as possible. This did not allow enough time for the body to "decompress," and, therefore, nitrogen came out of solution, formed bubbles in the bloodstream, and lodged in the abdomen, joints, or head.

The symptoms of decompression sickness vary, depending on a variety of factors, including the physical condition of the individual and where the bubbles or pockets of nitrogen form. Age, obesity, extreme fatigue, alcohol consumption, dehydration, extremely hot or cold water, even old injuries can make the formation of bubbles worse. If the bubbles form in the brain, symptoms can include dizziness, paralysis, unconsciousness, or blindness. If bubbles form in the lungs, asphyxia and choking may occur. Pain in the joints, muscles, or bones is a signal that bubbles have formed there. In some cases, death may result.

The "submarines," as they were called, who worked in the caissons of the St. Louis Bridge, eventually experienced all of these symptoms. But since some men apparently had no problems at all, and it was known that women seemed to be less susceptible to these afflictions than men, it was initially thought that the basic health or lifestyle of the individual was more to blame than was anything else. When severe cases began to crop up after the caisson reached a depth of sixty-five feet, several workers were sent to the hospital. The doctors there, not having any experience with the malady, were unprepared to provide proper treatment. The work, in any case, had to go on.

About the time that the first serious cases of decompression sickness began to be noticed, when the east caisson had reached a depth of about sixty-seven feet, a telegraphic instrument was placed in the air chamber. One wire led from the chamber to the office of McComas, the general superintendent, aboard one of the derrick barges, and the other led to Eads's office in the Virginia Hotel. A party of men and women soon went down into the caisson to observe Eads send messages to the barge, his office, and on to some of the directors of the bridge company then in New York.

Shortly before sunrise on the morning of February 28, one portion of the caisson cutting edge finally reached bedrock. McComas, an assistant to Ellet in the rebuilding of the Wheeling Bridge, recorded an immersion of ninety-two feet at 5:40 A.M. and added: "We will now commence to settle the caisson for the last time. I hope we shall be successful in landing it level." His sense of anxiety was understandable, given that the bedrock of the river sloped eastward, thus making it potentially difficult to level the pier. But within thirty-five minutes the task was accomplished and McComas could write, "East Pier rests on rock! The men are all in high glee and are preparing to fire a salute."[2]

Roberts presented McComas with a flag, which the superintendent hoisted over the pier. Other flags were affixed to the tugboat *Hewitt.* Cannons boomed and boat whistles shrieked, announcing to the world that the most difficult part of the project, or so it was thought, had now been accomplished.

Before the process of filling the caisson with cement began, Eads went down into the air chamber to examine the bedrock beneath. He found what he was looking for. The rock appeared worn and moderately polished. Despite what the board of engineers convened by Boomer had determined, it was Eads's guess that the rock had not only been exposed to the direct action of the current, but that such exposure had not been so remote as to be unlikely to occur again within the life of the bridge. Therefore, he had new confirmation that his decision to found the piers on bedrock had been correct.

The next week or so was spent washing all the stones and loose gravel that had been screened out of the sand, and removing all refuse from the chamber. Cement and aggregate was brought into the caisson and mixed with the sand that remained in the chamber to form concrete. The process of filling the chamber, air locks, and shafts with this mixture began the first week of March.[3]

The submarines begun experiencing greater and more frequent discomfort upon reaching bedrock and many had to be sent to the hospital during the month of February. Workers were ordered to climb the stairs slowly, and it sometimes took them fifteen or twenty minutes to do so. When they reached the top they were stripped, rubbed, treated with a "magnetic battery," given a hot bath, and wrapped in warm blankets.[4] Shifts had to be shortened to only one hour, followed by two hours of rest before returning to work.

To ward off the mysterious effects of decompression sickness, about a third of the men began using "galvanic" bands of metal, usually composed of silver lined with zinc. These bands of "voltaic armor" were first worn as bracelets around the wrists, arms, and ankles, beginning about a week after the process of filling the air chamber began. Later the bands of metal were wrapped around the waist or placed next to the soles of the feet inside the shoe. Other remedies were tried, and the use of "abolition oil" became quite popular. Associate chief engineer Roberts claimed that it "worked like a charm."[5]

Eads had determined, based on discussions with Brereton concerning his experience of sinking the piers of the Royal Albert Bridge, that shortening the amount of time the men spent in the air chamber was the only solution to the maladies being suffered. But the workmen begged to be allowed to work longer shifts because the effort of transitioning through the air lock and climbing or descending the stairs of the access shaft was widely disliked. Almost their entire one-hour shift could be occupied with the process of treatment. Eads, therefore, gave McComas his approval for a resumption of two-hour shifts, followed by four-hour breaks.

At about 10:00 A.M. on the morning of March 19, after working two hours in the east pier chamber, a man named James Riley emerged from the center access shaft. He told a friend that he felt well, but fifteen minutes later he gasped and fell over. A few minutes more and he was dead. McComas recorded in his diary, "I was fearful it would have a bad influence on the men, but they did not appear to mind it in the least."[6] Later that day James Moran, thirty-five years old, who visited the chamber for two hours on March 14 without performing any work just to see if he could stand the pressure, also died. John Sayers, twenty-two years old, died on March 22. Theodore L. Baum, twenty-one years old, died the next day, as did Henry Klausman, twenty-seven years old.[7]

The Knapp brothers, true to their contract with the bridge company, tried to keep the news out of the *Missouri Republican.* There were several other newspapers in town, however, including the German-language *Westliche Post,* and several of the workmen taken to the hospital were German. It wasn't long before even the *Republican* had to start covering the story.

On March 24 the coroner held an inquest on the death of Baum. One of his fellow submarines testified that he saw Baum on the evening of the twenty-first, "lying in the sitting room of the boat insensible," and that he would "lie quietly for a while, then turn over and grunt, and try to bite." The witness added, as though it was a relevant fact, "He used to drink a good deal of beer, and used to get drunk." McComas testified that they didn't seem to have any problem with the men who had been in the chamber before; the trouble was generally with the new men. He added, "I think it depends upon the habits and condition of the person." Dr. Louis Baur, who assisted in postmortem examination of the body, stated: "Perhaps the mode of life may have something to do with it. I should think that the use of ardent spirits would be highly prejudicial under these circumstances."[8]

With no more information than this to go on, the verdict of the coroner was that Baum had died of "apoplexy," the cause determined in all the other deaths.[9] Dr. E. A. Clark, physician in charge of the city hospital, demonstrated his complete ignorance of the problem by recommending that in the future the men be brought out of the caisson as rapidly as possible.

On March 30 the *Missouri Republican* reported, "there has been no workman disabled for a week or so. In fact the fashion of the 'Grecian bend' has almost disappeared from the pier population. There is no doubt but this to be attributed to the voltaic armor now worn by nearly all the men." McComas purchased a large quantity of the material for this armor, and even though it took some time to convince the skeptics among the crew to use it, he claimed, "The armor undoubtedly will facilitate the work on the pier, and may probably save the lives of some of the men."[10]

That same day, David Kennedy, a young man from Omaha who had initially been rejected for work by McComas, put on the armor and spent two hours in the east pier air chamber on his first day of work. He died fifteen minutes after emerging from the shaft. The coroner, as usual, attributed the death to apoplexy.[11]

The following day Eads appointed his trusted family physician, Dr. Alphonse Jaminet, to supervise the medical treatment of men assigned to work in the air chambers. At this point, there had been no significant cases of the mysterious illness reported by men working in the west pier caisson, on which the first masonry was laid January 15. Jaminet, therefore, set up a floating "hospital" just below the east pier in order to render swift aid to distressed workers emerging from that structure.

Dr. Jaminet was no stranger to the effects of decompression sickness. He was one of those visitors who frequently ventured into the air chamber of the east pier during its descent. Shortly before 3:00 P.M. on February 28, the same day the cutting edge first rested on bedrock, Jaminet and Eads began to leave the air chamber after a visit of approximately two and three-quarter hours. The discharge valve was opened to its maximum, as customary whenever the always-busy chief engineer was in transition, and Jaminet began to feel the familiar and unpleasant loss of heat that always accompanied the process. But this time there was a new sensation. A terrible pain shot through his head and he asked that the valve be closed. Within three and one-half minutes of entering the lock, however, the process was complete and the men crawled out into the shaft. Jaminet crept up the stairs with great difficulty, noticing, as only a physician might, that his pulse rate was 110. He took the first ferryboat back to the levee and barely managed to walk the one hundred yards or so from the landing to his buggy. His home and office were a half-mile distant, and he drove himself there despite dizziness and sharp pains in his abdomen. Paralysis set in shortly after he staggered into his office and for the next three or four hours he believed his end was near. Although he could not speak, he signaled his wife to place him on his back with legs slightly elevated. Any attempts at movement during the next three hours brought about great agony. Gradually, over the course of a week, his health returned.[12]

This personal experience, terrifying as it was, provided valuable knowledge of the workmen's suffering and Jaminet became determined to find a way to eliminate or ease their pain. At first he required men finishing their second shift to lie in bunks on the hospital boat for at least an hour. But the men, accustomed to doing as they pleased after ending their shifts, preferred drinking in the saloon of Irish-born prizefighter Mike McCool. The workmen were generally a rough and ignorant lot, fond of alcohol, and not given to taking orders they thought unnecessary. They noticed that newer men seemed to suffer most from the strange malady, as did those who appeared weak or in ill health. Since women seemed to suffer less than men did, it became somewhat a test of one's manliness to shun treatment while also continuing to work hard and carouse after-hours. Soon Jaminet reported that the workmen refused to obey him, a fact that not only irritated him but probably also increased his tendency to agree with those who claimed that the life-style of the men was a great part of the problem. Although not untrue, this somewhat judgmental belief did little to advance a scientific solution.

During the process of filling the east pier air chamber, the river rose to a point more than twenty-six feet above low water, thus requiring an increased air pressure within the caisson to keep out the water. This also caused an increase in the suffering of the submarines. Finally, on April 2, they went on strike. McComas had successfully put down previous rebellions and he intended to do the same this time. The men received $4 for a day consisting of three shifts of two hours each, and they wanted $5 for two shifts of two hours each. McComas responded by telling them all to go ashore. When the next crew reported they demanded the same and were told the same. The next day there were only five or six men at work in the chamber. But the corporation held its position, and four days later most of the men were back at work.[13]

Shortly after the strike ended, a visitor with a particularly strong interest in air lock and caisson design descended the spiral staircase, passed through the lock, and entered the east pier chamber. Washington Roebling was then in the process of building a much larger caisson for use in construction of a great suspension bridge over the East River in New York. Roebling's father, John, had twice submitted plans for a bridge at St. Louis, first in 1857 and again in 1868. Now, less than a year after John Roebling's death, his son stood on the bedrock of the river.

Washington Roebling had already educated himself regarding the theory and practice of air locks and pneumatic caissons, including the use of air locks as part of a patent process of sinking pneumatic piles used by Boomer.[14] But he lacked Eads's practical experience. No one had ever employed caissons of the design, size, or to the depth of those used in sinking the St. Louis foundations, and Roebling learned much from his two-day visit. Perhaps he learned too much. Eads later sued Roebling for stealing his caisson design, and the two men carried on a nasty fight in the pages of *Railway Gazette* and *Engineering*. Roebling, in ill health from the effects of decompression sickness during the period in which the debate raged, eventually agreed to a cash settlement without admitting any legitimacy to Eads's claim.

About a week after Roebling departed St. Louis, around 5:00 on the morning of April 13, the iron envelope surrounding the east pier ruptured. Water rushed in and flooded the top of the pier, nearly twenty feet below the surface of the river. A man emerging from the central air lock had to fight a cascade of water pouring down the access shaft as he ascended the stairs. The other men in the chamber were signaled to come up the ladders through the small shafts. McComas suspended work on the east pier and the men moved over to the west pier.

That structure reached bedrock on April 2, which was only about eighty-six feet beneath the water and sand at that location. Filling of the caisson and shafts began two days later. The process was still under way when transfer of the east pier crews took place. With their help, the west pier was completely filled by May 8.

On May 11, the work of filling the air chamber of the east pier resumed. A well-built thirty-year-old German named William Sayler, who had already worked for three months in the west pier without apparent illness, transferred to the east pier crew. He was not the type of man expected to suffer from decompression sickness. He was older, experienced in working under pressure, fit and healthy. He worked a one-hour shift in the morning and a one-hour shift in the afternoon. At 2:00 P.M. he entered the air lock, apparently feeling well and ready for a return to the fresh air above. The bottom door was pulled shut and secured, the valve-cock opened, and as the highly compressed air in the little iron room hissed out he began to feel sick. When the upper hatch to the shaft was flung open he found that he couldn't ascend the stairs. His legs would not work; his body was paralyzed. His fellow workers carried him up the winding spiral staircase to the barge above. He became insensible while being taken to the hospital. Never having regained full consciousness, he died at 4:20 in the afternoon.

The postmortem examination by Dr. Jaminet recorded that the stomach was "normal *and entirely empty; no traces of food were found,* which confirmed my opinion that this man had not taken any dinner, and probably a very light breakfast, but had been drinking beer and whiskey quite freely, as it was afterwards ascertained."[15] According to Jaminet, since Sayler was a drinker who neglected to eat he was the agent of his own death. The work would go on.

There were, of course, dangers associated with the project other than decompression sickness. On March 25 an air hose leading to the east pier air chamber burst. Peter Sheridan, one of the masons working on that pier, was caught in the recoil of the hose and flung against the stone with great force. He was taken to the city hospital with little hope of recovery.[16] Another worker, Patrick Shirley, sued the company for $10,000 as a result of injuries suffered by another burst air hose.[17]

The official response of the company to claims resulting from injuries was that it had no legal obligation to pay. Unofficially, settlements were usually reached for as little as the company could get away with paying. Widows, orphans, and those without recourse to legal counsel were totally at the mercy of the executive committee, and usually got less, if any, than did those with greater negotiating power. For example, on October 4, 1871, the executive committee sanctioned Taussig's offer of $100 to Catherine Riley, widow of the first decompression sickness fatality, in exchange for her release of the company from any further claims.[18] She could have received a better settlement.

On April 18, the executive committee had agreed to pay another air chamber worker, Henry Intoll, who had become paralyzed and wished to go to Europe, $1,000 for a release of his claim against the company. It appears that it was worth ten times as much to the company to permanently dispose of the claim of a live worker than it was to settle the claim of a dead worker's widow. Patrick Shirley's claim was disposed of in similar fashion by giving him the equivalent of 100 pounds sterling and a one-way ticket back to Ireland.[19] Such were the economic and moral considerations of a corporation operating in the Gilded Age of unregulated business.

Despite death, injury, flooding, and a variety of other problems, the air chamber of the east pier was finally filled on May 27, 1870. The air locks and shafts were similarly filled, and the iron envelope surrounding the now-solid mass of masonry dismantled. A wood dam constructed in its place served to keep water out of the work area as masons labored to complete the remaining stonework.

Altogether, there were at least twelve deaths attributable to work in the east pier caisson, although some of these men, like Sayler, worked in both the east and west pier caissons. One death resulted from work in the west pier caisson, two men were crippled for life, and there were many serious cases of illness. These figures include only those men who sought medical treatment. There may have been other deaths or debilitations that went unrecorded, because the men afflicted often walked off the job before the seriousness of their injury was known.

Despite the deaths and calamities associated with the sinking of the river piers, Eads decided to use the pneumatic caisson method for sinking the east abutment during the fall and winter of 1870–71. He originally intended to found the masonry on piles driven to a depth of fifty feet below low water and protected with riprap. Now he intended to take the abutment to bedrock, about 136 feet below the high-water mark, and the dangers posed were therefore much greater. Both Eads and Dr. Jaminet would have to devise new solutions to the problems of decompression sickness if they wished to prevent a dramatic rise in the death toll.

Problems associated with the pier caissons dictated a new design, and Eads had worked on it diligently until finally satisfied in March 1870. In April a steam-powered planing machine was set up in East St. Louis for the purpose of preparing lumber, because the new design called for a much larger percentage of wood.[20] In order to save money, less iron was used for the roof and walls of the air chamber. According to Eads, this was acceptable because the abutment would be subject to much less oscillation than the river piers. In his third report to the president and directors of the bridge company, dated October 1, 1870, Eads provided details of his new design.

Projected to cover five thousand square feet of surface when resting on bedrock, the base of the caisson was to be about one-quarter larger than that of the east pier. The entire abutment would be about 25 percent larger than the east pier. As eventually constructed, the roof of the caisson was made of timber four feet, ten inches thick to ensure stiffness. The sides were also composed of timbers, being eight and a half feet thick at the top and eighteen inches thick at the bottom, with some placed vertically, some horizontally, and some at a forty-five degree angle. All were solidly connected together with iron bolts and large white-oak pins. The sides of the chamber were about ten feet high, and the two interior trusses, which divided the chamber into three smaller compartments, were ten feet thick at the top, three and a half feet wide at the base, and nine feet high.

The outside of the structure was covered with thick sheets of iron, with the sides at the bottom made thicker by riveting together four plates. This iron work did not extend as high up the sides as with the previous two caissons, only being twelve feet above the roof of the air chamber, but extended ten inches below the sides to form a cutting edge. The top of the air chamber was covered with iron, through which passed the shafts and several small holes for pumping air, water, and sand.

One notable change in the new caisson involved the design of the shafts and air locks. The main shaft, which carried twice as far into the chamber as the shafts of the other two caissons, had two locks at the bottom, each about eight feet in diameter. There were only two other shafts, each four feet in diameter and terminating in an eight-foot-diameter lock. It was not intended to use these smaller shafts regularly, but only in cases of emergency. The most novel innovation was the incorporation of an elevator into the main shaft. Eads believed that this would lessen the effects of decompression sickness, when actually it could only make things worse by speeding the rate of decompression.

New lamps were also designed to illuminate the air chamber, each composed of a candle within a sealed glass globe. An outlet pipe, one inch in diameter, vented into the access shaft. This allowed for combustion at the more normal air pressure of the shaft, while also keeping soot and carbon out of the work area. Eads decided to whitewash the interior walls of the chamber to improve illumination and lessen the gloomy feel of the place.

The new caisson would not be ready to launch until November, but there was much masonry work yet to be performed on the existing structures. During the spring and summer the river piers and west abutment were built several feet above water level and faced with granite. The original contractor from Virginia, the Richmond Granite Company, proved to be unreliable after providing about seven hundred cubic yards of stone, and much delay was caused by a lack of granite with which to cover the underlying limestone. Not wishing to experience further delays, the company had sent W. Milnor Roberts to Portland, Maine, to supervise loading of granite from new quarries owned by Thomas Westcot and Son.[21] Roberts could not control ocean storms, however, and two ships bearing the much-needed material sank off the coast of Florida on the way to New Orleans. An old friend of the project, B. Gratz Brown, had signed a contract to provide more easily obtainable Missouri red granite on April 7, but it took some time before that stone could be cut and shipped to site.

In order to give the structure a more pleasing appearance, the executive committee decided to face both piers and abutments with granite almost to the top, thus adding about $73,000 to the cost of the project. The company could afford the additional expenditure, however, thanks to the newly developed bond-selling abilities of their junior partner from Pennsylvania, Andrew Carnegie.

9

Golden Eggs

Eureka! Here's the goose that lays the golden eggs.

—Andrew Carnegie

As was common practice with railroad corporations during the post–Civil War period, the Illinois and St. Louis Bridge Company began raising capital for initial construction by issuing stock, to be paid fully in installments as needed. Subscriptions were opened locally at first, but after the primary investors had their opportunity subscriptions were opened to people outside the region. This was a necessary step in the funding process because there was insufficient capital in St. Louis to cover the entire cost.

The bridge company also followed the lead of railroad corporations in issuing stock to suppliers of essential goods and services in lieu of cash payment. This was to the advantage of the bridge (or railroad) corporation because it involved no expenditure of cash. It was an advantage to the contractor or supplier because the stock-issuing company often offered several dollars in stock for every dollar's worth of good or service. The disadvantage of stock was that it was only as valuable as the corporation's ability to make a profit.

The stock of some western railroads, built through relatively unpopulated areas, would never amount to much. Therefore, much of the capital for speculative railroads came from bond sales, which carried interest obligations that were independent of earnings, and thus more attractive to risk-avoiding investors.[1]

The Illinois and St. Louis Bridge Company was a corporation with unknown potential. Although it was assumed to have bright prospects, it would have to depend on construction loans secured by a mortgage on the property owned by the corporation in order to attract investors. And it would have to depend upon the connections of the Philadelphia interests to sell bonds in Europe.

The successful sale of $3 million in stock subscriptions in New York and St. Louis during February 1869 provided the necessary funds to begin sinking the piers of the bridge. But toward the end of that year, with the east caisson well on its way to the bottom of the river, the officers of the bridge company began to turn their attention to the bond sales necessary to finance the remainder of the project.

This was the moment Carnegie had been waiting for. Only the closing of a construction contract with the bridge company was more important. Since receiving his first dividend from capital investment in the Adams Express Company, a step that he reluctantly took at Scott's urging, Carnegie had been enthralled by the idea that one could make money without really working for it. For him, capital investment was the goose that laid the golden egg.[2] And the opportunity of receiving stock with real profit-making potential in exchange for his services in selling bridge bonds in London, which did not involve much real work, was intoxicating.

The bridge company bonds, which were considered to be essentially the same as railroad bonds, would be placed on the market at a time of uneven but dramatic growth in British railroad investment. During the Civil War, new British financing of American railroads virtually ceased, and confidence in American railroad companies remained low for several years after termination of the conflict. The reputation of American railroad securities as safe investments received another blow in 1868 as a result of the renewed and intensified struggles of Daniel Drew, James Fisk, Jay Gould, and Cornelius Vanderbilt to control the Erie Railroad. This provided an opportunity for Dutch and German companies, who were willing to handle riskier investments, to move into the market. William Taussig had already been contacted by one German banking house regarding the bonds of the bridge company. But the British, who were generally more desirable business partners, seemed to be slowly improving their attitude.

In 1868 there were only three new issues of American railroad securities brought out in London, but in 1869 there were four, and in 1870 there would be ten. Yet, despite indications of growing interest, London was still a bit leery of investing in western railroad companies, or in companies building bridges across western rivers. To offset this cautious attitude, the Pennsylvania Railroad pioneered the use of a form of unconditional guarantee based on a traffic agreement. Of course, only railroad companies as large as the Pennsylvania had enough control of the market to provide reliable traffic guarantees.

Another form of guarantee becoming increasingly common about 1870 was the endorsement of bond issues by the merchant banking house through which the securities were placed on the market. Jameson, Smith and Cotting, the New York firm holding stock in the bridge company, was willing to provide such guarantees based on its expectation that Carnegie and associates (as Carnegie referred to himself and those joining him in a business deal) would help in arranging binding contracts with railroad companies for use of the bridge.[3] At the end of 1869, however, the relationship of the bridge company to the Philadelphia interests was less than secure.

McPherson sent Carnegie a sharply worded letter on December 2, 1869, which revealed his suspicion that contracts for use of the bridge by the railroads were being held up by Carnegie and associates as a lever to win the superstructure contract. Having assumed that "this was the way the cat was jumping," McPherson obtained authority from the board of directors to give Carnegie and associates a margin of $250,000 on the superstructure contract, without regard to Carnegie's success or failure in negotiating the bonds. He acknowledged that this was not as much as he and Carnegie had talked about, "but on this you can rely so no more of your delays in the matter."[4]

While Carnegie mulled over the letter from McPherson, the bridge company received a request from Marx and Company of New York for a thirty-day option on the exclusive right to sell the bonds, and an offer from a company in London to arrange a short-term construction loan. In response Carnegie offered to arrange a $400,000, sixty-day loan if the bridge company agreed to give him a ninety-day option for sale of the bonds. The bridge company board of directors decided to give Marx and Company the option for sale of the bonds up to January 20, 1870, with 10 percent of stock ($400,000) payable as a bonus. If they should be successful in selling the bonds, a 10 percent stock bonus would also go to Carnegie in consideration of his effecting the short-term loan and obtaining other advantages for the company.

In an effort to motivate Carnegie, a memorandum of agreement was also drawn up between the bridge company and Carnegie and associates stating that Carne-

gie would have until March 20, 1870, to negotiate sale of the bonds. Twenty percent of the stock of the company (about $800,000) would go with the bonds as a
bonus, unless the bridge company was able to negotiate issuance of the bonds itself by January 20, in which case Carnegie and associates would receive only 10
percent stock ($400,000).[5]

As soon as the deal was made, Carnegie sent to E. W. Clark and Company, one
the largest banking houses in Philadelphia, $150,000 in notes of the bridge com-
pany to be immediately discounted so that $40,000 could be drawn that month
against a short-term loan.[6] A few days later, on December 29, 1869, Carnegie informed the banking house that in a formal resolution the board of directors of the
bridge company had agreed to give Carnegie and associates the contract for the
superstructure, although, in fact, the agreement had not yet been executed. Pre-
suming that Carnegie and associates, as superstructure contractor, would have
some influence on who supplied the steel, Carnegie offered to try and throw the
contract to E. W. Clark and Company. Moreover, he promised them that if he could
not get them the contract, he would pay $6,250 as a commission for arranging the
short term loan.[7]

Since E. W. Clark and Company was a banking house and not a metal fabrication company, Carnegie was really suggesting that the contract for steel would be
given to a Philadelphia firm, William Butcher Steel Works, via J. Hinchley Clark
and William Sellers. Clark and Sellers had financial interests in both the banking
firm and the steel company and would benefit by tying the award of the steel contract to the provision of the loan.[8]

Sellers, the most important connection between the two companies, was well
known to both Eads and Carnegie. He was the president of William Sellers and
Company of Philadelphia, maker of tools for machinists, founders, smiths, and
boilermakers, and sole manufacturer and licensee of Giffard's injector, the pump
for feeding boilers that Eads used as a model for his sand pump.[9] This firm's development of a specially designed machine for testing full-sized structural members
allowed Linville to conduct a series of tests, from which he derived the data required to design the Ohio River Bridge at Steubenville and another constructed
about the same time across the Monongahela River at Pittsburgh.[10] The Keystone
Bridge Company purchased this machine and moved it from Altoona to Pittsburgh, where it contributed to Keystone's preeminent position among bridge-
building firms as a leader in advancement of bridge technology. William Sellers
and Company also produced a patent steel anti-friction roller (a mechanism lo-

cated at one end of the bottom chord of a truss bridge that allowed for contraction and expansion of the metal) that was later used in the Keokuk Bridge.[11]

Having arrived at an agreement concerning bond sales, it was time for the bridge company board of directors and Carnegie and associates to solidify terms of the contract for superstructure erection. Carnegie wrote a memorandum of agreement on February 3, which stated that Carnegie and associates (not, it should be noted, the Keystone Bridge Company) would erect the superstructure of the bridge in conformance with Eads's plans and specifications. Carnegie and associates would be entitled to a bonus of $250,000 if erection was complete by December 1, 1871. In exchange for receiving the construction contract, Carnegie and associates would secure a contract for perpetual use of the bridge by the St. Louis, Vandalia and Terre Haute Railroad Company and the St. Louis, Alton, and Terre Haute Railroad Company. Within a certain number of days (the number to be filled in later) from the date the contract was signed, Carnegie and associates would effect the negotiation of $400,000 first mortgage bridge bonds at ninety cents net to the bridge company per dollar. On February 5, Carnegie met with the bridge company executive committee in McPherson's office and signed the agreement.[12]

Since this agreement was essentially a means of securing the project management assistance of the Philadelphia interests, terms of a separate formal contract with Keystone Bridge Company for erection of the superstructure were worked out on February 7.[13] The first clause stipulated that Keystone would build the bridge in conformity with the plans and specifications of Eads and complete the work within seventeen months of receipt of working drawings, provided workers were not delayed waiting on masonry after March 1, 1871. The second clause stipulated "all workmanship and material to be subject to the tests, inspection, approval & acceptance of the Engineer," meaning Eads. The third clause set the amount to be paid to Keystone at $1,460,418, the same amount that Eads estimated as the cost of construction in his 1868 report to the company.[14] Ten percent of that amount would be retained by the Illinois and St. Louis Bridge Company to secure the faithful performance of the work, and if the work was not completed on time, the company could retain one half of that reserve.

Carnegie returned to New York a few days after the second signing to begin making preparations for a trip to London sometime in March. On February 25, 1870, he sent Eads a request for a summary of the work performed to date and any other information that might help sell the bonds in Europe. "I expect to sail on the 9th of March," he wrote, and added that "parties here, & in Philada., seem

afraid of anything in the shape of a Bridge—Railway Bonds with not a title of assured revenue are preferred. This may operate against us abroad, but we will give
it a hard trial anyhow."[15]

Carnegie also informed Eads that William Sellers had made a bid for the steel
tubes, provided that Eads accept some design changes in the coupling joints. Sellers wanted to avoid the use of screws, which were costly due to loss of material and
increase in time of fabrication in cutting threads. Sellers and Piper were also very
leery of using cast iron for the couplings. Unfortunately, Sellers may have created
a greater problem for his company in suggesting grooved steel couplings because
William Butcher Steel Works later experienced great difficulty in fabricating the
parts.[16] Three days later, Carnegie wrote to George Rogers, fourth vice president of
the Pennsylvania Railroad, to acknowledge receipt of a bridge use contract with
the St. Louis, Vandalia and Terre Haute Railroad (the Vandalia line). They were still
meeting resistance from the St. Louis, Alton and Terre Haute (the Alton line), but
Thomson had "advised" them to execute a contract, and Carnegie expected one
would be forthcoming.[17]

Although the Pennsylvania Railroad held a majority of the shares of the Vandalia line, under terms of a lease of the Pittsburgh, Ft. Wayne and Chicago Railroad effective July 1, 1869, it also became possessed of one-half the shares of the
Indianapolis and St. Louis Railroad Company, which had a lease on the Alton line.
This meant that the Pennsylvania Railroad had an interest in two parallel railroads
extending west from Indianapolis, built through country that was at the time
barely able to support one.[18]

Carnegie and associates had other interests at the time that involved the Vandalia line. In April 1867, Carnegie organized the Keystone Telegraph Company
under a charter from the Commonwealth of Pennsylvania. It soon acquired a fran-
chise from the Pennsylvania Railroad granting the right to erect two wires on any
utility poles of the company located within the state. With this concession as leverage, Carnegie managed to swap shares in Keystone Telegraph for a one-third
interest in the Pacific and Atlantic Telegraph Company the following September.
At that point, he had not yet strung a foot of line for Keystone Telegraph, but he
began to aggressively expand the lines of the Pacific and Atlantic. By January 1869,
he was ready to string lines on the poles of the Vandalia line (and eventually, he
hoped, over the St. Louis Bridge) as a means of invading the territory of Western
Union, and he asked Scott to help him negotiate an agreement with the railroad.
At the end of the year, those negotiations were still underway.[19]

Early in 1870, Carnegie drafted a prospectus for the Illinois and St. Louis Bridge

Company that he planned to present to the financiers of London. The Vandalia, the Alton, and the Decatur and East St. Louis Railroad (the Decatur) were listed as three of six railroads located east of the Mississippi River that were expected to provide traffic over the bridge. The others were the Ohio and Mississippi; the Rockford, Rock Island and St. Louis; and the Belleville Railroad.[20]

The Decatur was then in the process of constructing a 109-mile line from Decatur, Illinois, to East St. Louis with connections to the Illinois Central Railroad. Before expiration of the year, however, this relatively small railroad was taken over by the Toledo, Wabash and Western Railroad, which, along with the Pennsylvania Railroad, had contracted to use the bridge at Keokuk in January 1869. This contract did not, however, necessarily preclude the Pennsylvania interests from profiting by an additional connection through St. Louis. Azariah Boody, the president of the Toledo, Wabash and Western, also must have seen the benefits of multiple connections across the river because he held five hundred shares of stock in the Illinois and St. Louis Bridge Company.

The Ohio and Mississippi Railroad continued to be a vitally important potential source of toll revenue. The Eads group had no control over this railroad, however, aside from the influence exerted by one of its New York directors, William Whitewright Jr., who owned 250 shares in the bridge company. This influence might be somewhat offset by one of the company's St. Louis directors, Lewis B. Parks, an incorporator of the Boomer-organized Illinois and St. Louis Bridge Company. Having been forced out after Eads's takeover, Parks was not likely to support a bridge use contract unless the rewards of doing so were substantial.

The Rockford, Rock Island and St. Louis Railroad and the Belleville Railroad were less important than the other eastern railroads, but they ran lines through rich coal-producing areas in Illinois. Both were expected to pay significant tolls for hauling this valuable commodity across the bridge.

The railroads located west of the river mentioned in Carnegie's draft prospectus were the St. Louis and Iron Mountain, the North Missouri, the Missouri Pacific, and the Southwest Pacific (Atlantic and Pacific). The St. Louis and Iron Mountain was controlled by men generally opposed to the bridge company, but the Eads faction had had some success in gaining control of the North Missouri and the Atlantic and Pacific. And they expected soon to strengthen their position with the Missouri Pacific by election of bridge company investors to the directorship of the railroad.

In Carnegie's preliminary draft of the prospectus, he wrote that the bridge was designed to connect these railways with each other so that freight and passengers could be transferred without a change of car and without ferriage, thus providing St. Louis a permanent and uninterrupted connection with the East.

The draft sent to the printers later that month, however, showed significant changes. Specific railroads were no longer enumerated, and the prospectus merely stated that the object of the bridge company was the connection "of the railway system of the south-west of the United States, which centers on the city of St. Louis, on the west side of the Mississippi River with the important lines on the east side of the river."[21] The wording of this document, both in draft form and as printed, is important because it signals a shift in the perceived function of the bridge as one component of the national rail system being constructed by the Pennsylvania interests.

Perhaps the parties involved had already begun to concede the trade of the upper Mississippi and Missouri River valleys, irretrievably lost to Chicago following completion of bridges at Rock Island, Clinton, Dubuque, Burlington, Quincy, and Kansas City. They certainly knew that the Keokuk Bridge would be completed long before the St. Louis Bridge, thereby providing the Pennsylvania Railroad with a connection to the West and the Pacific Ocean. Given that reality, the St. Louis Bridge would function better as part of a transportation system designed to reestablish St. Louis's traditional trade links with New Orleans and the South, and to open entirely new markets to the Southwest via a connection with Scott's planned Texas and Pacific Railroad. Whatever their thoughts, the prospectus was changed in a manner that still made the bridge seem like a good investment.

Just days after drafting the prospectus, Carnegie sailed for London to negotiate the bonds with Junius S. Morgan and Company. If he found no success there, he planned to try the more risk-prone firm of Sulzbach Brothers in Frankfurt.

Carnegie presented Morgan with the bridge company prospectus on or about March 24 and then returned the next day to find Morgan ready to make a purchase offer. Morgan's lawyers, however, demanded certain changes in the wording of the bonds. Knowing that Carnegie planned to go to Scotland for three weeks, Morgan suggested that he first write the bridge company in St. Louis for its approval. There would be time enough to finalize the deal upon Carnegie's return to London. But Carnegie, as he later recalled, "had no idea of allowing the fish to play so long." On March 25 he used the Atlantic cable to transmit the changes to Cotting in New York, who immediately telegraphed St. Louis for a reply. The bridge company held an emergency meeting that evening and agreed to the changes. This response was sent back to Cotting, who sent it on to London. On March 28 Carnegie offered the following: until April 2, J. S. Morgan and Company could purchase $1 million of the first mortgage gold bonds at 70 percent of face value, with an option until May 1 on the remaining $1.5 million at 72 percent, with the bonds bearing interest at 7 percent from April 1. This was subject to certain alterations being made in the bonds, such as a change in the sinking fund to one and three-eighths percent instead of one percent.[22] Three days later, J. S. Morgan and Company accepted the offer, with the stipulation that the stockholders not release the $1.5 million they were holding off the market without J. S. Morgan and Company's consent.[23]

Carnegie cabled McPherson the next day and said he thought the deal was a good one for an unfinished structure, and he added, "Don't refuse compliance."[24] He also cabled the terms to Thomson, who replied on April 2, "Price low. If best you can do, accept."[25] Thomson, of course, thought the price low in comparison with their previous assumption, which was that Morgan would take the bonds at 85 percent of face value, thus yielding a 20 percent stock bonus to Carnegie and associates of about $800,000. But, given the conservatism of the London market at the time, coupled with the slow pace of bridge construction, Carnegie realized that Morgan's counteroffer was the best he could do and he took it.

According to Carnegie, the speed with which he did business so impressed the capitalists of London that his reputation as a bond salesman was made with that first negotiation. He was later told by his friend and business partner George Pullman that Morgan related the story of Carnegie's use of the Atlantic cable to some guests at a dinner party and predicted, "That young man will be heard from."[26]

Partly because Carnegie told the skeptical financial editors and solicitors of London that Congress had declared the bridge a post road, meaning, "only the Supreme Court had direct jurisdiction," the bond sale was a great success. Within two hours of being placed on the market they were all re-sold. In Carnegie's view, his triumph virtually guaranteed future success with other bridge bond sales. "This one has turned out so finely it has been quite a pleasure to talk it up."[27] With his coup accomplished, Carnegie sailed for home on May 14.

Carnegie's victory made a big impression on Taussig. On April 16, he sent a letter to an old friend concerning his jealousy over J. S. Morgan and Company's role in the matter. "The profit for the London office [Morgan] is enormous. They took over the bonds at 72, and within 10 days they have re-subscribed the entire issue at 90. Now that the succulent roast has been grabbed away from them, the gentlemen in Frankfurt who spurned them contemptuously for years, will throw up their hands . . . and see how short-sighted they have been."[28] The "moral of the story," as he put it, was not lost on Taussig. If the New York brokerage house with which he was associated, Taussig, Fischer, and Company, had a branch office in

Frankfurt-am-Main at the time the bonds were being placed overseas, he could have made a considerable fortune on their placement. He resolved, therefore, to establish such a company in order that the future sale of any bridge or railroad bonds with which he might be associated would provide him profits beyond those realized from owning stock in the venture in question. After some delay due to outbreak of the Franco-Prussian War, the firm of Gempp and Taussig was duly established in Frankfurt and began soliciting business.

Shortly after he returned from Europe, Carnegie began to seek favors from the bridge company he had served so well in negotiating bond sales. On June 2, he asked the executive committee of the bridge company to defer the last $200,000 payment on Carnegie and associates' purchase of $2.5 million in bonds, subject to the deposit of such marketable collateral security as the committee might approve. As Carnegie stated in his request, "We have occasion to use funds, just now, for the completion of Keokuk Bridge." He offered to pay "such rates of interest as you receive for surplus funds from other parties or say 7%."[29] But the next day he wrote Henry Phipps to tell him, "I expect to have 200,000$ [sic] surplus belonging to Keokuk next week which I could invest in 2, 3, 4 & 6 months paper & if you can get 8 or 9%, I may send it to you for that purpose."[30]

As Carnegie's biographer Harold Livesay has noted, Carnegie was here manifesting the investor's mentality par excellence, "restlessly searching, thrusting for profitable employment for idle money, whether or not it was his own."[31] Of course, he was simultaneously preventing the bridge company from doing the very same thing with the available funds. But he felt that he deserved some consideration because without him the money would not be there to invest.

On July 13, Carnegie presented several different securities, from which the committee selected a combination of railroad bonds, City of Evansville, Indiana, bonds, and some bonds of the Pullman Sleeping Car Company. At the suggestion of Henry Vail of New York, the bridge company also asked for some Pennsylvania Railroad bonds. After these were thrown in, and the Evansville bonds taken out, the deal was eventually made on August 3. But, although the fifteen-month loan was due November 6, 1871, Carnegie and Scott talked to McPherson and Taussig and were told that they could get credit on their stocks and bonds for the $200,000, and "It is not to be repaid."[32]

The good relationship that existed between Carnegie and the bridge company during the summer of 1870 was not to last, however. Even before Eads had announced his decision to alter the method of constructing the river piers, everyone connected with the project had assumed that sinking the foundations to an unprecedented depth would be the most difficult part of the project. By any measure, that task had been terribly difficult. But during the fall, with masonry work on the piers and west abutment essentially complete, and the launch of the east abutment caisson pending, attention was increasingly directed to the superstructure.

Problems had begun to arise with the fabrication of steel components, with the overall design of the structure, and with the determination of which company should bear the financial burden of cost overruns. Before long, these problems would begin to threaten not just the already shaky relationship between the Philadelphia interests and their partners from St. Louis, but also the success of the entire project.

10

Untried Methods

It is the very nature of genius to devise new, untried methods even
when old ways meet all practical requirements.

—Andrew Carnegie, December 1870

As with his methodology of sinking the piers, conversations with European engineers had suggested to Eads certain changes in design of the bridge arches. The first published plan of the bridge specified that the upper and lower ribs of the arches would be made up of two parallel steel tubes, each nine inches in diameter. By early February 1870, one tube of thirteen inches in diameter had been substituted for the two smaller tubes in each member of the rib, and the depth of the rib had also been increased.[1] By the time Eads made his third report to the president and directors of the bridge company in October 1870, he had decided to make the tubes eighteen inches in diameter.

At the end of March, the central span of the bridge was still designed to be 515 feet in length, with each of the side spans being 497 feet in length. The rail deck was still designed to pass eight feet below the crown, or center, of the arch.[2] At some point during the following three weeks, Eads decided to raise the rail deck four feet and drop the crown of the arches four feet, thus bringing the rail deck level with the center of the span. The deck would now form a tangent with the curving line of the arch. As Eads told the *Missouri Republican,* "this modification in the plan will materially add to the beauty of the bridge, and give an uninterrupted view of the arches."[3] The most compelling reason for the change, however, was probably the need to improve the gradient of the tracks as they passed over the approach spans.

Although he never addressed the issue in his reports, Eads must have decided to change the span lengths at the same time he made changes in the design of the arches. The center span would now be 520 feet long, and the side spans would each be 502 feet in length. Since it was too late to move the piers and abutments, he provided for the increased length of the spans by simply slicing two and a half feet off of both sides of the river piers and each face of the abutments.

After new preliminary sets of working plans were made available to Keystone in April and May of 1870, John Piper traveled to St. Louis to discuss details with Eads and his assistant engineers. Piper had been instructed by Carnegie to do what he could to alter the design in ways that would make the bridge components easier to fabricate, thus reducing cost and increasing Keystone's profits. Eads was initially amenable to these suggestions, recognizing in Piper a man who had far more experience than he in the business of building bridges. But neither of them was prepared for the complexities of manufacturing and erecting structural members made of steel.

Shortly after Carnegie returned to New York from his bond-selling trip to Europe, somewhere at the very end of May 1870, he met with Eads and Butcher to discuss the contract for steel fabrication. Eads specifically forbade the use of Bessemer steel, due to quality-control problems and its tendency to break under sudden strain. But he seemed to be pleased with the selection of Butcher as a contractor, having extensively tested the crucible cast steel produced by Butcher's foundry in April. Carnegie made it clear to Linville, however, that he would rather pay a penalty to E. W. Clark and Company than buy the steel from Butcher if the price turned out to be too high. There were several other firms interested in the contract, and Carnegie sent such drawings and specifications as he had in his possession to J. S. Morgan and Company so that English manufacturers could examine them.[4] Eads did not furnish complete working drawings, however, until the first of July.[5]

In typical Carnegie fashion, he tied award of the contract to the manner in which the funds derived from bond sales were distributed. He sent Butcher a note on September 15 recommending that he ask the bridge company for a $50,000 advance, with 6 percent interest paid by Samuel Huston (president of the Butcher

Steel Works), Clark, Sellers, and Butcher himself until the loan could be repaid with deliveries of steel. As a postscript he added, "They might want interest at 10% I don't know, but they have the funds."[6]

The next day Carnegie demonstrated his duplicitous nature by writing Eads, "You will see by the enclosed that steel contract still hangs fire upon that Fifty thousand advance." Reminding Eads that Butcher had promised to begin delivery of rods and other materials within fifteen days of signing the contract, he assured Eads that the advance would soon be worked out. "If you can arrange this I hope you will do so & telegraph me so we can get contract executed. I am now satisfied if we had time we might get out of Butcher's power, but he has us at present."[7] The bridge company made it very clear, however, that contractors had to take care of their own financial affairs and would be held to strict accountability in performance of their contracts, especially in terms of time. The bridge company executive committee would not pay the $50,000.

Perhaps due, at least in part, to failure of the bridge company to approve the loan, no contract for steel was forthcoming. Butcher claimed that Eads's specification of tests was incomplete, and Butcher Steel Works wanted to know before it signed the contract exactly what Eads intended to require. This greatly distressed Carnegie. After having solicited bids from virtually every potential steel fabricator in the United States and Europe, Carnegie found Butcher to be the only firm willing to bid that could meet the specifications. In frustration, Carnegie finally agreed to pay the advance from Keystone funds in order to get the contract for steel fabrication signed. As he wrote Eads in October, "If no one will contract to make it we will all be in a pretty fix."[8]

Carnegie's sense of impending disaster was apparently so great that he informed Eads that he thought Butcher unreliable, and it would be far better to "use Iron, Cast or Wrought or <u>something</u> that you know can be obtained from more than one source." Having said that, however, he urged Eads to go to Philadelphia and try to smooth things over with Butcher and Sellers. "It may be," he wrote, "that your specifications & the general air of unusual severity that characterizes them, have frightened Messrs. Sellers & Co. & that a personal interview will satisfy them that you look for nothing impracticable. I think it would judging from the effect you always exercise on our people, but at all events if the St. Louis Bridge interprise [sic] is to be triumphantly completed in proper time, & this is so essential, it will be by your prompt attention, in person, to this matter."[9]

Carnegie did have reason to worry. Butcher may have been the only steel manufacturer not completely scared off by Eads's specifications, but his firm didn't even have a rolling mill. It proposed to erect one after receiving the contract. No wonder that Carnegie wrote to McPherson on October 5, "I wish the Captain's genius could devise some plan in which Iron could be used. We would then be independent." He added, "You may think self interest comes in here as we Manfr. Iron but if so you are simply wrong. I have a much deeper interest at stake in rendering St. Louis Bridge a success, & we are not likely to be in want of Iron to make."[10]

Finally, on or about October 17, the steel contract was signed and Butcher began construction of a rolling mill, even though there was still some confusion over exactly how the testing of materials produced by Butcher Steel Works would be conducted.[11] From this point forward, Eads's incessant demands for procedures and standards that exceeded any then commonly acknowledged by leaders in the metal fabrication and bridge-manufacturing business served to cause delay and boost the cost of the project.

Carnegie, a businessman out to make a profit, was concerned about the cost of Eads's perfectionism. But his fundamental emphasis on profit did not mean that he was opposed to the adoption of new procedures and methodologies. In fact, Keystone had a reputation for leadership in advancement of the art and science of metal bridge fabrication that stemmed from Linville's work on the bridge at Steubenville. The subsequent establishment of a testing program at Keystone, along with development by the Union Iron Mills of an iron particularly suitable for use in bridges, served as evidence of Keystone's progressive business practices. As far as Carnegie was concerned, Keystone Bridge Company built iron bridges that were more than just adequate; they were the best then being constructed in the world.

Yet Keystone's product was competitive without being extraordinary. The company built bridges that were somewhat different than all others in that it used a patent truss designed by Piper and Linville, but it was building essentially the same thing that everyone else in America was building—the vernacular iron railroad bridge. It had to be functional and cost efficient, but it didn't have to be particularly innovative. But as Carnegie was starting to find out, Eads wanted to build something else, something unique, and something grander. And he wanted to build it with steel, a metal little understood at that time by fabricators of bridge components.[12]

The day after the steel contract was signed Carnegie advised Katté regarding how he should reply to Eads's claim that the delay in the provision of steel should be charged to the manufacturer's requirement that the product be tested at the point of fabrication. As Carnegie put it, "you can justly explain to him that no Manufr. would agree to allow tests to be made except upon his premises, by his own agents, & under his own supervision. Had we departed from the invariable custom of the trade in this respect we should naturally have encountered difficulty. See that this is fully understood by the Captain please."[13]

According to Carnegie, Eads was also under the misconception that delays and charges of "extra cost" were due to his requirement that the manufacturer bear the cost of testing. But that wasn't the problem. Butcher was actually more concerned that the specifications demanded by Eads were excessively precise and costly. Eads, for example, demanded that all the steel be rolled within a certain tolerance. When he was informed that those tolerances could not be met by rolling, he demanded that every part be planed. That required a capital investment in new planing machinery, plus the expenditure of more time, and thus cut into profits. Eads did not care. He wanted what he wanted. But to the men of Keystone Bridge Company and Butcher Steel Works, this was evidence of inexperience and poor business acumen.

The conflict between the two perspectives is well summed up by another comment made by Carnegie in his letter to Taussig. "The St. Louis Bridge is one out of a hundred to Keystone, while to Captain Eads it is the groundwork of a distinguished life. With all the pride of a Mother for her first born, he would bedeck the darling without much regard to his own or others cost. Nothing that would please, & that does please, other Engineers, is good enough for this work. All right, say Keystone, provided he allows the Extra Cost & the extra time. I think this tendency needs checking."[14]

Yet, having said this, Carnegie also acknowledged Eads's essential nature and expressed his ultimate confidence in the man. "Keystone is only experiencing the fact that of all men your man of real, decided genius is the most difficult to deal with practically, but he will come out all right."[15]

Since the beginning of the project, Carnegie had been confident that Linville and Piper could educate Eads in the methodology of cost-effective bridge manufacturing. But Keystone, faced with erection of a bridge of unprecedented design, would also be in for an education.

The first important production task of the company was the provision of anchor bolts. Each rib of each arch terminates in a skewback plate, with each plate attached to a pier or abutment by anchor bolts held in place by the masonry. Since there are two ribs per arch, four arches per span, and three spans, there are 48 skewback plates. Each arch has a lower and an upper rib. Therefore, there are 24 upper skewback plates and 24 lower skewback plates. Four bolts attach each of the lower skewback plates. Three bolts, two on top and one below, attach each upper skewback plate. At some point, Eads determined that all of the bolts through the lower plates were to be made of crucible cast steel, as were the single bolts passing through the bottom holes of the upper plates. But it was assumed that the bolts passing through the two upper holes on the upper skewback plates, being subject to less strain, could safely be made of wrought iron, a less-costly material. Since there are 28 anchor bolts for each face of each abutment or pier, and six faces altogether (one for each abutment and two for each pier), a total of 120 steel bolts and 48 wrought-iron bolts, or 168 bolts total, were required in the superstructure.[16]

The fabrication of these bolts, particularly the ones made of steel, was no simple task. Yet progress of the entire project depended on speedy fabrication because once the laying of masonry for the piers and abutments reached a certain point, superstructure erection could proceed no further until the anchor bolts were placed into position. It was imperative that components of the superstructure be ready as soon as work on the east abutment was completed.

On November 3, shortly after the contract for fabrication had been signed with Butcher, the east abutment caisson was ready to launch. Although the ramps on which the behemoth slid into the river had been well prepared with tallow, when the blocks and lashings were removed the structure left a considerable trail of smoke behind as it swept into the river, its blunt side forcing a huge wave to rise. Sitting about ten to eleven feet low in the water, it rocked slightly in the current during its five-hour, seven-mile voyage to the abutment site. Whereas one steamer sufficed to tow the east pier caisson into position, it took three tugs to perform the task this time. Once at the construction site no guideposts were needed since the caisson was not in the stream, and cables alone held it in position.

On November 17, the process of laying masonry began. After November 22, the work continued at night under the harsh light of calcium lanterns, and the sand pumps were put to use beginning November 25. With ten workmen, three foremen, and one supervisor laboring in each compartment of the air chamber for ten hours a day, the excavation progressed rapidly. On December 2, work within the chamber was divided into three eight-hour shifts.

As in the case of the river piers, there were many curious visitors wishing to go down into the caisson. Engineers from both the United States and Europe partook of the novel experience, and Eads, Flad, or one of the other assistant engineers was usually available to give tours. In addition to those men with a professional interest in the work, a large group of Missouri legislators from Jefferson City came for an inspection. There were so many visitors that the crew on duty often suspended work in order that there be sufficient room for all the guests. Other guests, with an interest born of nothing more than idle curiosity, also took the elevator to the bottom of the caisson. Some received an experience beyond that wished for.

On December 3, there were two women in the air chamber when a blowout occurred. These events happened from time to time when the caisson settled unevenly or when there was an inequitable excavation of sand from different parts of the chamber. Construction superintendent McComas guessed that it was the latter cause that explained the rather forceful blowout that took place on December 3. Sand in the central portion of the caisson had been excavated to a depth of several inches below the cutting edge, and with tightly packed sand on the outside preventing a slow and gradual release of pressure, there was a sudden release when the pressurized air within finally forced its way out.

The danger inherent in these events came from a sudden and uncontrollable increase in the water level in the air chamber that usually followed the outrush of air. On this particular day, the water rose fourteen inches in a matter of seconds. Although no one was hurt, the young female visitors were quite alarmed, as were the masons and riveters working on top of the chamber who received a water bath when the escaping air boiled to the surface. The force of this event was so great that two men were blown from the adjacent scaffolding onto the roof of the chamber.

A greater danger arose from a shift in the position of the caisson that became very noticeable around December 9. The entire caisson had worked its way from the shore about three feet on the north side and about three feet, five inches on the south. Corrections ordered by Eads allowed the caisson to slip back toward the shore but also resulted in a very pronounced slant of the entire structure. It wasn't until December 18 that the caisson was once again level, but further efforts could induce it to move only slightly closer to the shore. Finally, it was decided to offset some of the masonry as a corrective measure.

Difficulties such as these didn't prevent good progress from being made, but cold winter weather, ice flows, and sudden changes in the level of the river slowed work considerably as the end of the year approached. From December 19 to December 30, the temperature was too low for the laying of masonry. As soon as the masons resumed their work, an ice gorge threatened both the protective icebreaker erected upstream and the pontoon boat *Gerald B. Allen*. That danger passed on January 11, but by January 17 the level of the river dropped so much that the *Allen* was grounded. Sand pumps were employed to remove sand from under its hull in order that it remain in proper position. But there were many days when ice in the river prevented delivery of additional stone, thus keeping the masons from performing their job.

Toward the end of 1870, however, problems in the process of manufacturing superstructure components were of greater concern to the project partners. In attempting to assign blame for the continuing delay, Carnegie was disposed to place most of the burden on the chief engineer.

Carnegie wrote Taussig a confidential letter on December 30, 1870, in which he complained that Eads had demanded all holes be drilled, "something unheard of in Bridge building here. Experiments satisfied him Keystone was right, that punched holes were just as serviceable, & he changed. Now Mr. Katté writes he intends to notify Mr. Linville he has changed again to drilled holes." Carnegie continued, saying, "if he is only made to understand that he can only require from Keystone 'the custom of the trade' & when he wishes anything beyond he must not only allow additional pay but increased time."[17]

Carnegie's position was reasonable, but in a sense, Eads was somewhat ahead of Carnegie on this point. In years to come, after bridges composed of structural members with punched holes had been in service long enough to evaluate the adequacy of prevailing shop practice, the bridge-building industry shifted from punched holes to drilled holes. This was particularly true for pin-connected trusses. The process of punching not only stressed the metal to an unacceptable extent, but the characteristics of the punched hole were such that pin connections made through punched holes tended to experience unacceptable wear. At the time, however, it was assumed that punching was an acceptable method.

Part of the tension between the two factions hinged on the issue of inspection. Eads originally assumed that he could inspect bridge components after they were delivered in St. Louis, and he instructed Flad to design a testing machine for this purpose. The machine was set up in the old Virginia Hotel between Main, Second, Green, and Morgan Streets, a building leased by the bridge company for use as offices, warehouse, and machine shops.[18] Butcher and Keystone, however, demanded that primary inspection first be conducted at the Butcher plant in Pittsburgh, as customary in the metal fabrication business. Butcher, therefore, requested that Eads send a man of his choosing to Pittsburgh to conduct the inspections. Eads first employed his old friend Paul Dahlgren in March 1870, but shortly before Dahlgren's resignation in July 1871, Eads applied to President Ulysses S. Grant for the temporary services of Henry W. Fitch, a United States Navy engineer. Grant agreed to the request and Fitch was appointed inspector in June.

This change in personnel may have accounted for some of the delay. It mattered little, however, who was in charge of inspection. The problems of fabrication were only partially due to methodology. The greater problem was due to the inability of crucible cast steel to meet the rigid specifications established by Eads.

In desperation Eads arranged for the American Tool Steel Company of New York to manufacture a six-inch bolt and make it available for testing. He also asked the company to supply some ingots of chrome steel in order to test the fitness of the material for the staves that would provide the internal structure of the arch ribs. Eads had apparently become knowledgeable concerning chrome steel as a result of his connections with engineers in the United States Navy, some of whom were enthusiastic about the material. In 1868 he sent thirty-two samples of chrome steel to David Kirkaldy in England for testing.[19] Encouraged by the results, Eads attempted to interest Scott in investing in chrome steel in 1869. Scott, in turn, asked Carnegie to speak with William Coleman of Pittsburgh about the material, as Coleman was known to be the most knowledgeable man then available concerning steel. Carnegie wrote Scott on March 8, 1869, saying that Coleman didn't think much of the chrome steel process and had no faith in it. Carnegie also enclosed a letter from a friend in England who was engaged in the manufacture of iron and had an interest in chrome steel. This man was but one of six who believed they possessed the secret of chrome steel manufacture, and according to Carnegie, they were all fools. As he cautioned Scott, "Don't be deluded into investing there. That there is to be a great change in the Manufc. [of] iron & steel some of these years is probable, but exactly what form it is to take no one knows. I would advise you to steer clear of the whole thing."[20] Scott was not convinced, however, and asked Carnegie to visit the shop of the American Tool Steel Company in Brooklyn, that firm being the parent organization behind the Brooklyn Chrome Steel Works. Carnegie reported his findings to Scott's personal secretary, R. D. Barclay, on March 29. Although he still could not recommend that Scott invest, he was generally impressed with the entire operation, reporting that "the steel I saw every where, looked well." Yet, the man who would become more associated with steel than any other American in history closed his report with the lukewarm comment, "Not pretending to know about the Steel Manufr. I do not give any opinion as to the process—It may be all that is claimed & it may prove in practical operation unable to hold its own with the old plan."[21]

Eads had more confidence than Carnegie, however, and sent his friend Commodore James W. King, chief of the navy's Bureau of Steam Engineering, along with Flad, to the Brooklyn plant to test the material the following April.[22] Eads was so impressed with the results of the test that he induced the bridge company board of directors to consider a memorandum of agreement that he had worked out with the American Tool Steel Company. In response, at a meeting held on May 12, the directors passed a resolution stating their preference for use of steel manufactured by that company.[23] Presumably, this steel would be sold to any subcontractor hired to fabricate the bridge components.

Keystone initially fought the agreement, however, because Carnegie wanted to award the contract for both manufacture and fabrication to Butcher in accordance with the secret arrangement worked out with E. W. Clark. After it became apparent that the crucible cast steel made by Butcher wouldn't work, Carnegie had no option but to let Eads pursue an arrangement for the supply of chrome steel. He had already executed his promise with E. W. Clark and Company by this time, and since it wasn't his fault that Butcher wasn't up to the job, he no longer owed Butcher any loyalty. He just wanted to see the project move forward as quickly as possible.

Therefore, an arrangement was arrived at on August 6, 1871, with the Brooklyn Chrome Steel Works whereby Butcher would be allowed to fabricate structural members, including the staves within the tubes and the sleeve couplings, out of the superior, but more costly, material. Since production of chrome steel was a patented process, C. P. Haughian, superintendent of the Brooklyn company, agreed to supervise production at the Butcher foundry and allow use of the patent for fifteen thousand dollars.[24]

Erection of the bridge was well behind schedule at this point. Almost all of the work necessary for the piers and west abutment to receive the first components of the superstructure had been completed, and the laying of masonry on the east abutment would soon be finished as well. This was in spite of a setback in sinking the east abutment due to a calamity that occurred on March 8, when the cutting edge was within four or five days' work of reaching bedrock.

The day had dawned bright but sultry. There were hints of rain all morning, and a few drops began spattering the crew at work on the east abutment around 1:00 in the afternoon. It began to grow darker to the south and west as a brisk, warm breeze blew over the construction site. Between 2:00 and 3:00 it began to rain more heavily, and the wind grew stronger, but there was no indication that anything other than a spring thunderstorm was in the offing. Suddenly, a few minutes past three o'clock in the afternoon, "the awful visitation," as the newspaper called it, appeared to the southwest, coming up the river in an easterly direction.[25]

Somehow, the tornado managed to miss most of St. Louis, but it struck the east bank of the river with considerable force. The roof of the East St. Louis Grain Elevator, the first building in the path of the storm, was "blown to ribbons," and the remainder of the structure was thrown in the river. The six-to-eight-hundred-foot-wide base of the funnel whipped into the adjacent railyards before most people in the little community even knew there was a tornado. John Bodkin O'Neil, purchasing agent of the Southeastern Railway, was standing in front of the passenger depot when a piece of lumber struck him in the head, killing him instantly. The station of the Belleville Branch Railroad vanished with nothing left to show were it stood except the piles on which it once rested. A twenty-five-ton locomotive of the Toledo, Wabash and Western Railroad blew over a fifteen-foot embankment, without touching the ground until it landed on its back at the foot of the slope. A lumberyard and a great number of houses were swept away, and railroad cars were scattered about the area. At least seven men on the east bank of the river were killed in the three minutes or so that it took the storm to pass, and more than fifty were wounded.

Of the twenty-two men at work in the east abutment air chamber and the one hundred or so at work on the surface, only James Halpin, a sheet-iron worker, sustained injuries that were immediately fatal. He was on the platform right outside of superintendent McComas's office when something massive struck him in the head and chest. One employee on shore was nearly killed when the twister dropped a house on him. Another worker, Joseph Clarke, had his arm and shoulder nearly torn from his body. He was taken to St. Luke's Hospital, where Dr. Jaminet made an examination and prepared for amputation on the following morning. Several other men were seriously hurt on the abutment, but none fatally.

Everything the bridge company owned above ground at the east abutment site received damage, including boats, barges, travelers, scaffolding, and machinery. Yet the greatest single loss was probably the bridge tug *Hewitt*. Its wheelhouse ripped off and thrown in the river, it quickly sank. With all its specialized equipment, it alone was worth much of the $15,000 to $20,000 in damage estimated by a still shaken McComas after the storm. Since the bridge company had no need to alarm already apprehensive investors by claiming large financial losses, figures provided at the time are probably worthless. In his history of the bridge, Woodward later estimated $50,000 worth of damage sustained by the bridge company. In 1912, the year before he died, Taussig claimed the company lost $250,000 as a result of the tornado. But as serious as the monetary damages were, the loss in time was just as severe.

As soon as the storm blew over, the men working down in the air chamber of the caisson were ordered to come up. With no pumps left operable to supply air to the chamber, it filled with water within a few hours. Although McComas was temporarily rendered unconscious, he soon recovered his senses and put his men to work clearing the site. In three days they were able to begin refilling the air chamber, and by the twentieth they were again laying masonry.

On March 28 the caisson reached bedrock, and by May all the filling of cavities with concrete had been completed. Only the task of laying masonry above the water line remained.

Everyone realized how important it was for superstructure erection to begin as soon as the substructure construction phase was complete. The piers and abutments would stand idle for several precious months, however, due to delays in the manufacture of superstructure components.

If there was any positive aspect to this delay, it could be found in the additional time allowed for planning a union passenger depot, new freight depots, new connecting rail lines, and all the other facilities necessary to make the bridge and tunnel part of a unified transportation system. It was imperative that these efforts move forward as rapidly as possible. The future of St. Louis was at stake.

11

Proper Facilities

Western Missouri, Kansas and Nebraska are still looking to St. Louis
for a market, and if proper facilities are furnished to and in St. Louis,
her trade must increase immensely from year to year.

—St. Louis Mayor Joseph Brown, 1872

After returning from his successful bond sale in London, Carnegie began pushing the bridge partners to advance plans for a central passenger depot in St. Louis. On June 29, 1870, Carnegie wrote McPherson that he had spoken with Thomson the night before concerning depot matters and Thomson suggested that Joseph M. Wilson, Chief Assistant Engineer, Construction Department, Pennsylvania Railroad, would be a good man to look over matters at St. Louis. "He has been in Europe recently & is 'up' on depots," Carnegie reported.[1]

With Wilson's contribution to the design, and with Carnegie's input concerning the financial arrangements, Taussig's plans were well enough advanced within three months of Carnegie's recommendation that he was able to send Carnegie a preliminary prospectus of the Grand Union Passenger Depot, "as designed by us, which I hope will meet your approval."[2] The pamphlet omitted any mention of financial arrangements or cost estimates, since Taussig felt the provision of such confidential information should be restricted to friends. "Counting you among them, you shall soon hear from me on the subject," he wrote.[3] About the middle of December, Carnegie gave a revised copy of the prospectus to Scott and promised Taussig that Scott would look it over.

It might seem that these gentlemen had started their planning rather late, given that the need for a central passenger depot had long been apparent to anyone traveling through St. Louis by rail.

The Missouri Pacific Railroad had two tracks running into the city, with a small yard located at Seventh and Tenth Streets, and a frame house fronting on Seventh Street that served as both passenger and freight depot. There was also a ten-foot by twelve-foot frame box and platform on Fourteenth Street that served as a local station for people living on the western edge of the city.

The St. Louis and Iron Mountain Railroad owned a small house and a few spur tracks at the foot of Plum Street, and a single track that passed through South St. Louis to Carondelet, where there were additional spur tracks. There was also a small passenger station at the foot of Poplar Street, the recollection of which Taussig would later claim "will always be a nightmare to those who, like myself, had to use it constantly."[4]

The North Missouri Railroad had a single line running into St. Louis from Macon City to the north, and that line terminated at North Market Street where a small frame building served as both a freight and passenger depot. This building was just a short distance from the levee.

These small stations were not connected by any of the numerous streetcar lines then operating in St. Louis, and passengers wishing to use them had to rely on the slow service of the omnibus, which made pickups and drop-offs door-to-door at a leisurely pace. Sometimes it would take hours for a traveler arriving in St. Louis to complete the trip between one station and another. Those persons traveling east had to board the omnibus an hour or two before train departure time and sit patiently as the vehicle meandered about the city picking up other passengers. Eventually, the omnibus would deposit its load on the street in front of the Planter's House Hotel on Chestnut Street between Fourth and Fifth streets. It was to and from this point that all passenger traffic in and out of St. Louis centered. Train schedules therefore provided departure times under the heading, "Leave Planter's House."

The east-bound traveler boarded a huge four-horse omnibus at the Planter's House that provided a jarring ride down to the ferry landing and, weather permitting, an often frightening trip across the Mississippi River to one of the many terminals established in East St. Louis by the eastern railroads. As Taussig would later observe, "It is a pity that Dante, when he wrote his 'Inferno,' had no knowledge of the tortures of the transfer between St. Louis and East St. Louis in those times. Had he known of it he would have let the condemned be taken across the dark waters by that method, instead of having them rowed over by Charon in a comparatively peaceful way."[5]

The plan prepared by Taussig for alleviation of these tortures called for erection of a grand structure of magnificent scale located between Washington Avenue and Green Street, from Fifth (later, Broadway) Street to Eight Street. No structure of any great importance ever stood on that site, except for the old Lindell Hotel, which occupied one portion of the tract. Before burning to the ground in 1867 it was one of the finest hotels in St. Louis. Because it had not been rebuilt, the bridge directors believed the site to be a prime location for a new hotel that would be more convenient for travelers than was the Planter's House.

The entire three-block area, including streets, would be excavated to the level of the tunnel, projected to run from the western terminus of the bridge up Washington Avenue to Mill Creek Valley, where some limited freight facilities would be constructed. The tracks, approximately twenty feet below the level of the streets, would be turned by gentle curves into the underground level of the new station. On the lower story of the main four-story building there would be waiting rooms, baggage rooms, ticket offices, a billiard and barroom, a barbershop, and other associated facilities.

Coke-burning, "smoke-consuming" locomotives would be used for the purpose of bringing trains in and out of the tunnel and depot. The construction of special sound-deadening floors, and the management of trains with signals instead of whistles, would prevent noise from unduly disturbing those persons occupying the upper floors.

The site would accommodate a first-class hotel, general railroad offices, insurance and commission houses, and similar businesses. The upper three floors alone would provide no less than 330 "large and commodious" offices, furnished with all modern conveniences. A banking house would be located on the corner.

Since the old Merchants Exchange Building constructed in 1857 was in need of replacement, it was thought that the proposed site would be an excellent location for a new headquarters. Most of the bridge and tunnel company directors and investors were members of the exchange and hoped to have offices in the new structure. All buildings would be fireproofed to some extent by making the maximum use of iron in construction of beams, joists, girders, partitions, and exterior walls.[6]

George I. Barnett, St. Louis's premier architect, designed the building in the French Empire style. The promotional pamphlet prepared by Taussig, which featured Barnett's detailed elevations and floor plans, was printed and distributed to both the public and the heads of the thirteen railroads expected to use the structure. Some of the best-known railroad men and engineers in the country, including Warren Colburn, engineer (and later president) of the Toledo, Wabash and Western, Jacob Linville, and Joseph Wilson, examined and approved the plans. The cost was projected at approximately $1 million.[7]

On January 30, 1871, former St. Louis wholesale grocer Henry J. Spaunhorst introduced Missouri Senate Bill No. 84, "An Act Authorizing the Formation of Union Depots and Stations for Railroads in Cities of this State." With Spaunhorst's sponsorship, Taussig easily won passage of the bill in the Senate. He had to return to Jefferson City on March 2, 1871, however, to prod the House into approving the legislation. Strong opposition and "formidable amendments" required his personal attention.[8] When the situation seemed in hand, Taussig again returned to St. Louis, only to find that a wildfire of opposition re-ignited as soon as he left the capital. On the morning of March 17, it looked like the bill was dead, but "by manipulation," and after acceding to an amendment introduced on behalf of the heirs of the Lindell estate, which exempted the Lindell property, the bill passed just before midnight on March 18.[9]

For the most part, it was a well-written piece of legislation. Its principal author, St. Louis attorney John H. Shepley, created a document that proved to have wide applicability. Under its provisions both the first and second union passenger depots in St. Louis were eventually constructed, and several other states incorporated the bill into their own statute books.

Taussig initially believed he had won a great victory against "narrow-minded property owners on our side [of the river] and 'slush' operators on the other," because he didn't regard the exempted Lindell property as crucial. He immediately made plans to write notices to the thirteen railroad companies designated in the prospectus; sent Carnegie a letter asking if there was anyone else he should write on the subject; and also inquired, "Shall I mention the tunnel?"[10] Carnegie responded on March 22, congratulating Taussig on his triumph and also remarking: "The tunnel is an inseparable part of the Depot Scheme and should be so treated. Total cost will be as we thought 2-1/4 millions. This at 8% isn't a very heavy tax for Passenger Accommodation and <u>Freight</u> line through the City."[11] As initially figured by Carnegie, the tunnel would cost about $800,000, the depot building about $750,000, and the land about $550,000; with another $150,000 thrown in for contingencies, the total came to $2,250,000. One half of all rents would go to the participating railroad companies, with the remainder going to the stockholders.[12]

Unfortunately, the entire plan was unworkable from the start. As Taussig later admitted, "in light of what should have been at that time apparent to thoughtful, practical railroad men, it is astounding that such an impractical scheme could have been seriously urged."[13] Since coke-burning engines were never truly smokeless, the depot building above the tracks would have served as a huge shaft for the escape of smoke generated by activities on the lower level. In addition, there would have been no way of disposing of passenger coaches after unloading except to back them out of the station, thus causing a switching problem at some other point. Moreover, it would have been difficult to provide for the safe crossing of passengers between inbound and outbound tracks in a dark tunnel illuminated only by flickering gaslight.

What killed the project, however, was the realization that the Lindell property was crucial to the design. This fact became apparent so soon after Taussig's return to St. Louis that he immediately went to work on plans for a depot beyond the end of the tunnel, located on the six-block tract bounded by Clark Avenue, Poplar Street, Eighth Street, and Eleventh Street. By March 29, Taussig had an option on the entire tract and Wilson was ready with a preliminary design.[14] On April 15, a meeting was held at Carnegie's New York office, located at 57 Broadway. Wilson submitted his plans and estimates and after a full discussion appointed a committee to prepare a plan and articles of association for a union depot company. The committee consisted of Taussig, McPherson, Thomas Allen (president of the St. Louis and Iron Mountain Railroad), Azariah Boody (president of the Toledo, Wabash and Western Railroad), E. W. Woodward (president of the Indianapolis and St. Louis Railroad), and W. R. McKeen (president of the Terre Haute and Indianapolis Railroad, which leased the St. Louis, Vandalia and Terre Haute).[15]

After obtaining the approval of Carnegie and associates, Taussig had a new prospectus printed on April 20. The plan now called for issuing $2 million in 7 percent gold bonds, with interest on the bonds and 8 percent interest on the original capital investment guaranteed by the contracting railroads through assessments on future rents. Taussig, wishing to slice off a piece of the bond sale commission, offered to go to Europe to finalize Carnegie's negotiations.[16] He also sent his cousin, Edward Taussig, to Frankfurt to open a branch of the Taussig, Fisher and Company commission house. As he told Carnegie, "If Frankfort [sic] promises to be a better market for such Bonds as we may wish to negotiate, he will be of great assistance to us."[17]

Despite all of Taussig's hard work, negotiations with the railroads were dragging by May. In order to win the support of those companies necessary to the depot plan, many of which were reluctant to participate, the bridge company decided to put one of the directors of the Ohio and Mississippi Railroad, Lewis B. Parsons, on the bridge company board of directors along with Azariah Boody.

Although McPherson and Hudson Bridge had already sold out most of their interest in the Missouri Pacific Railroad, much to Carnegie's dismay, they managed to retain their positions as directors in the elections held March 27. But the decidedly anti-Eads Joseph Brown was elected as the new president, and some of the other directors of the road were opposed to the depot plan. Participation of this company was crucial to the success of the depot scheme, and participation of the Atlantic and Pacific Railroad was almost as important. But although Eads, Scott, and Thomson were incorporators of the latter company, there were other incorporators who were against them, and none of the Eads or Philadelphia group were on the board of directors. Therefore, both the Missouri Pacific Railroad and the Atlantic and Pacific Railroad were only "considering" their involvement in the depot. The officers of the Chicago and Alton Railroad, which now had a line to East St. Louis, were reluctant to join in the venture because several of them had an interest in the ferry company. Moreover, even though the Eads group seemed to be solidly in control of the North Missouri Railroad, several of the directors and many of the stockholders were opposed to the new location for the depot.[18]

Taussig's growing frustration is reflected by a letter he sent to Carnegie on May 19, in which he complains (as he had in March) about all the unappreciated hard work he was doing, and about the prospects for disaster. According to Taussig, stockholders of the North Missouri Railroad who had lost control after the Eads takeover were allied with men from Chicago in opposition to "a connection through the tunnel with the Mo. Pac. & a transfer of freight over the Bridge, except by transfer boats which would, as they claim, give them and the No. Mo. advantages over any road." It was beginning to appear to Taussig "that between these upper and nether grindstones the Bridge investment would be crushed."[19]

Taussig, who eventually became more instrumental than any other citizen of St. Louis in the establishment of centralized railroad facilities in that city, expressed his vision of the future and indicated a principal factor in the eventual failure of the entire scheme, in writing, "We must have a Bridge for all roads and must therefore treat them all alike. Inasmuch therefore, as a contract to use the Depot and Tunnel involves out of necessity a contract to use the Bridge, one being inoperative without the other (a feature I designedly framed in the plan of organization) the Depot question, to those roads who have not yet contracted for the use of the Bridge, carries along with it the grave question of contracting for use of the bridge, a tender spot for a good many parties."[20]

Unfortunately, not all the parties involved were as wise as Taussig in comprehending the essential connectedness of the bridge, tunnel, and depot. An effort was made to convince Scott that the depot should be located along the track of the North Missouri in the northern portion of the city, a location that would have alienated both the Ohio and Mississippi and the Toledo, Wabash and Western. Other railroads continued to fight the proposed location for months. But even with the final location still undecided, a meeting of most of the interested parties, to be held in the offices of the bridge company, was arranged for June 10. In order to secure the support of the president of the Ohio and Mississippi Railroad, President Daniel Torrance, at that meeting, the executive committee approved a specific bridge use contract on June 9 with the railroad. The board of directors had already approved the general terms of the contract on May 10.[21]

Finally, at the meeting of June 10, articles of association were agreed to for creation of the Union Depot Company of St. Louis. Taussig was given the honor of serving as first president, and Scott was elected vice president. Eads, Scott, Taussig, Carnegie, Britton, Torrance, James D. Smith, A. N. Chrystie, and Lewis B. Parsons signed the original subscription list as individuals. In addition, officers of the Ohio and Mississippi (Torrance); Toledo, Wabash and Western (A. Anderson); St. Louis, Vandalia and Terre Haute (W. R. McKeen); Indianapolis and St. Louis (E. W. Woodward); North Missouri (Eads); Pittsburgh, Cincinnati and St. Louis (Scott); Pennsylvania (Scott); Chicago and Alton (John J. Mitchell); and the St. Louis and Iron Mountain (Thomas Allen) Railroads signed for their respective companies, as did McPherson (elected as president in May) for the Illinois and St. Louis Bridge Company. The railroads signed up for amounts ranging from 500 to 2,500 shares, and the individual subscriptions were for amounts from 50 to 1,050 shares.

Even though Eads was, by far, the largest stockholder in the bridge company, he took only fifty shares in the depot company, which may help explain why he later seemed so disinterested in the fate of the depot project. In dollar amounts, the subscriptions amounted to $1.5 million, with the Pennsylvania and allied interests taking $600,000 of that total. The Missouri Pacific Railroad, probably the most important of all roads then entering St. Louis due to its political influence, rail connections outside of the city, and ownership of existing right-of-way into the head of Mill Creek Valley, was conspicuously absent from the list of subscribers. The Atlantic and Pacific, which had previously consolidated with the Missouri Pacific Railroad via a long-term lease agreement, also declined to participate.

With the depot company formed, the next order of business was selection of a site. Although the company still held an option on the tract between Clark and Poplar Streets, there was a strong desire to find a location to which all parties could agree. Shortly after the meeting, Eads invited Scott to spend a night at his home on Compton Avenue. During the evening, Eads managed to persuade Scott that a long, narrow depot could be built along the side of the bridge on pillars forty-five feet above the ground.[22] Scott should have known better, but he championed this fanciful notion for a time until cooler heads convinced him of its impracticality. Such was the power Eads seemed to possess when dealing with men face to face. Carnegie noted this dangerous persuasiveness in expressing his frustrations with Eads. As he once wrote Taussig, "The personal Magnetism of the man accounts for much of the disappointment. It's impossible for most men not to be won over to his views for the time at least. Piper & Katté come to us after the sober second thoughts prevail to object & criticize, & give way to expressions of fear as to pecunious results, while the same men in St. Louis, seem incapable of telling the Captain how far he travels out of the safe practical path."[23]

Fortunately, Carnegie was able to talk Scott out of supporting this crazy scheme, but the incident served only to fuel his growing belief that Carnegie and associates had picked the wrong man to do business with. As he wrote Scott on June 25, "Capt. Eads is now in Phila. & I don't know what new fangled notion he may try next, but if we are to have the serviceable depot at fair cost, & in short time, I can tell you this[,] he must not superintend the plans. He seems unable to adopt anything that has been proved to be good, while anything new & untried captures his senses."[24]

The situation began to look much darker in August. Torrance became so disgusted with the lack of progress that he began to talk of disbanding the depot company, or at least living with a small depot suggested by Eads for the south side of the bridge.[25]

Since Brown's election as president of the Missouri Pacific Railroad, Taussig had become convinced that a site in the flat bed of the now-drained Chouteau's Pond was the best possible location, since this would make it easier to tie into the tracks of that railroad. That was what Brown advocated. This was also acceptable to Scott and Carnegie, and they assumed that McPherson and Brown could work out some sort of deal.[26]

The situation became more muddled on August 26, when inept management of the North Missouri Railroad under Bates and McPherson resulted in a foreclosure of the second mortgage. Scott, Eads, McPherson, and Britton were elected to the board of the reorganized company, now called the St. Louis, Kansas City, and Northern Railway, along with the New York financier Joseph A. Jameson and Solon Humpheys, a bridge company first mortgage trustee. Many other Eads supporters lost their positions, and a long-time Eads opponent, T. R. Blackstone, was elected president. John Mitchell was also elected to the board, and even though he subscribed to fifty shares of the depot company on behalf of the Chicago and Alton Railroad, he had no personal stake in the scheme and could jump either way. Taussig implored Scott to use his influence with the New Yorkers on the board to be content with their own independent track into the city if they couldn't support the Chouteau Pond location, but to stop fighting the issue either way.[27] Scott, however, seemed willing to let the matter drag.

By December, it began to appear that the Missouri Pacific and the Atlantic and Pacific would join the depot enterprise on the basis of Brown's suggestion concerning location. Thomas Allen was talking about having the St. Louis and Iron Mountain join the St. Louis, Kansas City and Northern in construction of independent approach tracks into the city, although the two railroads entered from opposite directions. Presumably, they could both run tracks along the levee, skip the tunnel altogether, and run a joint track into Mill Creek Valley to Chouteau's Pond. Although that meant that the tunnel would lose revenue from those railroads, at least they would be participating in the depot. Taussig gave himself a pat on the back for bringing the situation to this point. But there was a new problem on the horizon.

Delays in construction of the bridge led some parties to begin discussion of building a competing bridge at Carondelet. If that happened, the Missouri Pacific, the St. Louis and Iron Mountain, and probably several other railroads would likely abandon both the Illinois and St. Louis Bridge and the union depot. The key, as Carnegie told Taussig, was to show the depot parties that the Eads-designed bridge would be completed soon.[28]

The need for a general meeting regarding the union depot coincided with a need to sort out some problems that had arisen regarding the fabrication of superstructure components. Linville claimed that the adoption of chrome steel created a fundamental change that affected all of the various contracts, and that a renegotiation of those contracts was thus in order. A meeting was therefore scheduled at the Keystone Bridge Company offices in Pittsburgh for December 14, 1871. The arrangement agreed to at that time would be presented at a stockholders meeting to be held in Carnegie's New York office on December 20.

Taussig also set up a meeting of the depot company board of directors for December 19. He believed it essential that this board address certain fundamental issues before the bridge company stockholders met the following day.

As for Carnegie, he had no intention of waiting to see if the meetings set up for December would solve the problems associated with the bridge. In November he received an offer of $10,000 for 1,000 shares of St. Louis Bridge stock and he decided to take it, "because I am not in a position to invest more in that enterprise. I do not believe Capt. Eads will get through without trouble—at all events I wished to get rid of so much liability." He also advised Thomson and Scott to sell their interests in the bridge, "although it looks like a great sacrifice at present."[29]

Thomson and Scott trusted Carnegie's judgment in this matter and also began to unload those shares in the bridge company that represented money out of pocket. The bonds, which they received in exchange for services rendered in procurement of contracts or financing, were retained because they had nothing to lose from gambling on the possibility of eventual success when they held only bonds that had cost them nothing.

In the years to come, Carnegie's attitude about the bridge, tunnel, and depot would vary, improving somewhat when things were going better and sinking when difficulties arose. In his communications with J. S. Morgan and Company, however, he remained positive throughout, even when his true feelings did not support his written words. He had to maintain a facade of optimism in his dealings with J. S. Morgan and Company to avert an interruption in the flow of funds. But, after the end of 1871, he never regained enough confidence in the enterprise to risk any of his own money. As he wrote Thomson on November 27, "In short, I am disgusted with the affair, throughout, & may have sold at panic prices, still this day [next] year we may have to buy an unfinished Bridge, subject to the 1st Mtge. Bonds & let Linville & you, as Engineers, get a Bridge for us."[30]

Carnegie took money derived from the sale of St. Louis stocks and invested it in Missouri County bonds in support of the Missouri, Iowa and Nebraska Railroad enterprise. He suggested the same investment to Thomson and Scott.[31] This shift of funds represented more than just a rearrangement of an investment portfolio. It signaled the eventual shift of faith in a transcontinental railroad running through St. Louis to one running from Chicago through Iowa. At this early date, however, even Carnegie and associates were probably unaware of the long-term implications of such a shift.

In addition to the southern Iowa scheme that involved the Iowa Contracting Company, the Missouri, Iowa and Nebraska Railroad, and the Keokuk Bridge, Carnegie and associates were involved in a project further north in Iowa during 1871 that also threatened to divert their attention away from St. Louis. On May 17, 1871, Carnegie, Scott, Thomson, B. E. Smith, Thomas L. Jewitt, William Dennison (governor of Ohio), Oakes Ames, Oakes A. Ames (son of Oakes), John Duff, John H. Berryhill, and Hiram Price filed Articles of Incorporation of the Davenport Railway Construction Company in Scott County, Iowa.[32] Carnegie, Scott, Thomson, Dennison, Oakes Ames and his brother Oliver Ames, and Duff had all been elected to the board of directors of the Union Pacific Railroad on March 8, 1871.[33] That election dictated organization of the construction company in order to facilitate northern Iowa rail connections to the Union Pacific.

The construction company was created to finish a 150-mile road from Davenport, Iowa, to the Minnesota state line for the Davenport and St. Paul Railroad and to purchase that part of it already constructed by the Ames brothers. Price was president of the railroad, and Berryhill was on the board of directors. This railroad was created to carry traffic passing over the bridge between Rock Island, Illinois, and Davenport. At its eastern terminus, it connected with the Chicago, Rock Island, and Pacific Railroad, the Western Union Railroad, the Peoria and Rock Island Railroad, and the Rockford, Rock Island and St. Louis Railroad.

The office of the construction company was located at 57 Broadway, New York City. Four different parties, who each paid one-fourth the rent, shared the offices at that location. The other three were the Iowa Contracting Company, the Columbus, Chicago, and Indiana Central Railroad Company, and Carnegie and associates. The Columbus, Chicago and Indiana Railroad was leased to the Pittsburgh, Cincinnati and St. Louis Railroad Company, which was controlled by the Pennsylvania Railroad. B. E. Smith was president of the Columbus, Chicago and Indiana, and Dennison served on the board of directors.

The transcontinental possibilities associated with this investment represented an alternative to the more southerly connections that might be made via St. Louis. As Carnegie's biographer Joseph F. Wall has noted, despite Carnegie's well-known statement of business strategy that suggested putting all one's eggs in one basket and then watching that basket, in reality he scattered his investment "eggs" in many baskets and waited to see which one showed the greatest promise of hatching. At the end of 1871, it was beginning to look like the enterprise in St. Louis was an infertile egg.

It was with this attitude that Carnegie approached the crucial meetings scheduled for December.

12

A Little Mixture of Conciliation

Mr. Thomson honestly believes you will find it necessary to modify the present plans as you proceed. He has been informed that there is no Steel Mill in existence that can roll such sizes as you require. It would be very strange indeed, if mutual conference & a little mixture of conciliation, would not remove this obstacle from the path of an undertaking so imperatively demanded by general interests.

—Andrew Carnegie to James Eads, 1867

Andrew Carnegie had hoped that despite the rejection of Jacob Linville as consulting engineer at the beginning of the bridge project, the "subtle influence" exerted by the Keystone Bridge Company's president would manifest itself during the design phase and through the process of construction. Linville, however, having never believed the basic design selected by Eads to be appropriate, and having more work than he could handle in management of his company, had become a tangential figure in the years that followed.

It was left to Walter Katté, and to a lesser extent John Piper, to represent Keystone's position in matters relating to the engineering and mechanical aspects of the bridge. But these men had proved no match for the domineering intellect and personality of James B. Eads. Katté's objectivity may have already become suspect about this time due to his romance with Elizabeth Pendleton Britton, daughter of bridge company director James Britton. Eventually they married, making Katté son-in-law to the bridge company's second president.

By the end of 1871, Carnegie had had enough. As general superintendent of the Western Division of the Pennsylvania Railroad he had demonstrated his grasp of cold-blooded cost-benefit analysis by the manner in which he cleared wrecks. He either burned the cars that blocked the line or he built new tracks around the obstacle.[1] Now, more than four and a half years after inception of the bridge project, with the success of the enterprise seriously in jeopardy, Carnegie was determined to apply the same ruthless objectivity to the "obstacle" of James Eads. His intention was to go around the chief engineer by forcing upon him that which it was most in the man's nature to resist—authority over his greatest work by a consulting engineer.

The two most important issues presented for discussion at the stockholders meeting of December 20, 1871, held in Carnegie's New York office, were related to money and the control of the construction process. The available funds of the Illinois and St. Louis Bridge Company were clearly not enough to complete erection of the superstructure and approaches, and it was questionable whether additional financial support could be obtained given the endless delays.

In order to invigorate the project, Carnegie called for the appointment of a committee of stockholders, who would employ a bridge engineer "of eminence in the profession" with authority to make whatever changes were necessary to ensure swift and cost-effective completion of the bridge. The resolution further provided that should the recommendations of the consulting engineer fail to be acceptable to Eads, they would be submitted to the board of directors for adoption.[2]

Carnegie, as expected, immediately proposed Linville for the position of consulting engineer. The bridge company directors suggested Carnegie's competitor, C. Shaler Smith. Eads, for his part, probably believing that his friend Smith would be appointed, agreed to the resolution. His acquiescence temporarily put off Linville's request for a renegotiation of all the contracts. The New York stockholders, however, had ideas of their own. They placed James Laurie, the builder of a bridge over the Connecticut River for the Boston, Hartford and Erie Railroad, into the sensitive position as perceived savior of the project.

In regard to the need for additional funds, it was resolved to issue a call on the stockholders for additional payments on stock. The stock subscription at that point amounted to $3 million dollars, but only 40 percent of this had yet been paid. The board of directors also decided on January 12 to cut expenses by a reduction in wages and elimination of certain positions.

The board's actions, however, provided only a small boost to Carnegie's confidence in the project. On January 15, 1872, he wrote a letter to George B. Roberts, assistant vice president of the Pennsylvania Railroad, informing Roberts of his sale of 1,000 shares of stock in the bridge company (which included some stock held by Carnegie in Roberts's interest) and declaring, "It costs money to support an incompetent Engineer, but we have him tight at last I think."[3] On January 26, he sold another 500 shares of the bridge company at $20 a share, twice the amount received for his earlier sale. His intention, as he explained to Thomson, was to reduce his, Thomson's, and Scott's investment to no more than 1,000 shares each. The net amount due them from their bonus arrangement would be enough to cover any calls against these shares, and the result would be that without a dollar's investment they would each have 1,000 shares of full paid stock, and $50,000 worth of second mortgage bonds. Due to the uncertainties of the future, as Carnegie explained to both Thomson and Scott, he thought it best to arrange that Carnegie and associates never be called on to pay one dollar out of their own pockets for their investment. "All we make now will be clear profit."[4]

As they often had in the past, Thomson and Scott took the lead of their junior associate. The sale of stock was probably accomplished in March, prior to the decision of the bridge company board of directors on April 8 to issue a call of 5 percent on the capital stock, payable on May 10. Thus, Carnegie and associates used their insider's knowledge of the impending call on subscribers to unload stock in advance.

While Carnegie made plans for the sale, Laurie arrived in St. Louis and made a thorough examination of plans and the status of construction. He submitted his main report on April 10 and some additional suggestions, along with his letter of resignation and bill for services ($4,057), on April 30. If Carnegie had anticipated great changes as a result of Laurie's appointment he must have been greatly disappointed. Some relatively minor alterations were recommended that saved some money and changed the appearance of the bridge, such as elimination of iron cornices and the towers planned for erection on the approaches. He also recommended abandonment of tramways on the upper roadway, and some additional testing of steel components.[5] Nothing of any great importance was achieved by his efforts, however, and by May Eads was in an even stronger position than he had been in at the end of the previous year.

Carnegie may have decided to reduce his financial exposure prior to receiving the consulting engineer's report because he knew that Laurie could do little to solve the problems then being encountered in the manufacturing process.

The previous year, Butcher Steel Works had postponed manufacture of the 102 sleeve couplings needed until some of the problems associated with production of the anchor bolts and staves had been solved. Casting of the first chrome-steel ingot for couplings did not occur until November 1871. Butcher promised that it would begin producing the couplings on December 4, but various accidents and changes in shop personnel delayed rolling of the ingots until January 2. That day's work resulted in failure, as did every other attempt to roll acceptable couplings until July 9, when three couplings out of ten survived testing and proved suitable for use. The seven that were rejected exhibited a tendency to crack along the edges of the plane surface. Another batch produced at the end of the month was somewhat better; only nine out of seventeen were rejected.

On August 1, the open-hearth furnace being used to cast sleeve-coupling ingots gave out, and a general overhaul was necessary before it could be used again. The lower roughing-roll also broke on the same day. These equipment failures, and other problems, resulted in a suspension of rolling for twenty-seven days. In the meantime, Henry Fitch returned to his duties with the navy and several other inspectors came and went before Theodore Cooper, another navy engineer, took over the job around the first of August.[6] Destined to become one of the best known and most tragedy-stricken bridge engineers in the country, Cooper remained inspector of the shop work until completion of the project.[7]

Gradually Butcher's men improved their methodology of fabrication to such a point that by the first week of September Cooper was able to accept twenty-eight of forty-six couplings rolled. It appeared that the coupling problem was solved, but this slight success proved to have been deceptive. Later in the month, Cooper met Carnegie and Gerald Allen (the new bridge company president) in Pittsburgh to see how the couplings looked when finished. He was very discouraged. On September 24 Cooper wrote: "I was in Pittsburgh last week and saw the last shipment of couplings on the lathes and planers, and was not satisfied with the appearance of the material, shown after the tool. It was much honey-combed,—very few of the couplings appeared to be solid."[8] Allen ordered one of the couplings tested while he was there, and it proved to be of poor-quality steel. Apparently, Butcher was mixing regular carbon and chrome steel and using chrome scrap. This resulted in a lack of uniformity in the material.

On the same day that Cooper recorded his displeasure with the quality of the couplings, Carnegie wrote to J. S. Morgan and Company concerning his impressions of the visit to Pittsburgh. Although, as usual in his communiqués with Morgan, he attempted to put an optimistic face on the experience, he had to admit that the bridge project was held up by the inability of Butcher to manufacture couplings of the quality specified by Eads. If it weren't for that, he wrote, it would be safe to assume that the bridge would be open for traffic early in the summer of 1873 because all other aspects of the work were progressing rapidly. Carnegie also reported that Allen, "the only Mechanic connected with the work," was satisfied with the performance of Keystone following his visit to Pittsburgh, not mentioning Allen's less positive opinion of Butcher. "With such a man controlling the work there is no doubt of the result and after so long a struggle to obtain a practical man with whom to deal I find all our people quite elated. We shall cross by midsummer sure."[9]

Henry Flad also went with Allen to Pittsburgh to examine the couplings and again it was found that they failed the test applied. Allen suggested that the ingots be hammered prior to rolling as a possible method of eliminating the honeycombing that had become so much of a problem. That remedy was tried to no avail. After continued failures of rolled-steel couplings, cast-steel couplings manufactured by the Pittsburgh Steel Casting Company were tested. They did not work either. Nothing that had been tried worked, and it was beginning to look like nothing would work as far as steel couplings were concerned.

In his frustration, Eads became more demanding of the Keystone Bridge Company, and Linville responded on November 11 by sending Eads a list of resolutions adopted by his firm. One of those resolutions stated that Keystone did not consider it safe to erect the arches with the methodology devised by Flad, given the specifications dictated by Eads, if the strength required by those specifications be reduced.

Flad had developed an ingenious method of superstructure erection in 1870 that obviated the usual method of using falsework placed in the stream to support the work under construction. By use of temporary, fifty-foot-high wood towers constructed on top of the piers and abutments, it was possible to support the arches from above with a system of cables as they gradually extended outward, piece by piece, until the two halves met in the middle. Proper tension of the cables was maintained by the use of hydraulic jacks placed underneath the towers, and regulated by means of a system of gauges. In addition to the support provided by the overhead cables, the fixed-end arches would be partially self-supporting once construction moved past a certain point. Structural members of the bridge were placed on a barge that was then towed into position and anchored directly underneath the hoisting apparatus. Each part was then hoisted into position as needed.

Flad's method of erection, which he patented but never had the opportunity to use again, really wasn't the issue with Linville, however. He was more concerned with a loss of potential profit. The various changes in material and method of manufacture were costing money, and the time had come to decide who was going to pay for the unexpected costs.[10]

Having sent the list of resolutions, Linville retired to bed with a serious illness. In response, the bridge company requested a meeting of all interested parties for negotiation of a new contract, one that would provide a solution to the problem.

A meeting of Allen, Eads, Taussig, Carnegie, Linville, Katté, and representatives from the Midvale Steel Company (successors to William Butcher Steel Works) was held in Philadelphia on Saturday, December 7, 1872.[11] Although it was agreed who should pay what in regard to additional costs of fabrication, the most important aspect of the contract negotiated that day was a provision for use of cast-iron couplings if steel couplings could not be successfully manufactured.

This is what Carnegie had been wanting since the first problems with steel fabrication arose. As he wrote J. S. Morgan and Company on December 19, "Last week, I think we arranged to let Capt. Eads out of his difficulty about St. Louis Bridge Couplings. At least he & President Allen believed our concessions had removed every obstacle."[12]

The following week, however, Carnegie found out that the couplings were still not passing inspection. In fact, steel couplings continued to be tested until the latter part of January 1873 before it became apparent that iron couplings would have to be used. The attempt to manufacture steel couplings to Eads's satisfaction had consumed two years and four months, and it was still unknown how many of the five hundred steel couplings already made could be used, if any. Now, Carnegie, Kloman and Company, the firm that actually controlled the Union Iron Mills, could do what it knew how to do; fabricate well-made iron bridge components at a rapid pace.

Plans for superstructure erection were modified to relieve the couplings of some strain, and a meeting was set up for March 5, 1873, with representatives in attendance from the Illinois and St. Louis Bridge Company, Midvale Steel Company, and Keystone Bridge Company. A new contract was signed that recognized the failure of Butcher/Midvale to fulfill terms of the various contracts previously signed, and it also assessed a payment of $35,000 to Keystone to pay the costs of iron couplings and new erecting equipment required by the revised plans. Keystone was also released from the previous contracts. By April 18 work on the iron couplings was underway.

In anticipation of a solution to the coupling problem, Flad and Katté had already begun installing the first three sections of the inner pair of ribs on the west abutment and each side of the west pier on April 7, and work had begun on a fourth section before a parts shortage stopped construction for about a month. With a new contract for iron couplings in effect it looked like the process of superstructure erection was finally on track.

The annual meeting of bridge company stockholders took place on May 8, at which time Allen spoke of the delays caused by the inability of the steel contractors to deliver couplings of the required strength. He also announced that the chief engineer, with the consent of the board of directors, had abandoned the use of steel for couplings used in the upper members of the arches in favor of iron. He confidently stated that Carnegie, Kloman and Company was successfully fabricating these couplings "at a rate that will insure delivery of all required within two weeks." With the coupling problem now solved, and assurances from Keystone Bridge Company that it would prosecute the work with "all the vigor demanded by its importance to your interests," Allen felt comfortable in promising the stockholders that little remained in the way of a speedy erection of the superstructure.[13]

Allen also addressed the financial condition of the company, stating that the auditor's balance sheet showed $3,205,220 collected from payments on stock subscriptions, and $3,671,134 received from proceeds of sale of first mortgage bonds. Against the total receipts of $6,876,354, the company spent approximately $5,170,983 for masonry, superstructure, engineering, salaries, machinery, boats and general expenses; $695,204 for approaches on both sides of the river and for other real estate; $986,831 for interest on loans; and, $190,585 on charter account. Therefore, expenses had exceeded receipts by about $167,249, "which sum is represented by deferred payments on real estate, land damages, &c., not yet matured." When the projected need for future funds to complete the project was considered, the total deficiency was about $856,468. To meet this deficiency, it would be necessary to sell second mortgage bonds. Allen assured the stockholders, however, that projected revenues of the bridge were so great as to eliminate all worries concerning the mushrooming costs. Allen confidently predicted that before another year passed, a dividend would be paid to stockholders "large enough to give promise of a future that will amply compensate for the unavoidable delay in the construction of this great work."[14]

However much solace the stockholders may have derived from Allen's predictions, it was apparent that the bridge had already exceeded Eads's 1868 projections of cost by more than $2.5 million, and construction of the superstructure and that portion of the east approach beyond the arcade was still ahead.

Although the arcaded portions of the west and east approaches were similar, the sections extending beyond the point where the masonry stopped were quite different. The east approach would be very long, and there would be a complex division of rail and wagon decks at the grade level of connecting railroad tracks and city streets. Moreover, the ground on that side of the river was very poor in terms of foundation support. In fact, the area underneath some of the east arcade had once been free-flowing river. Therefore, the east arcade and approach had to be designed more carefully than the west approach, and the excavation for piers and footings required greater effort. The last factor had already caused the bridge company considerable delay.

Eads had originally intended to found the piers of the east arcade on piles, and to sink the piers by use of cofferdams. Just as with the east abutment, however, he changed his mind and decided to take the east arcade piers to rock with pneumatic caissons. He quickly came to believe that this was the right decision when the remains of an old and strongly built ferryboat were found underneath arcade pier number 2. It would have taken much longer to cut away the wreck if a cofferdam had been used. But still, the wreck delayed completion of this one pier by about three weeks.[15]

Originally to be constructed of timber, the east approach was now to be built of iron, from the eastern terminus of the bridge to the north side of Dyke Avenue, beyond which a short timber trestle and an earthen embankment would bring the decks down to grade level. Many contractors, including Keystone, had declined to bid on an all-wood trestle approach. But unlike the other contractors, who probably neglected to bid because they were uncomfortable with the specifications and plans prepared by Eads, Keystone was more concerned by the possibility of Eads's supervision of the work. As Carnegie wrote Linville, "the more I think of it the firmer I am convinced that we should not take that work, or any other work, in which Capt. Eads is the authority in charge."[16]

After Eads produced a new set of specifications for a wood and iron approach in March 1873, with considerable help from Katté, bids were received from several of the top bridge-building firms in the country. Although each bid was based on differing assumptions about what would actually be built, after some discussion the contract was awarded to the Baltimore Bridge Company for $377,900. However, to that figure Allen added another $75,000 for land damages and $40,000 for the wood trestle, making the total estimated cost of the east approach about $492,900.[17] The total projected cost of the east approach, therefore, came fairly close to the $520,397 estimated by Eads in 1868 for both approaches and a toll station on Third Street. Once again, design changes made by the chief engineer had delayed the project and increased costs.

To finance the work of building the approaches, the company made a separate issue of bridge approach bonds with Carnegie's help. Due to a shortage of cash, during the spring and summer of 1873 the bridge company paid the owners of property condemned for the approaches with these bonds.

Due to Carnegie's dependence on the capitalists of London for the east approach bonds and others that might be needed in the near future, he continued to represent the project in glowing terms to J. S. Morgan and Company. In a letter dated May 8, 1873, however, Morgan expressed his growing frustration with the delays and false promises. "We are glad to hear there is some prospect of the St. Louis Bridge being ready for traffic during the present year," he wrote Carnegie. "We have been told the same story the last <u>three</u> years; we shall therefore not encourage too strong hopes of the accomplishment of what we have been so long anxiously waiting for."[18]

Morgan could little imagine, however, just how far Carnegie's predictions of completion would miss the mark. For unknown reasons, the contract for construction for the east approach would not be signed until the following August. And at the other end of the bridge, the tunnel project was in serious trouble.

13

The Elements of Commercial Supremacy

With a direct rail communication eastward to the Atlantic, southward to the Gulf, and westward to the Pacific, all the means necessary for St. Louis to draw to itself all the elements of commercial supremacy will be accomplished facts.

—*Missouri Republican,* February 2, 1872

Even though construction of a tunnel under the streets of St. Louis was a necessary part of the bridge project from the very beginning, the officers of the bridge company had no desire to build it. They had first hoped that the Pennsylvania Railroad, already committed to construction of a similar project, the Baltimore and Potomac Tunnel, would do the job for them.

Begun on June 1, 1871, the 7,519-foot-long tunnel ran under the streets of Baltimore until emerging at the city limits. The project included about 1,057 feet of true tunneling, with the remainder constructed by the "cut and cover" method. Later used for the St. Louis tunnel, this method involved excavation of a trench from street level, construction of the masonry-and-iron tunnel, and reestablishment of the streets and walkways. Buildings located along the line of the tunnel had to be purchased and removed, or shored up with heavy timbers.

The Baltimore job, costing the railroad about $100,000 a month, was projected to total $2.3 million before completion. Numerous problems had been encountered, including underground springs and damage to adjacent properties. The railroad, already saddled with this unexpectedly difficult task, had no interest in attempting another such effort in St. Louis. Therefore, it appeared that the bridge company had no choice but to accept the burden of another construction project.

At an executive committee meeting on August 28, 1872, Eads presented a financial proposal signed by E. D. Morgan and Company and by J. Pierpont Morgan, among others. With this indication of support in hand, the committee directed Eads to immediately prepare plans and specifications. As soon as the meeting adjourned, Eads instructed the Knapp brothers to place an item in the next day's *Missouri Republican* announcing that the chief engineer would advertise in a few days for bids to construct the tunnel.[1]

The notice stated that the tunnel would be 4,000 feet long, including about 900 feet of curve, and would consist of two continuous brick arches, with side walls and center wall of stone. The open-cut excavation would reach a depth of 30 feet below street grade, and the project would require about 180,000 cubic yards of earth excavation, more than 30,000 cubic yards of rubble masonry, and 15,000 lineal feet of sewer construction. The contract would have to be completed by May 1, 1873, or as soon as the bridge could be opened for traffic.[2]

Having prepared the specifications, Eads left the country, departing New York on September 11, 1872, to arrange financing for the tunnel in London. Carnegie was not available to act as bond salesman in this instance because he was in Frankfurt-am-Main, engaged in a three-month battle with Sulzbach Brothers over the bonds of the Davenport and St. Paul Railroad. That draining experience would be his last effort as a bond salesman.

Soon after Eads left St. Louis, the bridge company awarded a construction contract to William Skrainka and Company for $788,701. Skrainka began working in the vicinity of Eighth and Poplar Streets on or about the first day of October.

On October 2, Eads wired Humphreys in New York to report that J. S. Morgan and Company had agreed to loan 100,000 pounds sterling, on notes issued by Drexel Morgan and Company in New York, in quarterly advances at 12 percent interest payable upon completion of the tunnel. J. S. Morgan and Company also suggested that a separate company be organized to build it.

Eads immediately returned to St. Louis and made arrangements for formation of a new corporation. On October 31, 1872, he and nine of his partners in the bridge scheme appeared before a notary public for St. Louis County and submitted articles of incorporation for the St. Louis Tunnel Railroad Company. The stated purpose of the organization was the construction, maintenance, and operation of a railroad running about two miles from the terminus of the bridge at Third Street to a place where a suitable connection could be made "with the track of the Missouri Pacific Railroad and the track of any other railroad."[3]

Taussig was placed in the position of president, but no attempt was made to open the books to outside subscribers or to effect a formal corporate organization. Despite the fact that the association was created as a railroad company, there was no expectation at this time that the organizers would actually build, maintain, and operate a railroad. The designation was merely a formality, necessary in order for the company to be able to lease its two-mile line to other railroads.

The city of St. Louis had already granted the bridge company the right to build the tunnel by ordinances passed on March 14, 1868, and July 11, 1872, which carefully specified the alignment. But several springs and a quantity of quicksand had been discovered shortly after excavation began along the path of the original route, thus making it virtually impossible to safely and economically construct a tunnel where first intended.

At the time this problem was discovered, the company was still in negotiation with J. S. Morgan and Company, and that firm placed a clause in the draft contract for financing that required a strict conformity to all laws and ordinances. Therefore, a new city ordinance would have to be passed authorizing the new alignment. Moreover, the authority granted to the bridge company to construct the tunnel would have to be transferred to the new tunnel company. But the city council initially seemed to be in no great hurry to pass the new ordinance.

After considerable delay, a man showed up at Taussig's office one day and informed him that several thousand dollars would have to be paid to him and his associates before the required ordinance would be passed. The president of the city council at the time was Lewis Bogy, archenemy of the bridge and tunnel companies due to the threat those organizations represented to the Wiggins Ferry Company.[4] The previous July, when the bridge company requested an amendment to the original 1868 ordinance that gave it the right to construct the tunnel, Bogy had vehemently opposed it. Not only was the bridge poorly located, claimed Bogy, but the stockholders of the bridge corporation would be men from outside St. Louis, "foreigners whose interests were not identical with us, yet we give them the right to penetrate the city." In so doing, he claimed, they might destroy the lives of hundreds of innocent persons. Furthermore, "the proposal to build a grand depot in the city was an absurdity as could be demonstrated. The whole scheme was impractical."[5] When one of the other council members said that he might feel the same way if he were a large stockholder in the Wiggins Ferry Company, Bogy replied that he owned no stock in that company. Whether or not anyone then present believed that the man who served as president of the Wiggins Ferry Company for eighteen years had no stock in it is unrecorded. But clearly, if the new amended ordinance was to be passed the continued hostility of Bogy and other bridge company foes would have to be addressed.

Taussig immediately asked Allen to call a special meeting of the board of directors. When Taussig reported the blackmail to the board, Allen said that he didn't understand what Taussig was saying, called for an immediate adjournment, and ordered that no mention of Taussig's comments appear in the record. Several days later, Allen gave Taussig the requested sum in cash and told him to make the payment.[6]

Mayor Joseph Brown was in attendance at the regular meeting of the city council in November. Brown, as president of the Missouri Pacific, was actively working on a scheme to build a competing bridge at Carondelet so the railroad could boycott the bridge being built by Eads. Yet he delivered a flowery speech in favor of the project. In speaking of those who were then engaged in construction of the bridge, he stated, "It is but due and fitting that we should grant all the support possible to sustain and encourage them in their efforts to complete this gigantic enterprise, not merely on account of its great importance to St. Louis, but in view of the peculiar difficulties connected with its execution." He then noted that in immediate connection with the great bridge was the "Union Depot," and "any temporary inconvenience resulting from the building of the tunnel" to connect the two was, in his opinion, "a matter of small consequence, and should create no public dissatisfaction."[7]

On November 29, the city council passed a new ordinance transferring the right to build the tunnel to the St. Louis Tunnel Railroad Company and allowing the route of the tunnel to be changed so as to pass under Eighth Street, past the proposed post office and custom house site on Locust Street, to the south side of Clark Avenue. From this latter point to Spruce Street the continuation of the tunnel tracks would be in a permanent open cut.[8] Apparently, the payoffs had done the trick.

With the appropriate ordinances in hand, J. S. Morgan and Company's legal representative allowed the bond sales to move forward. On January 1, 1873, Barton

Bates and Charles Edward Tracy were made trustees of 1,250 first mortgage bonds amounting to 250,000 pounds sterling, bearing 9 percent interest and issued at par value.[9]

However vexatious the process of securing proper authority for the tunnel project had been, the construction phase would prove to be equally frustrating. As winter set in, the ground froze to a considerable depth, making excavation more difficult. More springs were discovered and water had to be continually pumped out. Excavation of the trench, approximately fifty feet wide from curb to curb, required that a number of buildings and sidewalks be shored up. Property owners began suing the tunnel company for damages, either real or perceived. A commission set up to award compensation approved generous awards. In addition, accidents began to occur.

On Saturday, April 8, one of the contracting company's supervisors, Edward Riley, was overseeing the transfer of large stones from a pile in the center of the excavation to the adjacent wall. Somehow, he became caught between a seven-ton stone and the derrick lifting the stone. Although badly injured, he was taken to his home instead of to the hospital.[10]

Two days later, William Skrainka and Company decided that the work was proving to be too difficult and threatened to abandon the job. An arrangement was therefore made whereby Skrainka agreed to finish that portion of the work south of the south line of Market Street, and James Andrews, the contractor for bridge pier and abutment construction, would complete the remainder.[11] After that the project moved forward at a faster pace, but not without additional difficulties.

On May 9, about eighty teamsters employed in hauling dirt from Skrainka's division of the tunnel project struck for higher wages. They were told when they first hired on that they would be paid $4.50 a day, but they were required to haul eight loads a day in order to earn that amount. Because the distance from the tunnel to the dumpsite was considerable, many of the teamsters found that they could haul only enough dirt to earn $3.50 or $4.00 a day. But instead of asking for a greater per-load payment, they demanded $5.00 for eight loads. The contractor responded by replacing the strikers with new teamsters. On May 20, there was another strike. Once again the contractor refused to change the rate, and new drivers were hired. Advertisements in St. Louis newspapers continued to offer the misleading rate to lure replacement teamsters into the city from the countryside. As was the case with the striking air chamber workers, there were always enough new men to replace those who struck.

The tunnel project was similar to the bridge project in another way; accidents and death were not allowed to slow down the pace of construction. On June 12,

Patrick McAndrew was working in the tunnel trench when a heavy piece of timber fell from a derrick and struck him. Although no bones were broken he lost several days of work. This near-tragedy, along with the previous accident, was just a foreshadowing of accidents to come.

On June 21, at about quarter to seven in the morning, Peter Johnson and his brother Louis were working on scaffolding erected over a small bridge that crossed the portion of the tunnel excavation at Chestnut and Eighth Streets. Suddenly the framework gave way and both men were hurled to the ground nearly twenty-five feet below. Louis's right leg was broken at the knee and he also received several deep cuts on the head and face. His brother was more unfortunate, receiving internal injuries that resulted in his death at about 1:30 that afternoon.[12]

At about the same time that Peter Johnson expired, Patrick Tirrell, who was working in that portion of the excavation where the Johnsons fell earlier, narrowly escaped death when the wall of an embankment collapsed, burying him. Fortunately he was soon unearthed with only bruises to show for the experience.[13]

The accidents on the tunnel project were mirrored by events on the bridge. At about 2:00 in the afternoon of July 12, a portion of scaffolding attached to the west pier gave way, dropping three men into the river. One of the men managed to grasp a rope thrown to him, and a skiff picked up another. The third man, John Piatt, a bachelor from Ohio, slipped beneath the water before anyone could reach him. His body was never recovered. When the incident was reported to Eads, he gave orders that the foremen would be held responsible for the safety of their men, whatever that meant.[14]

In an age when work-related death and mutilation was accepted as an unavoidable fact of life, it is not surprising that the bridge and tunnel corporations were not unduly concerned with worker safety. The most pressing consideration was the need to finish the entire project. The various delays, difficulties, accidents, and even the fatalities might all be forgotten when everything was complete and the tunnel connected the bridge to a union depot. By the summer of 1873, however, it was apparent that even though the bridge and tunnel projects were behind schedule, virtually nothing was being accomplished in regard to construction of the depot.

The rumor being passed in the halls of the Merchants Exchange and on the streets of St. Louis was that the depot enterprise had been abandoned. This was substantiated in the latter part of May 1873, when a reporter for the *Missouri Republican* went to see Taussig, president of both the tunnel and union depot companies, to ascertain the truth of the rumor.

Taussig informed the reporter that there had been no meeting of the Union Depot Company for a year and a half, but occasional conferences of members had been held. At a recent conference in New York, Taussig had urged the parties involved to keep the organization alive and take some steps to secure a site, but he was told that it was almost impossible to determine where the central residential portion of the city would be in the future. As he further explained, "the Union depot was to be located with a view to residence and not business, and they thought that in time the passenger depot might be located further west than Fourteenth street, and still be nearer the central residential property than was the location that was contemplated two years ago."[15] It would have been located there, he continued, if the managers of the Missouri Pacific Railroad at that time had been friendly to the project. But they said the time had not yet come to determine the location of the depot because land east of Fourteenth Street was too expensive. With the cost of land and improvements considered together, the outlay of money required would be greater than could be justified by any future return on investment. In time, they claimed, the residential heart of the city would move west of Fourteenth Street, where the land was less expensive.

Taussig also stated that present intentions were "to establish a temporary depot on the other side of the river, at the end of the bridge, and wait." The existing depot organization was to be disbanded, and as far as the temporary wood-frame depot in East St. Louis was concerned, Taussig said, "I have not anything to do with it, it being on the other side of the river." He also added that the existence of this depot, to be constructed by "the railroad companies," and the abandonment of plans for a union passenger depot would not cause any changes in plans for the tunnel, "nor will it affect in any wise [sic] the volume of business which will pass over the bridge and through the tunnel."[16]

Given Taussig's previous statements to associates engaged in the bridge-tunnel-depot enterprise about the necessity of a union depot, it must be assumed that he was presenting a view to the newspaper reporter, and thus to the public, to which he did not adhere in private. Otherwise, he must be thought a fool, as anyone would be who wished to see the bridge and tunnel succeed, and who also thought it made sense to let the eastern railroads construct a "temporary" wood passenger depot in East St. Louis and then just wait as property values in St. Louis increased. If those interests desiring construction of a union passenger depot waited until the residential center of the city moved west of Fourteenth Street, they would find that the value of the land, the cost of constructing associated switching facilities and yards, and the cost of relocating rail lines through a more densely packed city would have grown to astronomical levels. But, as Taussig certainly knew by the summer of 1873, the men in control of the Missouri Pacific and the Atlantic and Pacific Railroads didn't really want a union depot, at least not if it aided the bridge and tunnel companies. They had their own plans.

On January 30, 1872, the St. Louis city council appointed a special committee to report on an ordinance granting permission to the Missouri Pacific Railroad Company to lay and maintain a railroad track through Carondelet, which had been incorporated with the city of St. Louis in 1870. On February 4, 1872, the committee, accompanied by an assistant city engineer, Richard Southerland, met David Rankin of the Missouri Pacific Railroad, A. L. Berfeld of the Carondelet Savings Bank, and Daniel Garrison to go over the proposed route. The new line was planned to leave the existing Missouri Pacific road at either Kirkwood or Laclede station. It would terminate at a point near Carondelet where a rock foundation had been discovered that stretched all the way across the river at a depth no greater than sixty feet on the Illinois side. There a bridge would be constructed, thus allowing a connection with the narrow-gauge East St. Louis and Carondelet Railroad in Illinois.[17]

The pressing need for a rail and bridge connection to the East at Carondelet was basically a result of the charter granted to the St. Louis and Iron Mountain Railroad by the Missouri legislature in 1851. The purpose of the company was to construct a line from downtown St. Louis to the iron deposits south of the city at Pilot Knob and Iron Mountain. The following year the Pacific Railroad of Missouri (Missouri Pacific) proposed to build an alternative route to the ore fields that would traverse the lead mines of Washington County, thus promising stimulation of a lead-smelting industry in addition to iron manufacturing. With its great political influence in the legislature, the company managed to secure the necessary charter for such a branch road in December. Following a period of spirited public debate, however, the Pacific was persuaded by members of the legislature to relinquish its right to build the branch line in favor of the more direct route suggested by the St. Louis and Iron Mountain.[18]

Shortly after the railroad commenced service in 1856, a German from Pennsylvania named Schalk opened up Carondelet's first ironworks. Other businesses followed, and by 1870, the year that Garrison broke ground for the Vulcan Iron Works, there were several foundries and three zinc works in operation.

When the members of the special committee made their excursion in 1872, Garrison made a point of showing them his foundry, which by then had a daily manufacturing capacity of 200 tons. They also stopped at the zinc works of Martindale and Eddy, where three furnaces turned out about 5,000 tons of metal per day, shipping most of it back east.

Although most of the ore utilized by these manufacturers came from Missouri, almost all of the coal used to fuel the furnaces came from Illinois. The cost and uncertainty of transporting that coal across the river by ferry would be lessened by construction of an expanded rail network and a bridge at Carondelet. Of course, a bridge would also make shipment of iron ore and finished products across the river to points east much easier, and there were entrepreneurs in both St. Louis and Pittsburgh who wished to see such shipments facilitated.

The Union Iron Mills, for example, began to make very large purchases in 1872 of iron ore from the Pilot Knob mines owned by Lewis Bogy. Carnegie's chemists had determined that the low-phosphorus, high-silicon ore produced by that mine was undervalued because other firms believed that it obstructed their furnaces. If properly fluxed, however, the ore could be used successfully in the new "Lucy" furnace constructed by Carnegie between 1870 and 1872. Carnegie would later write that the Union Iron Mills bought a great deal of ore from Pilot Knob "and received the thanks of the proprietors for rendering their property valuable."[19]

There was more at stake, however, than just visions of Carondelet as a second Pittsburgh or Birmingham. The grain business in St. Louis was also thriving, and a new grain elevator had recently been established in East St. Louis in competition with the St. Louis Elevator Company, whose president was John Jackson, a St. Louis and Illinois Bridge Company stockholder. Several St. Louisans, determined to make their city a leading cotton market, had decided to invest in construction of a cotton compress that would allow twenty-three thousand pounds of cotton to be loaded into a single freight car. They believed that much of the cotton shipped to New York would soon be sent via St. Louis instead of New Orleans.

The businessmen behind these and other commercial efforts were among a growing number of railroad-oriented entrepreneurs who accepted the fact that St. Louis had already lost most of its old trade area to Chicago. They saw new possibilities, however, in the establishment of trade corridors linking the East to areas not yet exploited by Chicago-based railroads, via St. Louis. In particular, they anticipated benefits from construction of a snow-free southern rail connection to the Pacific Ocean, and from construction of new railroads to Texas and the Gulf of Mexico.

The officers of the Missouri Pacific Railroad sought to exploit these opportunities by the extension of the Atlantic and Pacific Railroad and by connecting it to southern-oriented lines such as the St. Louis and Gulf Railroad, and the Missouri, Kansas and Texas Railroad.

The Knapp brothers may not have fully appreciated how plans for a new rail line to Carondelet might affect the economic health of the bridge being built by Eads. They may not have realized that connection of the proposed extension with the narrow gauge East St. Louis and Carondelet Railroad, via the existing ferry, was just a temporary arrangement. Eventually, the ferry would have to be replaced by a bridge, and new connections with standard gauge eastern railroads would erase much of the need for the Illinois and St. Louis Bridge. Otherwise, it is difficult to understand why, in their February 5 article on the Pacific railroad branch line to Carondelet, they would claim, "It is on such enterprises as this that the best hopes for St. Louis must be based."[20]

The next day, on February 6, 1872, while James Laurie considered what measures to take to rectify problems with the edifice being erected by Eads, Congressman John B. Hay of Illinois introduced a bill in the United States House of Representatives authorizing the St. Clair and Carondelet Bridge Company to construct another bridge across the Mississippi River at St. Louis.[21]

As expected, the steamboat interests immediately voiced concerns about the bridge, and the St. Louis Board of Trade appointed a committee to look into the matter. On the night of March 28, the committee met with representatives of the new bridge company and a variety of interested citizens. They were told by Samuel R. Dickson of New York, chief engineer for the company, that the combination rail and wagon bridge would be composed of four main spans, each four hundred feet long, and the bottom chord would be situated sixty feet above the high-water mark of 1844. Only one pier would have to be placed in the main channel of the river.[22] No action was taken on that night, but on the evening of April 19 the committee reported favorably on the bridge, remarking that whatever hazards to navigation it threatened, its value to the manufacturing interests of the community was greater.[23]

In May the *Missouri Republican* reported that a contract for construction, thought to be in the neighborhood of $3 million, had been signed with "some Eastern parties," and that the project was expected to be completed in no more than two years.[24] The signing of the contract was apparently enough to bring the *Missouri Republican* out in opposition to the bridge. In an editorial published later that month, the paper stated that the bridge would constitute such an obstruction to navigation, such a death-blow to river commerce, that the city might never recover from its erection.[25]

The opposition of the paper had no effect on the associated rail project, however. By November the Kirkwood branch was nearly complete and it appeared that the final cost would be only slightly over $200,000, much less than the $300,000 originally estimated. Arrangements were also made to transfer freight across the river during construction of the bridge by purchase of the Carondelet Ferry Company for $33,000. Although the Kirkwood branch was created mainly for freight service, some accommodation for passengers had also been made. A small station established on the farm of Ulysses S. Grant, along the line of the Gravois road, was named Grant Station in honor of the president. The railroad also built another small station in Carondelet. The entire line was expected to be in operation by the middle of the month.[26] The next step was construction of the bridge.

Early in January 1873, an old nemesis of Eads reappeared in St. Louis, checking into the Southern Hotel for a few days. The American Bridge Company, created by Lucius Boomer in 1870 as a consolidation of and successor to his separate wood and metal bridge-building firms, was the previously mentioned "Eastern interest" contracted to build the St. Clair and Carondelet Bridge.

Ostensibly, Boomer was on his way back to Chicago after having inspected work being carried out by his company at Booneville, Missouri, for the Missouri, Kansas and Texas Railroad, and at Little Rock, Arkansas, for the Cairo and Fulton Railroad. He was really in St. Louis, however, to examine the site of the proposed bridge, and to even up some old scores.

The contract Boomer previously held with the Union Pacific Railroad for a bridge across the Missouri River between Omaha and Council Bluffs, the biggest job his company ever attempted, had hit a snag. For reasons not of his making, Boomer had been forced to abandon the job before its completion. The railroad decided to finish the project with the help of Keystone Bridge Company, under direction of Theophilus E. Sickels, a Union Pacific staff engineer.

On June 26, 1872, James J. Goodwin, a Union Pacific Railroad trustee and an Illinois and St. Louis Bridge Company stockholder, had asked Eads to travel to Omaha to examine the bridge, approaches, and appurtenances and to "make report whether the same are entirely constructed and completed, or if incomplete specify what further is required to make them complete, and what would such further work cost." Eads was also requested to "associate with yourself some other Engineer who will join you in the examination and report."[27] He took Walter Katté.

The report, dated July 12, 1872, confirmed Sickels's estimate to complete the bridge and also estimated that Boomer was owed only about $1,000 under his contract. Boomer, however, claimed that the railroad owed him $10,000 in patent fees for use of the Post trusses and for materials ordered years before from Chouteau, Harrison, and Valle.[28] Eads ridiculed the claim in his report and generally treated Boomer uncharitably.[29]

Now, six months later, Boomer was back in St. Louis with an opportunity to get even with Eads, Keystone, and everyone else who had run him out of St. Louis years before. The new bridge would be a magnificent, cost-effective structure and would have the longest Post trusses ever erected. Moreover, it would announce to the world that Lucius B. Boomer was *the* man to whom the first shot at erecting a bridge in St. Louis should have gone in the first place. St. Louis, however, had one last slap in the face to lay upon Mr. Boomer.

The Merchants Exchange voted in February to recommend that no bridge be permitted below St. Louis with spans less than five hundred feet or an elevation less than seventy-five feet above the high-water mark of 1844.[30]

On February 22, 1873, shortly after Boomer returned to Chicago, the House of Representatives passed the St. Clair and Carondelet Bridge Bill, notwithstanding vigorous efforts by the St. Louis delegation, the steamboat interests, and the Eads faction to prevent its passage. They needn't have worried.

In the Senate the bill was amended to require two main channel spans of not less than five hundred feet in the clear at low-water mark, and the elevation of the bridge over the main channel could not be less than one hundred feet. This requirement would make the approach spans extremely long and costly in order to lessen the gradient of the tracks. The House concurred in the amendments, and the Senate version was voted into law on March 3, 1873.[31] Although the bridge backers were persuaded at the time to accept the amendments in preference to having their bill voted down entirely, the impracticality of the bill's requirements put a halt to their project, and to Boomer's plans for redemption.

For the moment, at least, the Illinois and St. Louis Bridge Company had survived another challenge.

14

The Texas Trade

The Texas Trade is worth looking carefully after. Much of it may come to St. Louis of its own accord; nearly all of it may be attracted hither if we make the proper efforts to secure it.

—*Missouri Republican,* November 8, 1872

hortly after the Senate passed its version of the St. Clair and Carondelet Bridge Bill, Eads began preparations for a three-week trip to Texas and the mouth of the Mississippi River. The trip resulted from an effort begun earlier in the year by the St. Louis Merchants Exchange to host a convention of western and southern congressmen in May. The purpose of the conference was to select the best plan by which the western rivers could be improved to facilitate cheap transportation of the grain, tobacco, hemp, and cotton produced by the states of the Mississippi Valley. In addition, the transportation of foreign goods and products consumed in the West was to be discussed.

As part of that conference, an excursion was planned on the newly opened railway from St. Louis to Galveston, via the Missouri Pacific Railroad (Atlantic and Pacific Railroad) and the connecting Missouri, Kansas and Texas Railroad (MKT). The return trip would take the voyagers up the Mississippi River by steamboat from New Orleans back to St. Louis. Arrangements for the convention and excursion were entrusted to an executive committee, of which Eads was a member.[1]

Some of the river-oriented businessmen of St. Louis, while mourning the loss of upper Mississippi River valley trade to Chicago, also desired a strengthening of those traditional commercial connections that St. Louis had enjoyed with the South, particularly New Orleans, before the Civil War. Others desired more than just a recapture of that which had been lost; they wanted a new economic order.

Eads, despite his railroad speculations, was primarily a man of the river. But unlike his river-bound brethren he was thinking in global terms. His prewar dream of maximizing the commercial possibilities of the western rivers by removing obstructions to navigation had now expanded to include removal of obstructions at the mouth of the Mississippi.

Ships destined for New Orleans often had to wait until a change in water level made it possible for them to clear the numerous alluvial sandbars that blocked their path. Upon attempting the passage, they often grounded and had to be refloated by tugboats, or had to wait for a rise in the river to do what tugs were unable to accomplish. As the size of ocean-going ships increased, the problem became even more acute.

Sometime in 1873, after it was apparent that completion of the bridge was just a matter of time, Eads increasingly began to turn his mind toward a cure for the problem. By the end of the year he had determined to construct a system of jetties that would channel the river and increase its flow rate to a level sufficient to scour out the sandbars.

If other obstructions on the lower Mississippi could also be cleared, ships from as far away as Europe and South America could sail right up the river to St. Louis. With the vast commerce of the world brought to its levee, the city could achieve the trade status promised since first being declared a port of entry in 1831. It was in consideration of this great vision that Eads planned his visit to New Orleans and the mouth of the river.

Unlike Eads, Thomas Scott was little interested in improving navigation on the Mississippi River. He was a railroad man, through and through. The first part of the trip, which took the travelers to Austin, Texas, and then on to Galveston, was of greater interest to him.

Although Scott had been elected president of the Union Pacific Railroad on March 1, 1871, both his financial stake in that company and his control over it were limited. His deepest desire was to construct a transcontinental rail network over which he had complete control, thus providing the opportunity for greater profits. In pursuit of that goal, Scott managed to take over the Texas and Pacific Railroad in 1872. The southernmost and the next to last railroad project aided by Congress (the Chicago and North Western being the last), the railroad was chartered to run 2,000 miles along the thirty-second parallel from the eastern border of Texas to San Diego via El Paso. In addition, two branches were authorized: one from the eastern terminus near Marshall, Texas, to New Orleans, a distance of 300 miles; the other from a point 100 miles from San Diego, connecting with the Southern Pacific of California. The company had a federal land grant of 13,440,000 acres and also received land donations from the State of Texas.

Shortly before the convention and excursion were scheduled to begin, the *Boston Globe* reported that the convention had greatly excited the railroad interests throughout the country. The paper also claimed that as a result of this excitement, a plan had been hatched by "that crafty manipulator, Col. Tom Scott, which will have the effect to capture the entire convention and nullify the objects for which it was called."[2] By taking the congressmen on an excursion to Texas, during which they would be treated in high style, Scott would presumably divert attention from the true purpose of the conference. "Where," the *Globe* stated, "in the programme as thus announced, the cheap transportation issue comes in for discussion, is not clearly seen."[3]

Soon after returning from the trip, in July 1873, Scott was elected president of the Atlantic and Pacific Railroad (J. Edgar Thomson was elected a director at the same time). The St. Louis and Gulf Railroad, a branch of the Atlantic and Pacific, ran from Missouri to the Gulf of Mexico at Sabine Point in Texas. Since Scott's election came almost exactly one year after the Atlantic and Pacific Railroad leased all the lines of the Missouri Pacific Railroad for a period of 999 years, it looked like St. Louis would soon have a rail connection to both the Gulf and the Pacific Ocean. As the *Missouri Republican* editorialized, "the prosperity of St. Louis as a business point receives a grand impetus from this move [Scott's election], and the whole Western and Southwestern people may be congratulated."[4]

There was another railroad, however, that competed for the loyalty of St. Louis business people. The Missouri, Kansas and Texas Railroad Company was organized April 7, 1870, as a consolidation of the Union Pacific, Southern Branch, and the Tebo and Neosho Railroad. Judge Levi B. Parsons, president of the Land Grant Railway and Trust Company of New York, one of the first directors of the Atlantic and Pacific Railroad and a former incorporator of Boomer's Illinois and St. Louis Bridge Company, was president of the MKT. With the help of such powerful eastern railroad financiers as J. Pierpont Morgan, Parsons began to lay track through southern Kansas and on into the Cherokee Nation toward Texas. He also provided for rapid erection of the numerous bridges required along the route by signing a contract with Boomer's American Bridge Company.

The Tebo and Neosho Railroad connected the main line of the MKT at Fort Scott, Kansas, with the Missouri Pacific line at Sedalia, Missouri. Parsons immediately began to exploit this connection by forming the Land Grant Railway and Trust Company of Missouri, an extension of his eastern corporation. This corporation developed townsite projects through a continuing succession of small subsidiary companies. Parsons also worked out an agreement with the Missouri Pacific whereby MKT traffic was carried from the Sedalia terminus into St. Louis.

By 1871, however, Parsons began to hear rumors that the Atlantic and Pacific directorship, in league with Governor Fletcher of Missouri and certain St. Louis interests led by Joseph Brown, was planning to gain control of the Missouri Pacific. Fletcher was reported to have said: "If we can once get ahold of the Missouri Pacific we can then command the trade of the Southwest, and will shut out the M.K.&T."[5]

As a response, Parsons first threatened the Missouri Pacific by signing contracts on January 1, 1872, for construction of a northeastern extension of the Tebo and Neosho Railroad to a connection with the North Missouri Railroad at Moberly, Missouri. Financial constraints, however, prevented much work from being done on this extension until after the MKT train crossed the Red River into Texas. Since no one in St. Louis believed that Parsons had the necessary funds to build the extension, the threat didn't work.[6]

Parsons also tried to gain direct control of the Missouri Pacific early in 1872 in order to make St. Louis the eastern terminus of the road.[7] He was defeated in that plan, however, by the Atlantic and Pacific general manager, Andrew Pierce Jr. of St. Louis. Pierce later served as vice president of the company under Scott. He also formed, along with Azariah Boody and others, the East St. Louis Stock Yard Company in October 1872 in anticipation of the arrival of Texas cattle. The yard was planned for East St. Louis, as opposed to St. Louis, because certain powerful businessmen in the latter city who were not part of the deal blocked construction of a union stockyard in that city.

Most of the citizens of St. Louis were unconcerned about the battle between Parsons and the Missouri Pacific Railroad, and enthusiasm was high in the city for the prospects of trade with Texas. Throughout 1872 the St. Louis newspapers had run a series of articles extolling the virtues of the Lone Star State. Reporters took excursions to that faraway land and sent back word that the natives were friendly, if a bit crude. As one writer to the editor of the *Missouri Republican* prophesied, what the Illinois Central had done for Illinois, the Chicago and North Western had done for Iowa, and the Kansas Pacific had done for Kansas, the MKT (in connection with the Houston and Texas Central) would do for Texas, "the Golden State of the Union."[8] The official position of the *Missouri Republican* was that the rapid approach to completion of both the Atlantic and Pacific and the MKT opened up a great area for St. Louis trade, and no effort should be spared to encourage that trade.

On March 11, 1873, the Houston and Texas Central Railroad made a connection with the MKT at Denison, Texas, completing a line that ran from St. Louis to the Gulf of Mexico.[9] On the previous day, Mayor L. S. Owings of Denison had sent a letter to Mayor Brown of his "sister city," celebrating the union of the South with the East, North, and West. In response, Brown telegraphed: "The event is hailed here with great satisfaction, and we invite you to an exchange of the products of the fertile plains of Texas for the manufactures and products of the Mississippi valley."[10]

One of the first products of Texas's "fertile plains" to arrive in St. Louis was cattle. In the previous year, approximately 100,000 head of cattle had been shipped from the railhead at Atoka at a cost of $120 a car. The cost from Denison, which was about seventy-five miles closer to St. Louis, was only $100 per car.[11] A revolution in the cattle business seemed to be in the offing, and the number of cattle shipped increased immediately. But Texans and Texas cattle were different in temperament from the Missourians and midwestern bovine more familiar to St. Louis.

Edward King, a visitor to the city around this time, wrote of the cosmopolitan nature of the motley crowd in East St. Louis awaiting transportation across the river. Among the German immigrants and English tourists stood "the tall and angular Texan drover, with his defiant glance at the primly dressed cockneys around him." An unending procession of wagons, loaded with coal, lined up for admittance to the ferry boats. The wagons were "constantly surrounded by the incoming droves of stock, wild Texas cattle, that with great leaps and flourish of horns objected to entering the gangways of the ferry, and now and then tossed their tormentors high in the air."[12]

By May, the situation was beginning to get out of hand. As the *Missouri Republican* noted on May 29, "Yesterday was a good day for Texas steers on the rampage. They could be met with almost anywhere in the city. A Texas steer when he is in good spirits can make things decidedly lively on a crowded thoroughfare. Several portions of our city were enlivened by this means yesterday. One very sprightly fellow with horns nearly a yard long, interviewed Mr. Lawrence Ford, (of Bridge,

Beach & Co.) on the corner of Chestnut and Commercial street, and was very sociable."[13]

Another Texas steer, on the corner of Main and Cherry, was "monarch of all he surveyed" and tried to force his way into a barroom. Yet a third of "the pestilent monsters" came running down Clark Avenue near Ninth Street, scattering people in all directions. Although the paper reported the breakout with considerable humor, it was later discovered that injuries were greater than first supposed. As these incidents became increasingly common, they became decidedly less funny.

Nonetheless, the presence of Texas steers on St. Louis streets was seen as a positive indication of the future because they served as physical manifestations of the newly realized potential of the city as the commercial center of the country. The entire city of St. Louis, therefore, seemed gripped by "Texas fever," and everyone wanted to get in on the action.

As the *Cincinnati Commercial* reported, "There are a great number, indeed a swarm, of St. Louis drummers now in Texas, and a man with a valise is very liable to be mistaken for that class of industrious persons."[14]

Anyone not a drummer was assumed to be looking for land. There was so much land for sale that a land buyer "is a popular individual for the time being." The truth of this fact was made apparent to the reporter from Cincinnati when an inquisitive Texan, from whom he had been seeking directions, asked: "You don't want to buy land, I 'spose. I can point you land for three dollars an acre that'll be worth twenty-five in four years. There's plenty of such trades as that to be had here all the time, and when you return to St. Louis."

"I don't live in St. Louis," the reporter replied.

"Oh, beg pardon; most all the strangers come from there. There's great excitement in that city about Texas lands. Maybe you're traveling for a house in some other city," the Texan continued.

"I'm traveling for a newspaper house in Cincinnati," the reporter responded.

"Cincinnati! Oh yeah; well, let me see; yes—fact is, one don't hear much of Cincinnati down here. It's sorter out of our beat. Cincinnati is so far the other side of St. Louis, you know. St. Louis is all the go here since the new railroad."

If Cincinnati seemed to the Texan to be located somewhere on the far side of St. Louis, Chicago must have appeared equally remote. Chicago drummers, whose overwhelming aggressiveness compared to salesmen from St. Louis had long been cited as one of the main factors behind Chicago's victory in the battle for commercial domination of the upper Mississippi Valley, were nowhere to be seen. St. Louis was thus in a position to dominate an entirely new, and potentially very lucrative, market. Whatever complacency may have earlier been evident in the behavior of St. Louis entrepreneurs, there was none to be seen in regard to Texas during the first half of 1873.

Completion of a bridge across the Mississippi River was an obvious and necessary step in the development of that potential. The bridge would be the key link in that chain of commerce between East and West, North and South, which St. Louis business people wished to forge. As Carnegie had first put it when attempting to sell the bridge company's bonds in London, the bridge would be "a toll gate on the continental highway."[15]

But after Eads returned from the excursion, and throughout the summer of 1873, it became increasingly evident that the bridge project was in a serious state. Many parts had been shipped to the site by Keystone far in advance of any need for them, while more crucial parts, such as the steel coupling bolts, had not yet been manufactured.

By the evening of July 3, only seventy-five additional tubes had been put in place, making the rate of erection about four tubes per working day.[16] The difficulty of fabricating parts had been far beyond anything anticipated by Piper or Linville, and their projections for completion subsequently suffered.

On August 11 Eads complained to Carnegie that Flad and Cooper had informed him of "the startling fact" that according to their latest calculations, "the arches of the bridge will not be closed before Sept. of next year. Mr. Katté has examined the estimate and I believe he fully concurs in it."[17] The board of directors was up in arms and called on Linville to order a duplication of the present tower and cable system so that the pace of erection could be doubled.

Originally, Keystone had proposed to use two towers and two complete sets of cables. The west span and one-half the center span would be erected simultaneously, and following closure of the west span arches the tower and cables on the west abutment were to be moved to the east pier. The eastern half of the center span and one-half of the third span were then to be erected, and the center span closed. Finally, the tower and all the cables on the west pier were to be moved to the east abutment, and the third span completed.[18] Eads, almost reluctantly, told Carnegie that he had been charged by Allen with the responsibility of cracking the whip on Keystone and demanding duplication of the tower and cable system.

Linville replied to Eads's demands two days later with the following: "Duplication of towers and cables can be made only at expense of your company; will call meeting to act on definite proposition to this effect. Have requested meeting Thursday morning."[19] That meeting, held in the Philadelphia offices of Keystone Bridge

Company on August 14, resulted in a new agreement whereby the bridge company would pay Keystone $35,000 if erection of the three arches was accomplished by January 1, 1874. An additional sum of $30,000 would be paid if the bridge was ready for rail and highway traffic by March 1, 1874. Another $250 would be paid for each day prior to March 1 that the bridge was opened for rail and highway traffic, provided that Keystone agreed to duplicate the towers, cables, hydraulic rams, and associated equipment needed for a speedier prosecution of the work. Keystone accepted the terms of the agreement, and orders for the new equipment followed immediately thereafter.

The increased cost, paid by the Illinois and St. Louis Bridge Company, was of secondary importance in light of the pressing need to demonstrate progress to the financial backers of the project. The capitalists of London, with millions of dollars already invested, simply refused to sink more money into the bridge until an arch was successfully closed.[20]

Unfortunately for the bridge company, it was at this crucial point that Eads's health began to fail him once again. The trip to Texas and New Orleans had exacerbated his respiratory problems and he began to cough up blood. His doctor once again recommended a trip to Europe, and the directors of the company agreed to give Eads a leave of absence. As he wrote Carnegie on August 11, "I have had several recent hemorrhages from my lungs and am on my way for a trip to England and back for the benefit of my health and am anxious to sail at the earliest moment."[21]

With the assumption that the agreement of August 14 provided a solution to the problems of superstructure erection, Eads appointed Flad as his surrogate and sailed for England on August 20. Almost immediately thereafter, Keystone informed the bridge company that it could not execute the terms of the new agreement. Its excuse was that its board of directors had met on the fourteenth without legal notice, but it was clear that the real problem was the risk involved. After the officers of Keystone had a chance to look at the agreement, they realized that any delays caused by weather or a rise in the river would jeopardize payment of a bonus. More important, they realized that if there were any problems with insertion of the closing tubes, the final act that would render the arches "completed," they would also suffer. Therefore, they demanded a change in the agreement that essentially required them to have the last interior arch ready for insertion of the closing tubes on January 1. That way, if the arches did not actually close due to mistakes in Eads's design of the tubes, or for any other reason, they could still demand the bonus.

The bridge company responded by dropping the requirement for closing by a specific date and merely asked instead that the necessary duplicate erection equipment be ordered. This was done, and the bridge company paid Keystone $35,000 just for doing so. In addition, it was agreed that the actual closing of each arch would be done under supervision of an Illinois and St. Louis Bridge Company engineer, instead of under supervision of a Keystone employee. Therefore, Keystone could escape blame if the arch could not be closed.

Following approval of the new agreement, Keystone vigorously prosecuted the work of erecting the arches until the first inner arch was ready to be closed about the middle of September. Absence of the chief engineer didn't seem to affect the pace of superstructure erection, unlike the situation during Eads's trip to Europe in 1868. The effort was far enough along at this point, and the experience of the assistant engineers great enough, that Eads's presence was no longer as crucial as had been the case during earlier phases of construction.

But on August 20, the same day Eads departed New York, the secretary of war took action that could result in irreparable damage to the enterprise and financial failure of the bridge company. And only Eads had the skills necessary to answer the new challenge.

Plate XVII

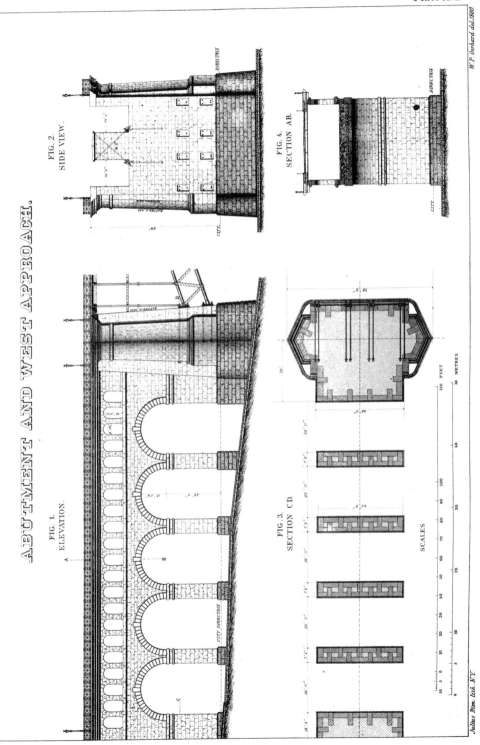

ABUTMENT AND WEST APPROACH.

FIG. 1.
A   ELEVATION.

FIG. 2.
SIDE VIEW.

FIG. 3.
SECTION CD

FIG. 4.
SECTION AB.

SCALES

FEET

METRES

W. P. Gerhard del. 1880.

Julius Bien. lith. N.Y.

Abutment and west approach

Plate XIV

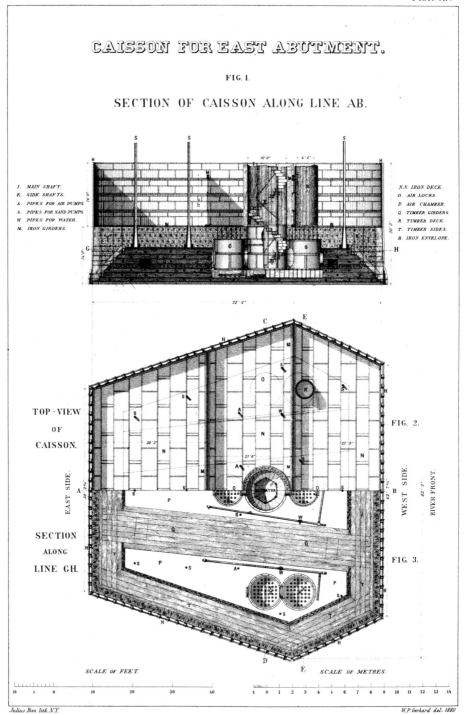

Caisson for east abutment

Plate VII

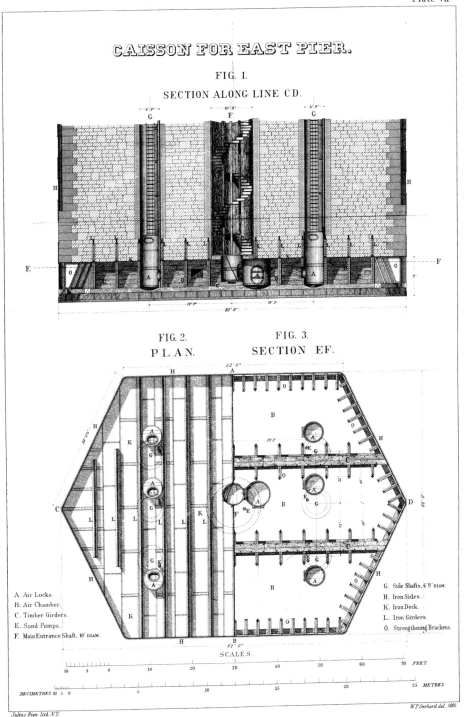

Caisson for east pier

Plate XIII.

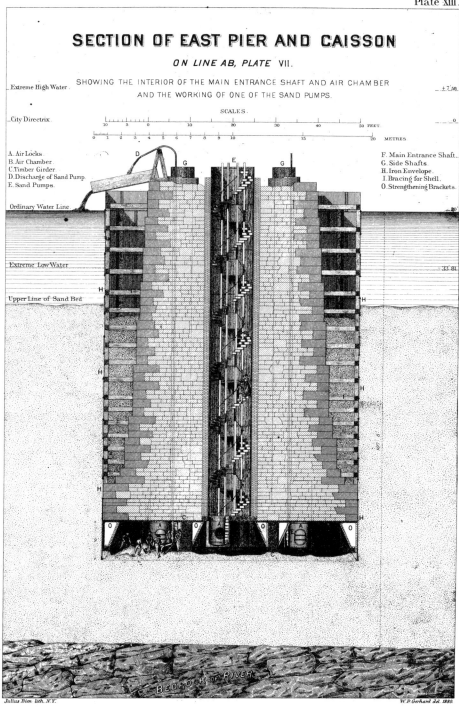

SECTION OF EAST PIER AND CAISSON

ON LINE AB, PLATE VII.

SHOWING THE INTERIOR OF THE MAIN ENTRANCE SHAFT AND AIR CHAMBER
AND THE WORKING OF ONE OF THE SAND PUMPS.

Extreme High Water.

± 7.58

SCALES.

City Directrix.

10 5 0   10   20   30   40   50 FEET.

0 1 2 3 4 5 6 7 8 9 10   15   20 METRES

A. Air Locks.
B. Air Chamber.
C. Timber Girder.
D. Discharge of Sand Pump.
E. Sand Pumps.

F. Main Entrance Shaft.
G. Side Shafts.
H. Iron Envelope.
I. Bracing for Shell.
O. Strengthening Brackets.

Ordinary Water Line.

Extreme Low Water

-33.81

Upper Line of Sand Bed

BEDROCK OF RIVER.

Julius Bien lith. N.Y.

W. P. Gerhard del. 1880.

Section of east pier and caisson showing the interior of the main entrance shaft and the working of one of the sand pumps

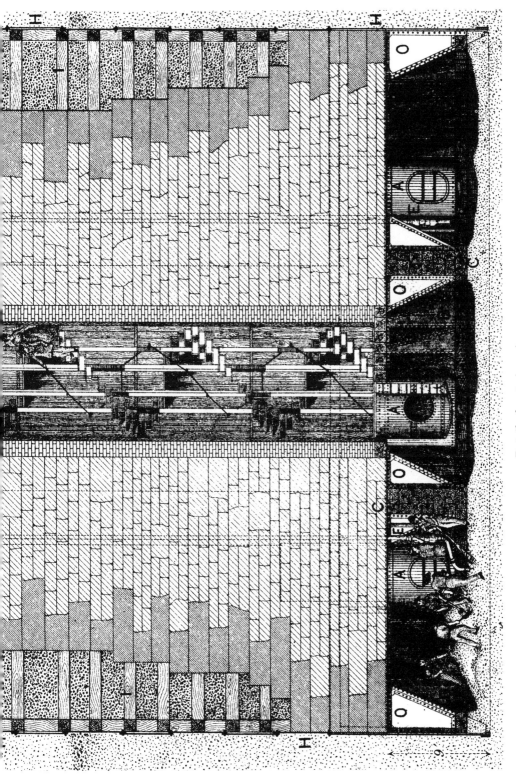

Detail of east pier caisson

Plate XV.

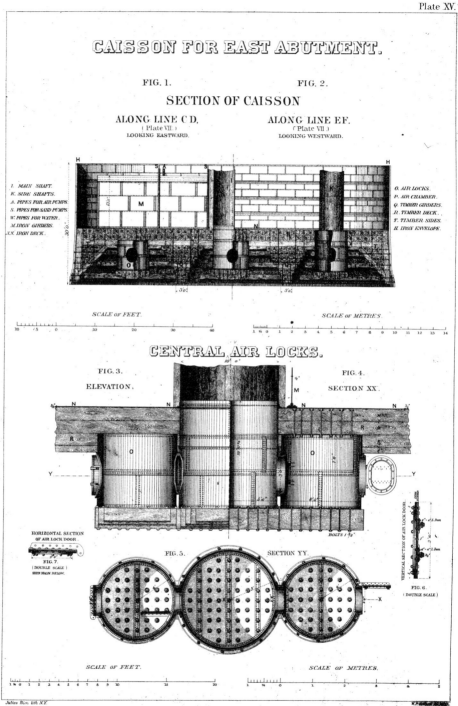

CAISSON FOR EAST ABUTMENT.

FIG. 1.   FIG. 2.

SECTION OF CAISSON

ALONG LINE C D,   ALONG LINE EF.
(Plate VII.)   (Plate VII.)
LOOKING EASTWARD.   LOOKING WESTWARD.

I. MAIN SHAFT.
K. SIDE SHAFTS.
A. PIPES FOR AIR PUMPS.
S. PIPES FOR SAND PUMPS.
W. PIPES FOR WATER.
M. IRON GIRDERS.
N. N. IRON DECK.

O. AIR LOCKS.
P. AIR CHAMBER.
Q. TIMBER GIRDERS.
R. TIMBER DECK.
T. TIMBER SIDES.
H. IRON ENVELOPE.

SCALE OF FEET.   SCALE OF METRES.

CENTRAL AIR LOCKS.

FIG. 3.   FIG. 4.

ELEVATION.   SECTION XX.

HORIZONTAL SECTION
OF AIR LOCK DOOR.

FIG. 7.
(DOUBLE SCALE)
SEEN FROM BELOW.

BOLTS 1 ⅜"

VERTICAL SECTION OF AIR LOCK DOOR.

FIG. 6.
(DOUBLE SCALE)

FIG. 5.   SECTION YY.

SCALE OF FEET.   SCALE OF METRES.

Julius Bien lith. N.Y.

Caisson for east abutment: section and air lock

Plate X.

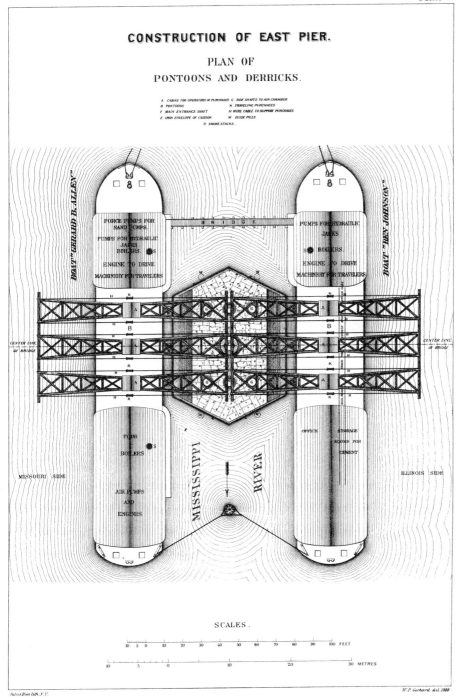

Construction of east pier: plan of pontoons and derricks

Plate IX.

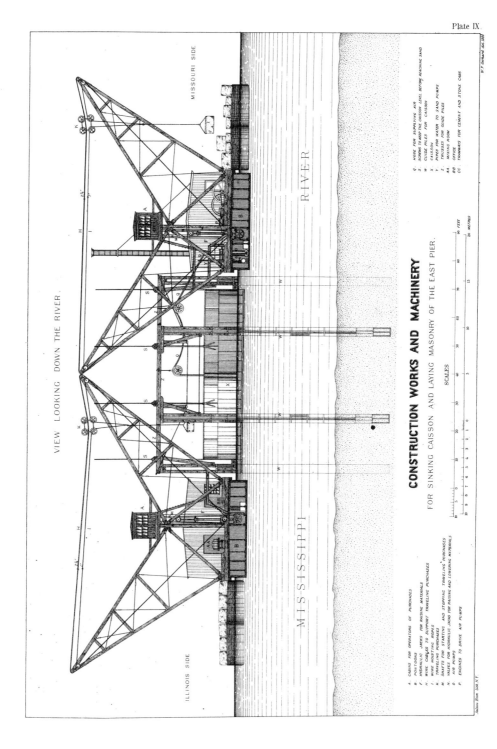

VIEW LOOKING DOWN THE RIVER.

ILLINOIS SIDE

MISSOURI SIDE

MISSISSIPPI

RIVER.

CONSTRUCTION WORKS AND MACHINERY

FOR SINKING CAISSON AND LAYING MASONRY OF THE EAST PIER.

SCALES

A   CABINS FOR OPERATORS OF PURCHASES
B   PONTOONS
F   HYDRAULIC   JACKS FOR RAISING MATERIALS
H   WIRE CABLES TO SUPPORT TRAVELING PURCHASES
I   WIRE HOISTING ROPES
K   TRAVELING PURCHASES
M   SHAFTS FOR STARTING AND STOPPING TRAVELING PURCHASES
N   VALVES FOR HYDRAULIC JACKS FOR RAISING AND LOWERING MATERIALS
O   AIR PUMPS
P   ENGINES TO DRIVE AIR PUMPS

Q   HOSE FOR SUPPLYING AIR
S   SCREWS TO KEEP THE CAISSON LEVEL BEFORE REACHING SAND
W   GUIDE PILES   FOR CAISSON
X   CAISSON
Y   PIPES FOR WATER TO SAND PUMPS
Z   TRUSSES FOR GUIDE PILES
AA MIXING ROOM
BB OFFICE
CC TRAMWAYS FOR CEMENT AND STONE CARS

Julius Bien Lith. N.Y.

W.F. Gerhard del.1881.

Construction works and machinery for sinking caisson and laying masonry of the east pier

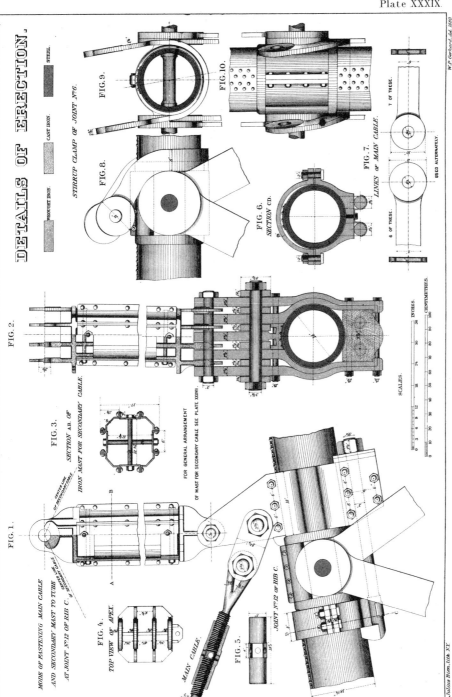

Plate XXXIX.

DETAILS OF ERECTION.

WROUGHT IRON. CAST IRON. STEEL.

FIG. 9.

FIG. 10.

STIRRUP CLAMP OF JOINT Nº6.

FIG. 8.

FIG. 7.

LINES OF MAIN CABLE.

FIG. 6.

SECTION CD.

7 OF THESE.

6 OF THESE.

USED ALTERNATELY.

FIG. 2.

FIG. 3.

SECTION AB. OF

IRON MAST FOR SECONDARY CABLE.

MODE OF FASTENING MAIN CABLE

AND SECONDARY MAST TO TUBE

AT JOINT Nº12 OF RIB C.

FOR GENERAL ARRANGEMENT

OF MAST FOR SECONDARY CABLE SEE PLATE XXXVI.

FIG. 1.

FIG. 4.

TOP VIEW OF APEX.

MAIN CABLE.

FIG. 5.

JOINT Nº12 OF RIB C.

SCALES.

INCHES.

CENTIMETRES.

Julius Bien, Lith. N.Y.

W.P. Gerhard. del. 1880.

Details of erection

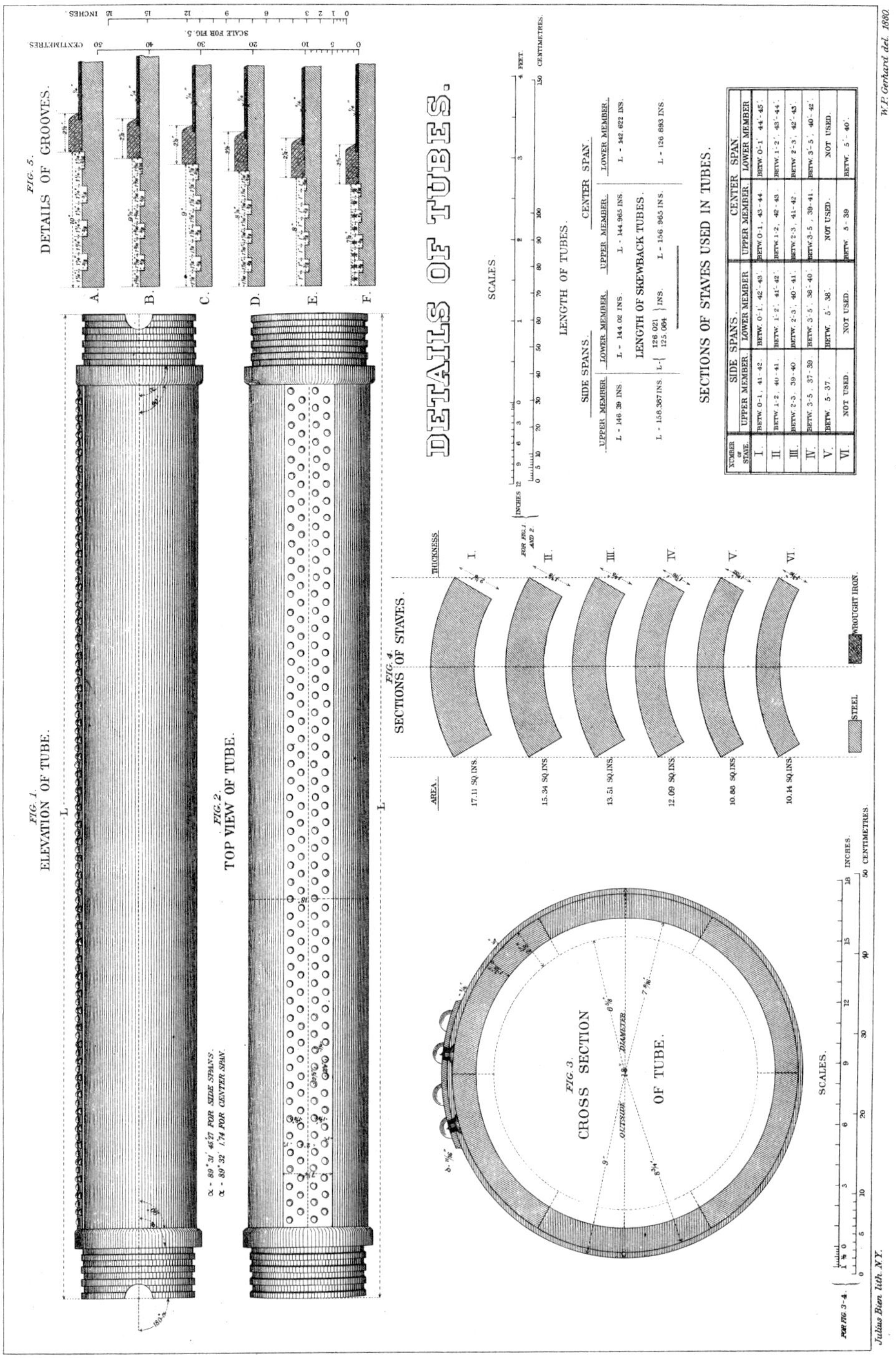

Plate XXIX.

DETAILS OF TUBES.

FIG. 5.
DETAILS OF GROOVES.

A. B. C. D. E. F.

SCALE FOR FIG. 5.

INCHES
CENTIMETRES

FIG. 1.
ELEVATION OF TUBE.

L

α = 89° 31' 45" FOR SIDE SPANS.
α = 89° 32' 1.74 FOR CENTER SPAN

FIG. 2.
TOP VIEW OF TUBE.

L

FIG. 4.
SECTIONS OF STAVES.

THICKNESS

I. II. III. IV. V. VI.

AREA

17.11 SQ. INS.
15.34 SQ. INS.
13.51 SQ. INS.
12.09 SQ. INS.
10.86 SQ. INS.
10.14 SQ. INS.

STEEL   WROUGHT IRON.

FIG. 3.
CROSS SECTION
OF TUBE.

DIAMETER
OUTSIDE

SCALES.

INCHES
CENTIMETERS

SCALES

LENGTH OF TUBES.

FEET
CENTIMETERS

SIDE SPANS.

UPPER MEMBER | LOWER MEMBER
L = 146.39 INS. | L = 144.02 INS.
L = 158.367 INS. L = { 126.021 / 123.006 } INS

CENTER SPAN.

UPPER MEMBER | LOWER MEMBER
L = 144.965 INS. | L = 142.422 INS
L = 156.965 INS. | L = 176.693 INS

LENGTH OF SKEWBACK TUBES.

SECTIONS OF STAVES USED IN TUBES.

NUMBER OF STAVE	SIDE SPANS		CENTER SPAN	
	UPPER MEMBER	LOWER MEMBER	UPPER MEMBER	LOWER MEMBER
I	BETW. 0-1, 41-42	BETW. 0-1, 42-43	BETW. 0-1, 43-44	BETW. 0-1, 44-45
II	BETW. 1-2, 40-41	BETW. 1-2, 41-42	BETW. 1-2, 42-43	BETW. 1-2, 43-44
III	BETW. 2-3, 39-40	BETW. 2-3, 40-41	BETW. 2-3, 41-42	BETW. 2-3, 42-43
IV	BETW. 3-3, 37-39	BETW. 3-5, 38-40	BETW. 3-5, 39-41	BETW. 3-5, 40-42
V	BETW. 5, 37	BETW. 5, 36	NOT USED.	NOT USED.
VI	NOT USED	NOT USED	BETW. 5, 39	BETW. 5, 40'

SCALE FIG. 3-4.

Julius Bien, lith. N.Y.

W. P. Gerhard, del. 1880.

Details of tube

Plate XVIII

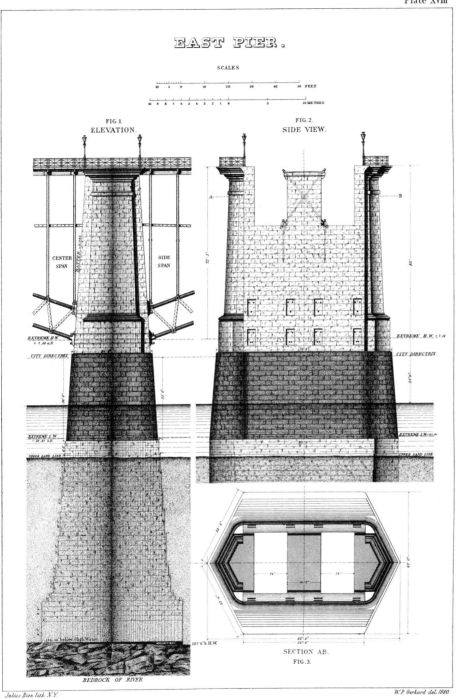

East pier: elevation and side view

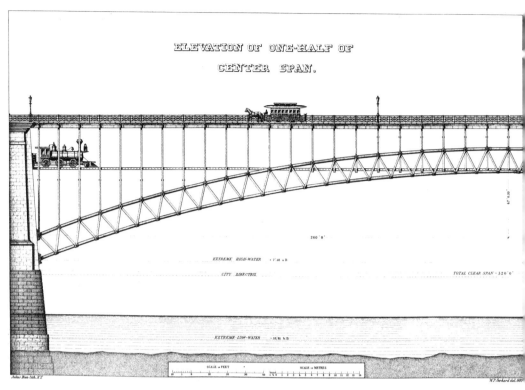

ELEVATION OF ONE-HALF OF
CENTER SPAN.

EXTREME HIGH-WATER · 7'48 × D

CITY DIRECTRIX

260 0'

TOTAL CLEAR SPAN · 520 0'

EXTREME LOW-WATER · 35'81 × D

SCALE OF FEET   SCALE OF METRES

Elevation of half of center span

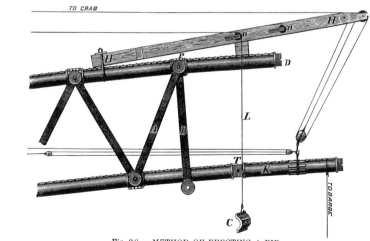

Method of
erecting a rib

TO CRAB

Fig. 28. — METHOD OF ERECTING A RIB.

Plate XI.

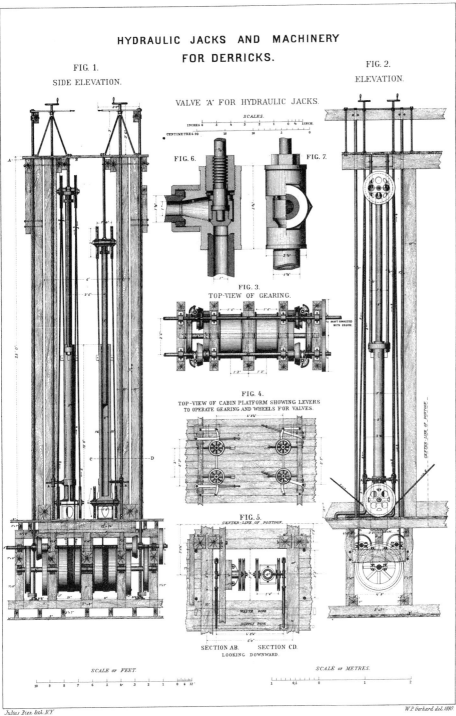

HYDRAULIC JACKS AND MACHINERY FOR DERRICKS.

FIG. 1.

SIDE ELEVATION.

FIG. 2.

ELEVATION.

VALVE 'A' FOR HYDRAULIC JACKS.

SCALES.

FIG. 6.   FIG. 7.

FIG. 3.
TOP-VIEW OF GEARING.

FIG. 4.
TOP-VIEW OF CABIN PLATFORM SHOWING LEVERS
TO OPERATE GEARING AND WHEELS FOR VALVES.

FIG. 5.

SECTION AB.   SECTION CD.
LOOKING DOWNWARD.

SCALE OF FEET.

SCALE OF METRES.

Julius Bien lith. N.Y.

W.P. Gerhard del. 1880.

Hydraulic jacks and machinery for derricks

Plate XXIV.

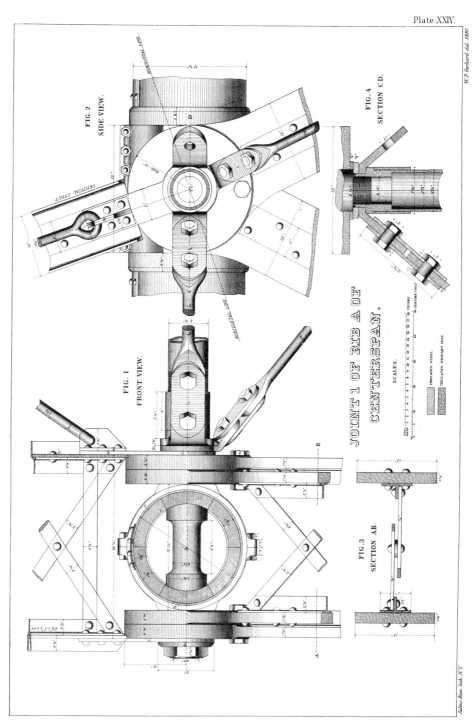

FIG. 2
SIDE VIEW.

FIG. 1
FRONT VIEW.

FIG. 4
SECTION CD.

FIG. 3
SECTION AB.

JOINT 1 OF RIB A OF
CENTERSPAN.

SCALES.

INDICATES STEEL.

INDICATES WROUGHT IRON.

W. P. Gerhard del. 1880.

Julius Bien lith. N.Y.

Joint 1 of rib A of centerspan

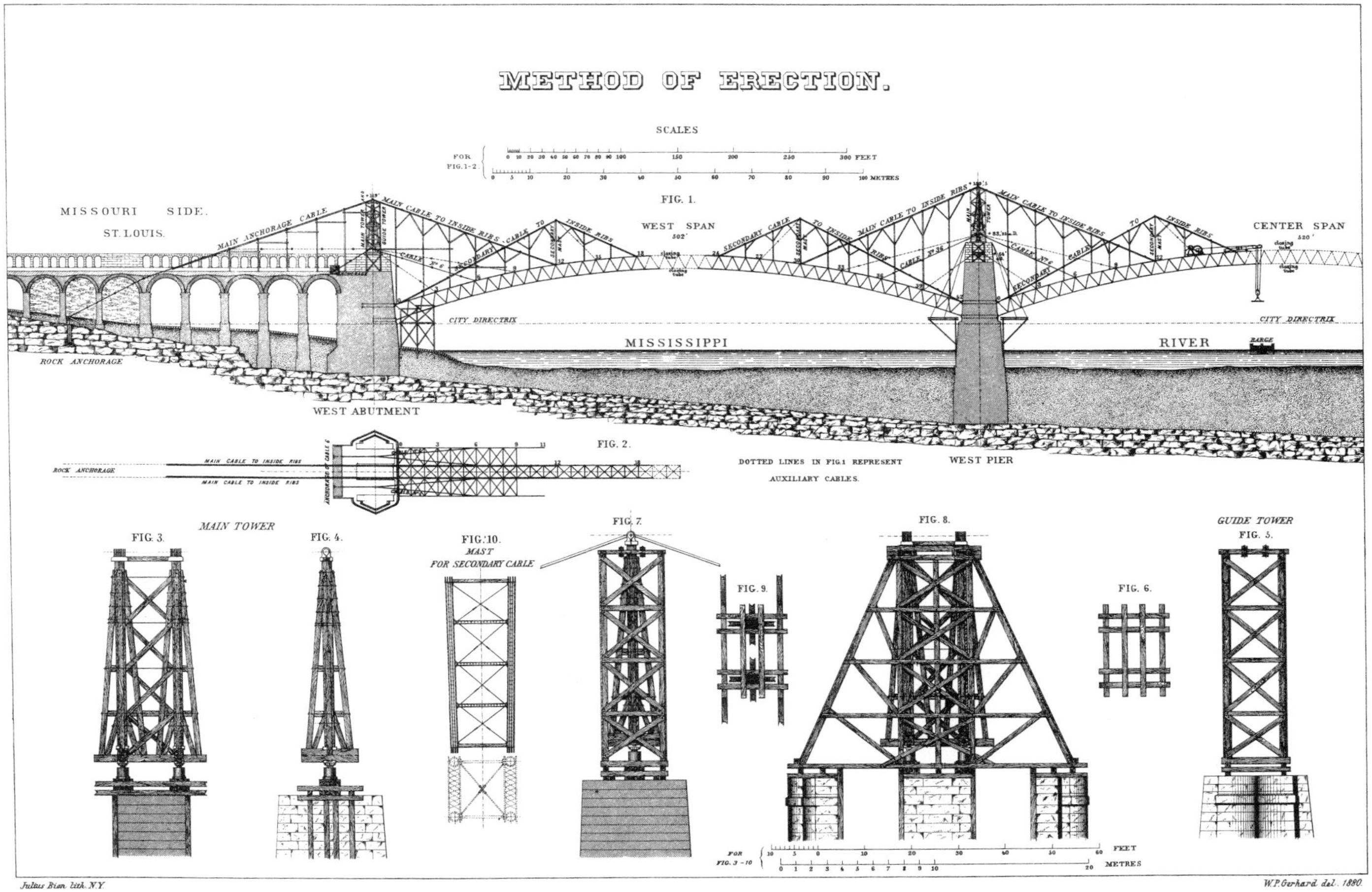

Method of erection

Plate XXXVII

Plate XXXVI.

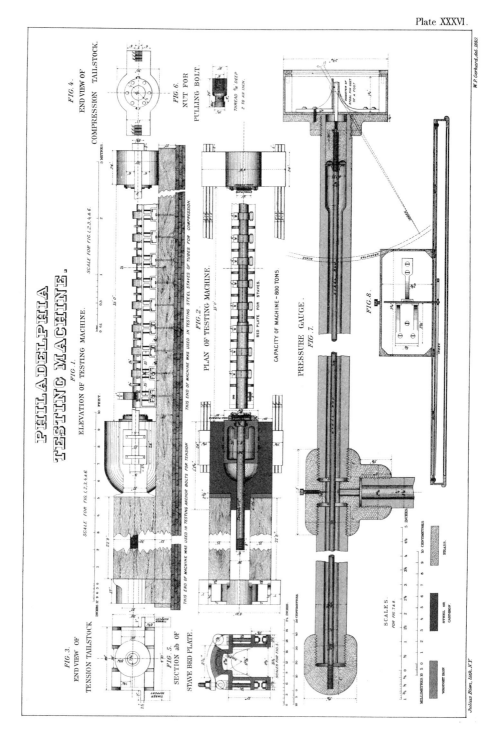

Philadelphia testing machine

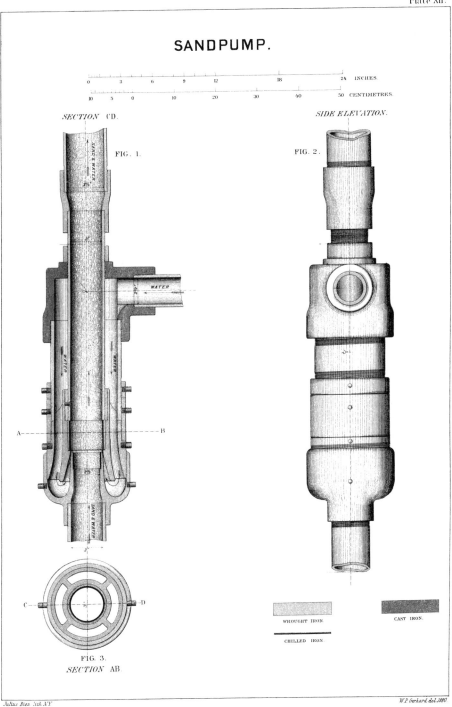

Plate XII.

SANDPUMP.

SECTION CD.

SIDE ELEVATION.

FIG. 1.

FIG. 2.

FIG. 3.
SECTION AB

WROUGHT IRON

CAST IRON.

CHILLED IRON

Julius Bien lith. N.Y.   W.P. Gerhard del.1880.

Sand pump

Plate XXXV.

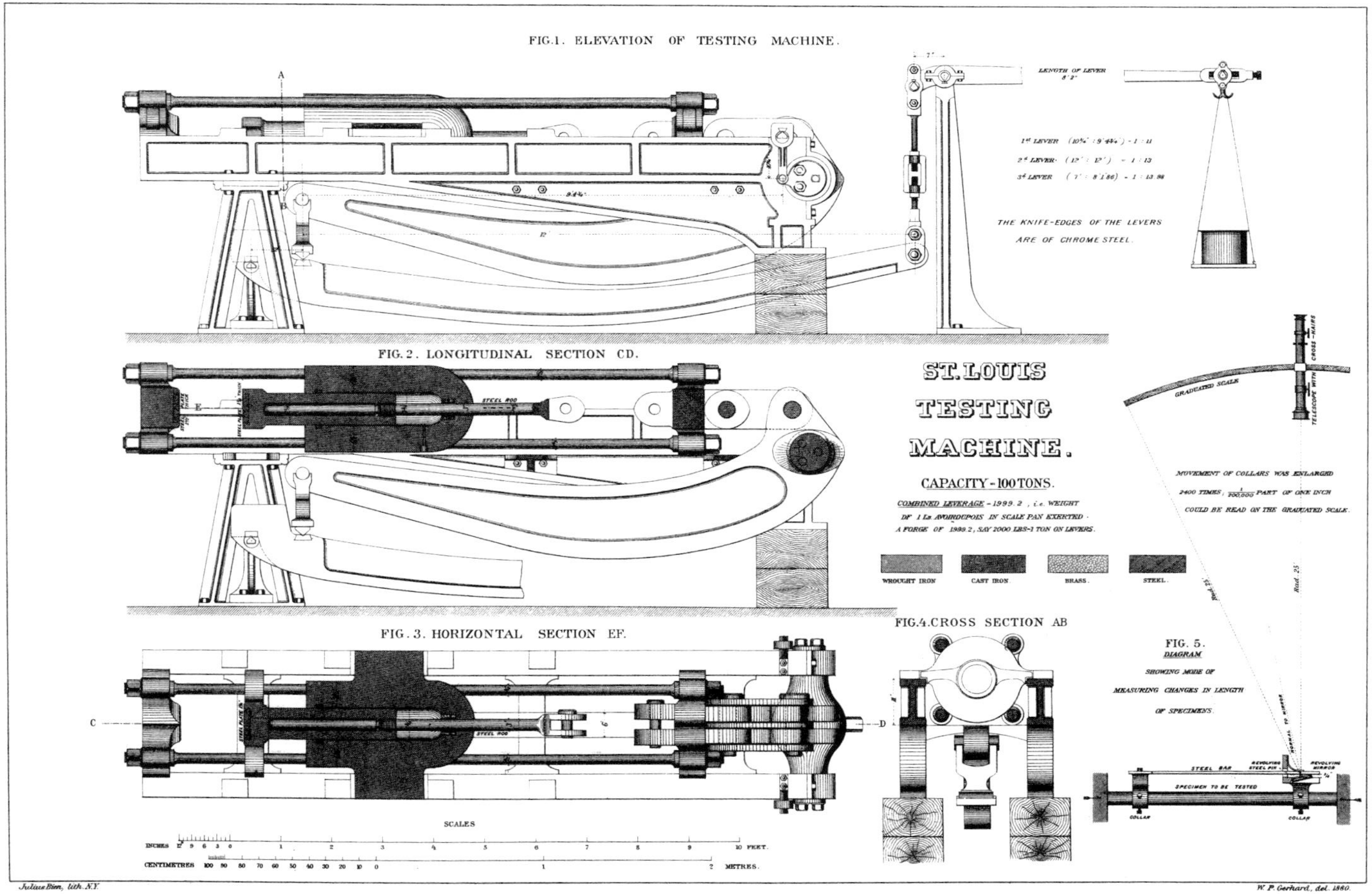

St. Louis testing machine

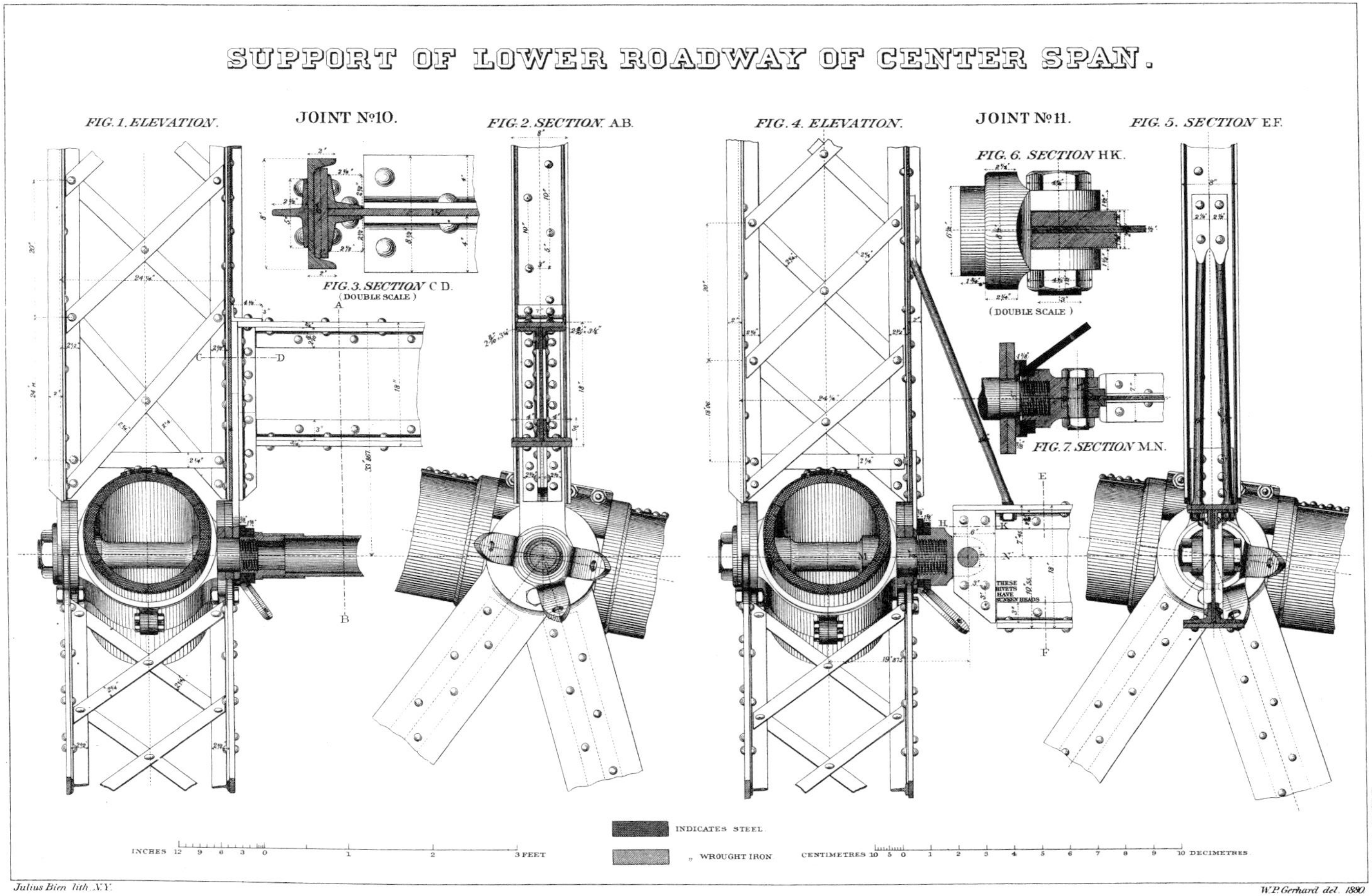

Plate XXVII.

SUPPORT OF LOWER ROADWAY OF CENTER SPAN.

JOINT Nº11.

FIG. 5. SECTION E.F.

FIG. 4. ELEVATION.

FIG. 6. SECTION H.K.
(DOUBLE SCALE)

FIG. 7. SECTION M.N.

JOINT Nº10.

FIG. 2. SECTION A.B.

FIG. 3. SECTION C.D.
(DOUBLE SCALE)

FIG. 1. ELEVATION.

INDICATES STEEL

WROUGHT IRON

CENTIMETRES

DECIMETRES

INCHES

FEET

W.P. Gerhard del. 1890.

Julius Bien lith. N.Y.

Support for lower roadway of center span

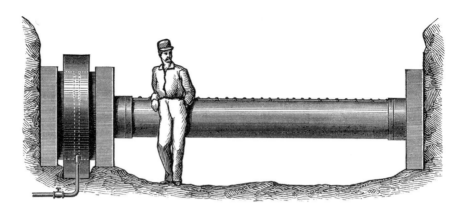

Fig. 17.—METHOD PROPOSED BY COL. FLAD FOR TESTING A LARGE TUBE.

Method proposed by Col. Flad for testing a large tube

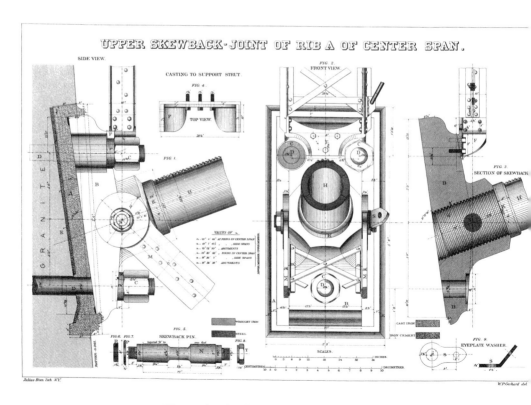

Upper skewback-joint of rib A of center span

Plate XX.

Vertical sections at pier between first and second ribs and between second and third ribs

Erection of the west and central arches

Erection of the west arch cables

Ribs complete and decks begun

Sinking the east abutment

Closing the center and east arches

The St. Louis Bridge after completion

Eads Bridge, 1999 (Photo by the author)

The west approach of the Eads Bridge, 1999 (Photo by the author)

Honor at the Stake

Rightly to be great
Is not to stir without great argument,
But greatly to find quarrel in a straw
When honor's at the stake.

—William Shakespeare, *Hamlet*

When the first tubes of the west arch of the bridge began to go up in the spring of 1873, many of the steamboat operators of St. Louis thought that they were part of the complex web of scaffolding. By July, however, it was clear that the tubes were actually part of the arch, and that the lower portion of each arch would be far closer to the water than indicated by previously published illustrations. Fearing the effect the lower part of the arches might have on free navigation of the river, the steamboat interests banded together and dispatched a letter to Secretary of War William W. Belknap requesting that this potential obstruction be investigated and reported upon by a board of army engineers. They also requested an injunction against the bridge company while the investigation was underway.

The complaining faction was led by John S. McCune, president of the Keokuk Northern Line Packet Company,

Carondelet Marine Railway and Dock Company, Illinois and St. Louis Railroad and Coal Company, Alton and Grafton Packet Company, and past president of the Pilot Knob Iron Company. According to McCune, when the committee of the Merchants Exchange chaired by Eads in 1866 sent its resolution to Washington regarding the proper restrictions to be placed on any bridge constructed at St. Louis, they understood that the lowest part of the bridge would be fifty feet from the high-water mark of 1844, as measured at the center of the span. Even when the law was passed with a provision stating that the span over the main channel would be only fifty feet above the city directrix, they were not alarmed because they assumed that a horizontal truss bridge with a straight bottom chord, similar to what had already been built at other points on the river, would be erected. And fifty feet was adequate clearance for that type of bridge.[1]

Nor did they become concerned when drawings of what was obviously an arch bridge were displayed at the Merchants Exchange, because those drawings showed the well-known *Eliza,* supposedly one of the largest boats of her day operating on the lower Mississippi, passing underneath the bridge with fifteen or twenty feet between the tops of her chimneys and the "under part" of the bridge. A number of other steamers were illustrated lying at the wharf near the western abutment of the bridge, their chimneys reaching up only to the foot of the arch. As McCune stated, "we supposed this was a representation of facts and not fiction. But you cannot imagine our surprise when he [Eads] commenced erecting the arch this summer to see the foot of which reach down even *below* high water mark."[2]

Although they acknowledged that the bridge was perhaps being built in accordance with the letter of the law, the steamboat interests said that they had misunderstood the ramifications of the language contained therein. Furthermore, the bridge violated the spirit of the law in that it would obviously obstruct navigation.

On July 24, the day that news of the controversy first hit the St. Louis newspapers, hundreds of people went down to the levee to see for themselves if the complaint had any merit. They could not discern much, of course, given the present state of construction, but they went to look anyway.

On July 30 General Foster of the Engineer Office in Washington declined to issue the requested injunction because he determined that the bridge was being erected according to law.[3] That did not end the matter, however.

On August 20, 1873, Belknap issued Special Orders No. 169, creating a five-member board of engineers to examine the bridge and determine if it would prove to be a serious obstruction to navigation and, if so, in what manner its construction could be modified.[4]

The members of the board were Colonel James H. Simpson, Major Godfrey Weitzel, Major William E. Merrill, Major Charles R. Sutter, and Major Gouverneur K. Warren. Simpson commanded the United States Army Engineer Office at St. Louis, and one or more of the other board members had been on every engineer board convened since the war to examine western river bridges.

On August 25, Simpson sent McCune a letter in which he asked for the names and dimensions of a number of the largest packets and towboats on the river in order to facilitate the work of the board. On the same day he went to see Henry Flad, notified him of the hearing, and received from him such drawings of the bridge as Flad thought necessary to present the facts of the bridge's design and placement to the board.

When the board met on September 4, Simpson informed the bridge company representatives that the board members wished to have the company represented by the chief engineer and officers, but they did not desire to have legal counsel present because they were not asked to consider questions of law. He also made a point of stating that the findings of the board would be based on "our own determination of facts."[5] By so doing, Simpson gave notice that the board members considered themselves qualified as professionals to examine the appropriate data and render an opinion that was based on objective analysis and not on the biased opinions of those who had reason to support or attack the bridge.

There were several witnesses and experts present for the steamboat interest and several for the bridge company, not including Eads, who was still in Europe. After hearing from five or six witnesses in opposition to the bridge, with much repetition of the same points, the board members announced that if there were no new points to be made they need not hear anyone else because they intended to examine the structure for themselves. They then asked the bridge company to bring forth its witnesses and experts, and the board spent considerable time going over the maps, sketches, and surveys presented by the experts representing the company. These men, and the witnesses for the opposition, were cross-examined by the bridge company's legal counsel, John W. Noble.

About noon on Friday Noble stood up and requested that the board adjourn until some time the following week, thereby giving him time to walk the streets of St. Louis soliciting signatures of all those in favor of the bridge. The board declined but stated that it would hear all the experts that the company could bring forward between that time and Saturday evening, the planned point of adjournment. The bridge company's counsel then abandoned the case without calling any more witnesses.[6]

The board issued its report on September 11, finding that indeed the bridge would be a serious obstruction to navigation. If the bridge was allowed to stand, the board could offer no remedy to the obstruction except construction of a canal around it on the Illinois side and placement of a drawbridge across the canal. The idea came from Weitzel, who enlarged the Louisville and Portland Canal with the world's largest locks between 1869 and 1872, thus allowing boats to pass the railroad bridge over the Ohio River at Louisville.[7] The board also recommended that lights and markers be placed on the bridge so that pilots could clearly see the position of the piers and judge the headway.

The findings of the report may have been determined, at least to some degree, by the testimony of steamboat owners who claimed that it would be difficult and expensive to lower the chimneys of their larger boats, and that some boats would have to have their pilot houses cut down as well in order to clear the arches. The high elevation of these pilothouses was considered necessary for pilots to have an unobstructed view. Boat owners also reported the problems experienced in regard to navigating past the draw spans of the upper Mississippi River bridges, which had generally proved to be serious obstructions to navigation. The difficulties of trying to pass under the exact center of the St. Louis main channel arch, a necessary maneuver in order to achieve the clearance required by the enabling act of Congress, were expected by steamboat operators to be much greater.

On October 15, the bridge company received notification that Chief of Engineers General Andrew A. Humphreys concurred in the report and had sent it on to the secretary of war with his recommendation that it be submitted to Congress for such action as that body deemed necessary.

Eads, who had just returned to St. Louis, responded to the board's report with a lengthy rebuttal addressed to the bridge company officers, which was published on November 19 in the *St. Louis Republican.* It was a typical Eads document: rational, articulate, persuasive, and misleading.

The primary thrust of his argument was that the correctness of the board's opinion rested entirely upon the reliability of the testimony received by the board, and upon the qualifications of its members as experts in river navigation. The board members were not experts in river navigation, according to Eads, because none of them had any skill or experience in the operation of steamboats. Therefore, only the validity of the testimony provided by "experienced boatmen" was of any relevance. Eads belittled the testimony of experienced boatmen who were opposed to the bridge in a detailed point by point analysis that cast doubt on every argument made. He also referred to letters of support by certain riverboat captains, letters not presented to the board on September 4, to demonstrate that one steamboat captain's opinion was as good as another.

In regard to the larger question of whether or not the bridge would constitute an obstruction to navigation, Eads stated that it had never been claimed that the bridge would not, to some extent, impede the free navigation of the river. In fact, he admitted, "it requires no great intelligence to discover that two piers standing in the main channel are an obstruction to navigation."[8] The real question to be decided, however, was whether or not the bridge was a *serious* obstruction, which was a matter of definition to be decided by "experienced boatmen," and not engineers.

What the board should have been authorized to consider, claimed Eads, was the degree of accommodation that steamboat operators and railroad operators owed each other in order to protect the rights of both. In defense of allowing bridges some degree of obstruction, Eads essentially used the same argument enunciated by Abraham Lincoln in defense of the Rock Island Bridge. "The right," Eads claimed, "of the traffic that flows east or west to cross the river is fully equal to that of the commerce on the river to go to the north or south. They are both in the interest of the whole country, the one cannot be favored at the expense of the other without loss to the nation. Both intersect each other at St. Louis in such volume that mutual concessions are imperative to insure the least delay to each other."[9]

In concluding, Eads wrote that those who still thought the bridge would be "a very serious obstruction to navigation" should wait until it was finished. Then they would see that it was built in accordance with the design parameters of the Merchants Exchange, as submitted to Congress in 1866 and contained in the authorizing legislation. What he intentionally failed to mention was that the legislation passed by Congress contained specific design constraints that were different than those recommended by the special committee of the Merchants Exchange.

In addition to defending the design of the bridge, Eads questioned the procedural correctness of the engineer's investigation by falsely claiming that the board had "refused to receive the rebutting testimony of the company."[10] He also stated, untruthfully, that the company first learned of the hearing by obtaining a copy of the special order from the *St. Louis Republican* on August 30.

Later, in a newspaper article published on November 30, Eads refuted another of McCune's charges by stating that the drawing exhibited at the Merchants Exchange was not meant to deceive anyone but was just a "fancy sketch." The name on the boat shown under the piers was placed there by the draughtsman as a compliment to Eads's daughter and was not meant to represent the real steamboat *Eliza,* which sank twenty-five years before.[11]

Simpson responded by asking the *St. Louis Republican* to print a copy of his August 25 request to McCune, a copy of the request he sent Flad on August 26, asking if the board could keep the drawings provided by Flad until the time of the hearing, and a copy of Flad's reply of August 27. The paper printed the letters, thus proving that the company did know of the hearing in advance of the date claimed by Eads.

On December 5, Simpson also responded to a letter and affidavit printed in the newspaper on that day in which Taussig made further unfair allegations against the board. After refuting Taussig's charges and reiterating his belief that the board had done its best to save the bridge while also protecting the interest of navigation, Simpson gave notice that he would no longer debate the issue in public journals.[12]

Although McCune was certainly prejudiced in the matter, he had previously written a letter to the newspaper that supported Simpson's claim to impartiality. In his opinion the board varied from its strict duty in that it tried to save the bridge "and not destroy or damage the beautiful structure" by rejecting recommendations, made by McCune, that would have required tearing part of the bridge down.[13]

There were many among the anti-Eads faction in St. Louis who agreed with McCune and thought that the board of engineers had been too timid in its suggestions for how to handle the obstruction. Much of the community, however, thought the call for a canal ridiculous. Eads, who had begun referring to the canal as "McCune's Ditch," was not hard pressed to point out the impracticability of the suggestion. A canal would have been extremely costly; would have destroyed East St. Louis; would have harmed the bridge; and would have required installation of a drawbridge, which no one really wanted. Carnegie's comments to J. S. Morgan and Company on December 5, 1873, pretty well sum up general reaction to the whole affair. "The report of Govt engineers has made them a laughing stock," he wrote. "It is simply ridiculous & the steamboat men see it in this light."[14]

The general public was certainly hard pressed to understand why, when the bridge was so close to completion after many years of delay, the question of obstruction was even being brought up. Fueled by biased newspaper coverage of the issue, the flames of rumor began to spread through the halls of the Merchants Exchange and on the streets of St. Louis—the board of engineers had been out to get Eads from the start.

It was true that army engineers, wishing to apply scientific methodology to management of the western rivers, were often opposed to the activities of civilian engineers in the service of private enterprise. It may be said that this position predetermined, to some extent, the findings of the board members. However, there were several factors working against them, in terms of public perception of their impartiality, over which they had no control. The most significant of these involved timing.

The fact that the bridge had been under construction for six years before the board of engineers was ordered to conduct its investigation was, ultimately, the greatest hurdle to overcome in the fight to win acceptance of its report. It simply did not seem fair to question the safety of a structure so late in the process of its erection.

Given what the steamboat operators had at stake, it certainly would have been worthwhile for them to have requested an examination and report on the design of the bridge when that design was first made public in 1867, rather than passively accept the information gleaned from a "fancy sketch." If they had taken such action they might have settled the issue at that time and spared the army engineers later embarrassment. But they did not take that action, and their complacency became grounds for questioning the credibility of men who could not have investigated the bridge before being ordered to do so.

Another major factor that contributed to impressions of partiality relates to the limitations of the inquiry. As stated in their first report, the board members confined themselves strictly to their instructions, which directed them to ascertain whether the bridge, as being built, would be a serious obstruction to navigation of the Mississippi River, and if so, what modification could be made in its construction.

The steamboat operators apparently assumed from the start that they could not successfully challenge the bridge in terms of its violation of the specific design parameters stipulated in the authorizing act of Congress, parameters inserted into the legislation to ensure that free navigation of the river be maintained. Their complaint to the secretary of war stemmed from the broader assumption that the bridge, in its entirety, was a serious obstruction and thus a threat to river commerce. It was this assumption that the investigation sought to test. And if the board arrived in St. Louis with preconceptions regarding this question no one should have been surprised. There could be no doubt that the bridge was an obstruction to navigation. Eads, as early as his first report to the officers of the bridge company in 1869, had acknowledged that the bridge would virtually cut the river in two.

In regard to the board members' execution of the second part of their charge, which directed that they consider what modifications could be made in the bridge's construction if it was found to be an obstruction, it could be said that they acted with considerable magnanimity. As McCune pointed out, they went out of their way to propose a canal rather than harm what they themselves termed a "magnificent structure." In so doing, they clearly went beyond what they were instructed to do in an attempt to make some provision "for allowing large boats to pass the bridge with safety whenever they find it necessary to do so."[15]

In January 1874 the board met for a second time to report on the survey and projected costs of the proposed canal, and to review Eads's published comments about its first report. The supplemental report produced by this second meeting, dated January 31, 1874, detailed plans and estimates for the canal but was primarily dedicated to a defense of charges made against the board by Eads, Taussig, and Noble. As might be expected, given the ridicule and disparagement that the engineers had been subjected to since their initial report, the tone of the second document was far less conciliatory.

The supplementary report stated that the many difficulties in construction of the canal had been noted by the board in its first report, "yet no other remedy for the obstruction to navigation has been proposed by the bridge company." Moreover, the report stated that if the canal was indeed costly, that "is something for which the board are in no wise responsible. It is the inevitable result of a badly designed bridge."[16] In calling the bridge "badly designed," the board was presumably referring to the use and placement of arches, which were much more restrictive in terms of navigation than were truss spans with straight bottom chords.

The board members did, however, admit that the canal was not a particularly good solution to the problem. The best solution, in their opinion, would be to substitute trusses with straight bottom chords in place of the arches. "This," the engineer's claimed, "is the structure apparently intended by law."[17]

The supplemental report also included a letter from G. K. Warren to Simpson, attached as an appendix, in which he defended himself against a claim of prejudice made by Taussig. The charge stemmed from a remark made by Warren at the hearing held on Friday, September 4. Taussig had requested that the board adjourn until Saturday, or perhaps Monday, so that the bridge company could assemble enough steamboat operators in its defense to counter the attacks of the opposition. Warren responded by saying, "If a thousand steamboat-men should come and say that this Bridge is no obstruction, it would not change my opinion."[18]

In his letter Warren explained that he had meant no disrespect to the steamboat operators, but that he simply did not need to hear their opinions to determine whether or not the bridge was an obstruction. Anyone with two eyes could judge that issue for himself. It was an undeniable fact.

Having said that, Warren also indirectly took issue with Eads's claim that engineers were unqualified to determine whether or not a bridge was an obstruction to navigation. At least as far as his own experience was concerned, Warren had good grounds on which to claim expertise.

In the seven years that passed since he conducted his first congressionally mandated survey of the upper Mississippi River from the falls of St. Anthony to St. Louis, Warren had dedicated much of his professional career as an army engineer to investigating how bridges could be erected across navigable western rivers without obstructing navigation.

In response to requests from the Senate Committee on Post-Offices and Post-Roads, he was ordered to study and report on the Clinton Bridge in 1867 and on the Steubenville Bridge in 1868. In both cases there were strong political divisions among pro- and anti-bridge factions, but his report was professionally objective. As one senator remarked regarding Warren's testimony before the committee, he "was careful in his statements."[19]

On July 10, 1869, the day after the secretary of war transferred authority over construction of the new Rock Island Bridge from the Ordnance to the Engineer Corps, Warren was put in overall charge of the project. In addition to executing his responsibility regarding the general plan of the structure, he personally located the piers and abutments with an eye toward lessening their degree of obstruction.

In 1870 Congress passed an appropriations bill for rivers and harbors that provided for the assignment of three army engineers to examine all the bridges erected or in the process of erection across the Ohio River. Warren was one of the three so assigned. He also served during this period as a member of several engineer boards studying the general subject of river improvements and was chief engineer on various specific river improvement projects.

Warren took on these additional assignments while continuing his supervision of the Rock Island Bridge project. The multiple responsibilities almost ruined his health, but he stuck to his tasks and performed admirably in executing all of them.

In addition to his personal experience Warren had carefully read the voluminous proceedings in the Wheeling Bridge and Rock Island Bridge court cases, both of which raised essential questions regarding the conflict between river and rail transportation. He had also sent a circular letter of inquiry to the members of the board of engineers convened by Boomer in 1867, requesting their views on the relation of span length to the necessities of river navigation.

Given this experience, it is fair to say that in regard to the specific issue of bridges as obstructions to navigation, Warren was far more of an expert than was James Eads. After all, Eads had never had to navigate a boat past a Mississippi River bridge because only one, the Rock Island Bridge, had existed for a few scant months prior to his retirement from the river in 1857. And unlike Warren, he had yet to build a bridge.

In his concluding paragraph, Warren stated that he was not indifferent to the need of St. Louis for a bridge, nor was he indifferent to the interest of those who had invested their money in the project. But he felt that a greater public interest, the free navigation of the river, should not be destroyed unnecessarily for the sake of those who were building the bridge. "I am convinced," he stated, "that a bridge suited to this great want, at an expense much less than has already been made, almost if not entirely unobstructing navigation, could years ago have been completed, upon designs well known and tried in this country, had not the authors of the present monster stood in the way."[20]

Warren's injudicious use of the term "monster" to describe the bridge, along with his earlier comment to Taussig at the September hearing, made him a lightning rod for criticism of the investigating board. His bias seemed apparent, and no consideration was given to the fact that he might have had reasons for being particularly defensive. But reasons did exist.

On the second day of the battle of Gettysburg, General George G. Meade said to Warren, then a brevet major general serving as Meade's chief engineer, "I hear a little peppering going on in the direction of that little hill yonder. I wish you would ride over and see if anything serious is going on, and attend to it."[21] The "little hill" was Little Round Top, and when Warren reached the crest he saw that there were no troops on it other than a few Union signalmen, and that the hill "was the key to the whole position."[22] Warren acted quickly to ensure the assemblage of adequate forces before the Confederates attacked. A fierce battle followed, which resulted in a successful defense. Warren's decisive response at a crucial moment in the most important battle of the war made him a hero, at least for the moment.

Less than two years later, while in command of an infantry unit, Warren arrived late in support of General Philip H. Sheridan at the battle of Five Forks, one of the last battles of any consequence in the war. Sheridan, in a fit of rage, relieved Warren shortly thereafter. Believing himself wronged by Sheridan's action, Warren spent much of the rest of his life attempting to clear his name. He repeatedly requested a board of inquiry to review the case. But Grant, who had the power to order such a review, wished to shield his friend Sheridan from criticism and blocked the inquiry.[23]

Warren was still engaged in his quest to regain his honor when the events in St. Louis transpired. It is no wonder, then, that Warren reacted emotionally to charges that he and his fellow officers acted improperly in regard to their investigation of the St. Louis Bridge. Sheridan had already questioned his personal honor and professionalism as a soldier, and Warren was not about to allow his honor and professionalism as an engineer to be similarly impugned, particularly when he knew he was right.

A bridge with equal utility to the St. Louis Bridge could have been built in less time, and at lower cost, had not Eads's ego required erection of a monument that would, in his words, "constitute a national pride, entitling those through whose individual wealth it has been created to the respect of their fellow men; while its imperishable construction will convey to future ages a noble record of the enterprise and intelligence which mark the present times."[24]

Of course, a lower-cost truss bridge, similar to the type suggested by Linville and others, might not have stood the test of time as well as the one built by Eads. But it would not have had to. Increased loading requirements of the railroads using those Mississippi River bridges authorized by Congress in 1866 eventually rendered all of them obsolete, even when they continued to meet their original design specifications. The bridge built by Carnegie at Keokuk, for example, continued in use until 1915, at which time a new superstructure was erected on the original piers. But the St. Louis Bridge, its superstructure only partially reconstructible in order to meet increased requirements, and its foundations too massive for economic removal, would remain standing in essentially original condition long after it ceased to function well as either a rail or a road bridge.

However valid Warren's claim might have been, it was certainly too late by the time he made it to construct a standard truss bridge from scratch. But since the arches of the St. Louis Bridge had not yet been completed, it was still possible for horizontal bottom chord trusses to be erected on the existing piers, as recommended by the board of engineers as an alternative to construction of a canal. Whether or not it would be prudent to do so was a matter of perspective. From the viewpoint of those who had invested in the bridge, anything other than completion of the structure as designed was unacceptable.

Concerned with the effect that the primary and supplemental reports of the board of engineers might have on members of Congress, Eads and Taussig decided to travel to Washington and appeal to President Grant in person. They did so not without some misgivings because Eads had opposed Grant's election to a second term in 1872, and Taussig thought that the president might still harbor a grudge because he had blocked Grant's appointment as a county engineer in 1859. But Grant, who had already received a petition from several bridge supporters alleging that the bridge faction had not been given a fair hearing, held no animosity for either man and was receptive to their complaint. In fact, he told Eads that he owed him for helping win the river war for the Union, and he told Taussig that he owed him a debt of gratitude for forcing him to find work to which he was more suited.

After the two men made their case, without anyone present in the chief executive's office to present the engineer's side of the argument, Grant called Belknap in and asked him point blank if the bridge was being constructed in accordance with the authorizing act of Congress. Belknap replied that he believed it was, and Grant then said, "I think, General, you had better drop the case."[25] With that, the red-faced Belknap backed out of Grant's office, and backed out of his support of the steamboat owners' cause.

The combined report of the board was transmitted to the House of Representatives Committee on Commerce on March 28, 1874, and published as House Executive Document Number 194. Without the support of the Grant administration, however, the recommendations of the board were ignored and the issue, as far as Congress was concerned, was dead.

The challenge of the steamboat interest had come to an end, at least for the moment, but the repercussions of the affair lasted for years. The army engineers came to feel that they had been unfairly abused for objectively carrying out their professional duties. This attitude undoubtedly poisoned their attitude concerning Eads, as later events would indicate. As for the steamboat operators, they became even more entrenched in their desire to maintain the status quo, which meant denying the bridge whatever business it was in their power to control while continuing to utilize the existing ferry and transfer system.

Unfortunately for the engineers, the steamboat operators and the War Department had mishandled the case from start to finish. Failure to address the fundamental legality of the bridge at the very beginning was a strategic error because it was not, in fact, being constructed in accordance with the authorizing act of Congress.

The main source of disagreement between the steamboat interests and Eads in regard to the degree of obstruction presented by an arch concerned the point above water level at which the height of the channel span should be measured. Much of the specific argument between McCune and Eads concerned the language of the recommendations submitted to Congress by the Eads-led Merchants Exchange committee in 1866. Those recommendations were not applicable, however.

The relevant portion of the authorizing act passed by Congress, which was applicable, stipulated that "the lowest part of the bridge or bottom chord shall not be less than fifty feet above the city directrix at its greatest span. Second, that it shall have at least one span five hundred feet in the clear, or two spans of three hundred and fifty feet in the clear of abutments. If the two latter spans be used, the one over the main steamboat channel shall be fifty feet above the city directrix, measured to the lowest part of the bridge at the centre of the span."[26]

The words "measured . . . at the centre of the span" relate only to the one span erected over the main channel if two spans of 350 feet were constructed, which is not the case with the St. Louis Bridge. Therefore, the lowest part of the bridge, or bottom chord, had to be less than fifty feet above the city directrix "at its greatest span."

Even if one accepts the definition of "bottom chord" to include the lower portion of the arches of the St. Louis Bridge, the lowest part of the bridge is the point at which measurement must be taken to assure compliance. This obviously does not mean that the measurement should be taken at the piers, because boats could not pass through piers, as the *Effie Afton* so well demonstrated in 1856. Instead, the measurement had to be taken at the lowest part of the superstructure of the channel span. Since the lowest part of the center arch of the St. Louis Bridge was much lower than fifty feet above the city directrix, the bridge was not constructed in accordance with the specific design parameters imposed by Congress. The bridge was, therefore, an illegal structure.

Eads had been wrong when he wrote in October that the degree of obstruction to river navigation allowable in accommodation of rail transportation was a matter for steamboat pilots, and not engineers, to consider. It was really an issue for Congress to decide. But, having already limited the obstructive nature of the St. Louis Bridge via the design parameters of the authorizing legislation, Congress was unlikely to revisit the issue unless presented with evidence that those limitations had been violated. But thanks to Grant's support of the bridge and Belknap's timidity in pursuing the issue, this was not done.

Moreover, by the time the combined reports of the army engineers were transmitted to the Committee on Commerce, the issue was largely moot in terms of the St. Louis Bridge. When Eads had suggested in November that anyone opposed to the bridge should wait until it was complete to determine if it was a serious obstruction, he knew very well that it would be too late at that point to do anything about it. The bridge would be a fait accompli. With this in mind, and with no injunction issued to stop construction, erection had continued while the debate raged.

16

Capital and Influence

Mr. Eads already stands prominent as one of the most enterprising and public-spirited citizens of St. Louis. . . . To him, and to the enlightened, public-spirited citizens who have pledged their capital and influence to sustain the enterprise, will justly belong the glory that will surely attach to the St. Louis Bridge.

—L. U. Reavis, *Saint Louis: The Future Great City of the World,* 1870

The need to push superstructure erection forward to completion was generated by more than just the threat posed by the board of army engineers. Lack of capital could stop the project as surely as any act of the secretary of war.

The directors of the bridge company had promised J. S. Morgan and Company that the first arch would be closed no later than September 19. This event had to take place before the London financiers would agree to provide a desperately needed loan of $500,000 to the bridge company. But as the two cantilevered sections of the first arch began to approach each other, one from the west abutment and the other from the west pier, it became increasingly apparent that the task would be difficult.

Each arch would be at its "normal" length when the

superstructure was complete, bearing the full dead load, or weight, of all the parts that it supported. Because fluctuation in temperature would cause a temporary lengthening or shortening of each completed arch, with a corresponding slight rise or fall in each deck, the normal length of a fully loaded arch was assumed to exist at an ambient temperature of sixty degrees Fahrenheit.

Each arch tube had been made about one-sixteenth of an inch longer than its normal length to provide for compression once a load was applied. Since the two unfinished sections of the arch were lightly loaded, each was a bit longer than it would be when connected and supporting the weight of the decks, sidewalks, and bracing. Initial calculations indicated that the length of an unloaded arch rib at sixty degrees Fahrenheit should be a little more than three inches longer than it would be after complete. Therefore, the space left for insertion of the last central tube at a temperature of sixty degrees would not be enough for a standard-length tube. Since the first arch would be closed in September, when the ambient temperature would be much greater than sixty degrees, the problem would be even more acute.[1]

Making space for the last tube by compressing the arch ribs with mechanical pressure alone was not possible because the great forces required would over-stress the tubes and supporting cables. Other means of contracting the ribs, such as running a stream of cooled, compressed air through the tubes, or packing them in ice, were also considered. But as the time grew near, no method of closure had been agreed upon.

Linville, not knowing exactly how insertion of the center tube would be accomplished, and wishing to avoid liability for any mishap or failure to execute the task, had announced that Keystone would not accept responsibility for closing the arch. When the cantilevered ends of the arch approached within a certain distance of each other, Katté would withdraw and Flad would take over supervision of the procedure.

Before he left for Europe, Eads ordered two sets of special tubes prepared. One set was similar to those tubes composing the arches but made the exact calculated length of the last remaining central space. The other set was fitted with an internal adjustable screw, by means of which the tubes could be lengthened or shortened to a limited extent. Although the adjustable tubes would presumably be easy to insert and adaptable to either a loaded or unloaded condition, they differed noticeably in external appearance from the standard tubes.

All four ribs of the arch were erected simultaneously as far as the tenth or eleventh tubes. At that point the outer ribs were discontinued and only the two inner ribs were continued toward the center. As the ribs approached each other the effect of temperature became more noticeable. Under the direct rays of the sun, the southern half-ribs expanded so much more than those on the north side that both arch ends tended to bend toward the north. It was therefore obvious that both ribs on the same horizontal line, either upper or lower, would have to be joined at the same time to prevent buckling or warping of the ribs.

On September 6, with the temperature at sixty degrees, it was discovered that the remaining space between the two ends of the inner rib segments was greater than had been anticipated. There had evidently been some mistake made in calculation of the finished length of the span, but since it now seemed that the process of closure would be easier than expected the engineers were pleased. However, as the two rib ends were gradually brought together during the next few days, it was observed that the western half of the arch was one foot lower than the opposite eastern half. Considerable experimentation with alterations of the tension of the cables finally brought the two ends into better alignment, and on the morning of September 14 Flad decided to take advantage of the relatively cool weather (forty-four degrees) to attempt closure. The final tubes were not ready, however, since completion of the arches had not been scheduled for that date.

From a plank spanning the gap, Flad nervously awaited delivery of the nonadjustable closing tubes as he watched the sun rise. Soon the ribs would heat to an unacceptable extent and the opportunity would be lost. About 9:00 A.M. the tubes were hoisted from the boat anchored underneath the arch, and the north tube was readily slipped into place. The south tube, however, became stuck. Considerable pounding with sledgehammers could not force it into position and if it stuck part way the consequences would be serious. Flad decided to take both tubes out and wait for a cooler day.

After two days of waiting it began to appear that the relatively cool weather that had prevailed on the fourteenth was not to return. Although Flad could have attempted closure with the adjustable tubes, he was determined to make the nonadjustable tubes work. His preference was apparently based on a desire for uniformity of appearance. Therefore, he ordered wood troughs built around each arch rib so that ice could be packed around the tubes, and this procedure was begun at 2:00 A.M. on the fifteenth. Ten tons of ice were broken, hoisted, distributed over the tubes, and wrapped in gunny cloth that was then wetted with water pumped from the river. After a warm night, the space remaining at sunrise on the sixteenth was still five-eighths of an inch too small. All during that day and the next night the process of packing the ribs with ice continued. An additional forty-five tons were used, but on the morning of the seventeenth the space was too small by almost an inch. The ambient temperature was climbing instead of decreasing, and Flad finally had to admit that the adjustable tubes would have to be used. The few men who remained on duty were so sleepy that they could barely keep their eyes open, and Flad was afraid that someone would fall in the river and drown. But no one did, and at 10:00 P.M., after sixty-five hours of constant work by a crew of about sixty men, two ribs of the first arch were successfully closed.[2]

Less than two weeks after the army board of engineers met for the first time, the event that McCune and others had so wished to prevent was an accomplished fact. Symbolically, at least, Missouri and Illinois were connected at St. Louis, and the commerce between upper and lower portions of the Mississippi River was partially blocked by the barrier of the bridge.

A notice was sent to J. S. Morgan and Company in London and forwarded on to Eads in Paris. The English capitalists, considerably anxious because of Keystone's unwillingness to assume any responsibility for closing the arches, were greatly relieved. With the deadline met, they agreed to issue 400,000 pounds sterling, 7 percent, second mortgage bonds at an issue price of 80 percent of face value, as soon as the remaining arches were closed.

Eads, on the other hand, claimed that he had not been concerned about the prospects of successful closure at all. His plans had been so perfectly made that failure was impossible, and there could be no doubt that the remaining arches would soon be successfully closed. In a note to Flad he stated, "I think good engineering will always give us this kind of feeling, and that disasters and serious accidents are always an evidence of bad engineering."[3] But good engineering could not prevent an event that took place the day after the closing of the west arch, an event that threatened the availability of additional financing, and thus the future of the entire enterprise.

On September 18, 1873, the New York office of Jay Cooke and Company, a banking house built on a foundation of speculative railroad investment, closed its doors. The offices in Philadelphia and Washington soon followed suit. Once the news hit Wall Street, railroad security prices plummeted. Railroad entrepreneurs and their financial backers were shocked and frightened. And no one had more reason for concern than J. Edgar Thomson and Thomas A. Scott, because they were in the mess up to their elbows. In fact, their business practices in attempting to develop transcontinental rail lines not passing through St. Louis had helped bring about the collapse.

The roots of the problem could be traced back to July 2, 1864, the date that Congress chartered the Northern Pacific Railroad Company to construct a line from Lake Superior to Portland, Oregon. The venture was supported with the largest land grant in United States history. But success in competition with other transcontinental routes depended on speedy construction, and construction was dependent on securing an adequate source of long-term capital. Knowing this, the incorporators of the railroad approached Jay Cooke and Company as early as 1865 for aid. The banking firm was at that time the most influential in the country due to its close ties to the federal government. But Jay Cooke was skeptical and refused to give his support.

Cooke was speculating in Minnesota real estate, however, and therefore more receptive when J. Edgar Thomson approached him in the summer of 1868 to help fund the 150-mile-long Lake Superior and Mississippi River Railroad, designed to connect Duluth, Minnesota, with St. Paul. Despite a large land grant, the railroad lacked the strategic position and support facilities necessary to divert the regional grain trade from its regular channels and therefore did not do well. In order to rescue the investment, Cooke began a detailed investigation of the Northern Pacific as a possible lessor of the Minnesota railroad. His research included study of a report prepared by Chief Engineer W. Milnor Roberts, which greatly underestimated the potential costs of construction.

On January 1, 1870, Jay Cooke and Company signed an agreement with the Northern Pacific that gave Cooke six of the initial eighteen shares in the company, although his ownership interest soon expanded to thirteen twenty-fourths. He also acted as financial agent and sold the securities of the company. Thomson's personal share was initially one-eighth of a one-twelfth interest. Thomas Scott and other members of the Philadelphia interests also invested.

Construction began on February 15, 1870, but rumors of corruption, extravagance, and mismanagement soon caused stock subscriptions to dwindle and land sales to lag. In need of additional funds, Cooke approached the banking houses of London only to find them uninterested. He then offered large commissions to firms in Amsterdam and Frankfurt, but the advent of the Franco-Prussian War, which began on July 19, 1870, doomed those efforts. By January 1871 the railroad company was overdrawn $600,000 on its account. Although Cooke forced the resignation of the first president of the company in 1872 and replaced him with the former president of a subsidiary to the Pennsylvania Railroad, Cooke had to continually advance large loans to the railroad using his depositors' money.

With bond sales lagging and capital becoming increasingly scarce, Cooke turned to Congress for help. With Thomson's support he joined Scott in requesting a $40,000-per-mile federal guarantee for the railroad's bonds. Despite the fact that the Crédit Mobilier scandal made it difficult for any politician to support what might be seen as a giveaway to a railroad, neither Cooke nor Scott abandoned their efforts. Cooke even went so far as to write, in forwarding his appeal to Congress, that "Scott, Thomson & all the big bugs of the Penna. R. R. & Texas & Pacific have signed below us on behalf of the Roads."[4] At approximately the same time, Cooke formed a syndicate in April 1873 to sell an additional $9 million of Northern Pacific bonds at 83 percent of face value, together with a 50 percent stock bonus for subscribers. But only a small amount of money was raised by formation of this syndicate.

Unable to meet its obligations, the company folded. Thomson lost approximately $50,000 due to his investment in the Northern Pacific, and Scott lost almost as much. The real damage to the Pennsylvania group, however, came not as a result of personal cash investment in the railroad, but as a result of the overall decline in railroad securities, and in the damage done to its transcontinental plans at just that point when it looked like those plans were going to pay off.

Prior to the financial collapse, Thomson and Scott controlled a rail empire that stretched from New England nearly to the Gulf of Mexico; into the Southwest; and across the northern Great Plains toward Oregon. In the early 1870s, when the Pennsylvania group appeared to be the strongest of all those competing groups of capitalists then vying for creation of a true transcontinental rail network, the ability of the Pennsylvania Railroad to honor its contractual obligations seemed to be beyond question.[5] On the eve of the panic, the Pennsylvania system had gross revenues of over $70 million, a 1,090 percent increase over the figures for 1860, and the company appeared to be strong.[6] But the aggressive expansion program carried out by Thomson and Scott caused the corporation to be financially overextended when the bubble of overcapitalization burst, and that factor would prove the undoing of their carefully constructed plans.

Scott was in Europe when he learned of Jay Cooke and Company's closure, and he quickly rushed home to salvage what he could of the empire that he had been building for so many years. James Ward, biographer of J. Edgar Thomson, identifies a type of entrepreneurial behavior common at the time among railroad and long-span bridge speculators when he states that Scott's "strategy at the onset of the depression was to secure his own personal situation to avoid default and then to support, if possible, his financial allies."[7]

In an attempt to cut his losses and save the Texas and Pacific, Scott first tried to resign as vice president of the Pennsylvania Railroad. But the board of directors refused to accept his resignation. Thomson, who chaired the meeting at which Scott offered to resign, encouraged the directors to reject the offer. Deeply disturbed by the results of Scott's risky speculations, Thomson had no intention of letting his protégé abrogate his responsibility to repair that damage to whatever extent possible. Some mistakes, however, could not easily be undone.

Scott had earlier organized the California and Texas Railway Construction Company to build the line of the Texas and Pacific Railroad. Thomson bought about 5 percent of the company, never expecting to have to pay the $500,000 represented by that purchase. But Scott maintained an aggressive construction schedule in order to meet the terms of the railroad's land grant, and this schedule soon exhausted the funds initially paid in by subscribers. By the fall of 1873 the company had about $7 million in unsecured debts. Scott's presence in Europe at the time of Jay Cooke and Company's collapse was due to his attempt to sell Texas and Pacific securities to keep the California and Texas company afloat.

While in Europe Scott sent a proposal to a special meeting of the board of directors of the Pennsylvania Railroad on August 18, requesting a purchase of $2 million in stock of the Pittsburgh, Cincinnati and St. Louis Railroad, held by the Pennsylvania Railroad Company, for use as security for a loan. In Thomson's absence, the board approved the purchase, paid for with a $2 million note of the California and Texas company and backed by $4 million in Texas and Pacific construction bonds. After the collapse of Jay Cooke and Company, the note of the California and Texas company, then being held in the vault of the Pennsylvania Railroad, became virtually worthless. There was nothing that Scott could do, in this instance, to ameliorate the loss.

Scott's general failure to meet his obligations in the crisis led to a permanent rift in his long relationship with Thomson. Thomson had been Scott's mentor. Now, with only eight months left to live, he started to lose faith in his protégé, and his dreams of a transcontinental railroad empire began to fade. Henceforth it would be all Thomson could do just to hold on to the presidency of the Pennsylvania Railroad.

As for Carnegie, he steadfastly refused to come to the aid of his mentor, Scott, despite Thomson's urging. Carnegie was in the process of building the Edgar Thomson Steel Works, a project begun in the previous year (1872), and he needed all the capital he could lay his hands on. This was partly because Thomson and Scott had failed to make more than a small investment of their own money in the project, which fact helped widen the breach between Carnegie and Scott. For the most part, however, Carnegie maintained his loyalty to Thomson, perhaps because Thomson offered to invest the only available capital he had at that time, the bonds of the Keokuk and Hamilton Bridge Company.[8]

Growing problems in the relationship of the three men, caused by the financial crisis, eventually led to serious trouble for the Illinois and St. Louis Bridge Company. But in the fall of 1873 there was one positive factor for both the St. Louis and Pennsylvania groups to consider. Pierpont Morgan, having heard that Cooke's company was in jeopardy, prepared his firm for the coming crisis by calling in all the notes of Drexel, Morgan and Company. Thus, in a better position to weather the financial storm than many of its competitors, Drexel, Morgan and Company took over much of the U.S. Treasury business after the failure of Jay Cooke and Company. An important source of financial support to the Illinois and St. Louis Bridge Company, Drexel, Morgan and Company not only survived the panic of 1873, it finished the year with a nice profit. This was important, because in the next year the bridge company would need all the financial support it could muster.

On October 7 the executive committee of the bridge company agreed to Drexel, Morgan and Company's offer, dated October 1, to advance the equivalent of 30,000 pounds sterling as a loan against a pledge of 250 second mortgage bonds.[9] The money would not be available in one lump sum but would be issued in increments over a period of time. This loan provided some funds for continuation of work on the superstructure, which proceeded without great difficulty. But the debt of the company had piled up to such an extent that the loan from Drexel, Morgan was not sufficient to pay all outstanding bills.

On October 18 Taussig reported to the executive committee that debts, just from the contractors alone, amounted to $120,000. But there was enough money in the company's account only to meet the most pressing demands of the contractors. It was resolved to pay the Baltimore Bridge Company and Keystone with the balance of the proceeds of the tunnel bonds, which were supposed to go toward construction of the tunnel.

Taussig went to Pittsburgh to meet with Andrew and Thomas Carnegie and to Philadelphia to meet with Linville in order to induce Keystone to accept $40,000 in promise of future payment as soon as draws against the loan from Drexel, Morgan and Company could be arranged. Taussig then met Eads in New York, where Solon Humphreys cautioned against asking the stockholders for any more calls on their subscriptions. The executive committee, with dwindling options available until issuance of the second mortgage bonds provided additional funds, voted to cut the salaries of all bridge company employees by 10 percent and to reduce costs as much as possible.[10]

As had been the case throughout the difficulties of the preceding years, Carnegie chose to present an unreasonably positive front to the financiers of London concerning both the fiscal health of the bridge company and the general economic climate in America. In a letter to J. S. Morgan and Company on December 5, 1873, he revealed his optimism regarding the financial crisis then threatening the nation by writing, "we are steadily outgrowing the foolish panic here—It is mostly a fright—& the spring will see things prosperous again."[11] But the bridge company could hardly wait for a season of renewed prosperity to arrive.

On December 6 Taussig reported to the executive committee that the company treasury was empty. Letters from Charles Tracy and Solon Humphreys in New York, advising payment of the sinking fund of the first mortgage bonds, were read along with a letter from an attorney, Samuel Glover, giving his opinion that the payments would have to be made.[12]

Eads was dispatched to New York to ask Drexel, Morgan and Company for another advance against the pending second mortgage, and the bridge company moved to call in what accounts receivable it possessed. But these actions were insufficient to meet the need. The executive committee therefore began to borrow more money from the National Bank of the State of Missouri, which it controlled.

This desperate tactic was only a stopgap measure, however. Every member of the executive committee knew that the long-term financial condition of the company depended on further progress in completing the superstructure. The option on the bridge bonds would lapse and the company would be unable to obtain additional capital unless the inner ribs of the east and middle arches were closed by December 18.

The alignment of the arch segments of the center span was relatively good, and closure was successfully accomplished on December 16. The east arch was more troublesome because the eastern segment was much lower and stiffer than the western segment. About noon on the seventeenth, the still absent Eads issued orders to Flad (by telegraph) to close the east arch by 7:00 A.M. on the morning of the eighteenth without fail. This was the first time that Flad was informed by Eads of the conditions attached to issuance of the second mortgage bonds. At that point the eastern half of the arch was still three inches too low, the main cables were highly strained, and the other cables were strained to the maximum extent. Flad tried every arrangement of jacks, cables, and blocking he could think of, but the closure attempt was not going well. About 10:00 P.M., however, a cold northerly wind blew in, making insertion of the inner tubes somewhat easier. After working all through the night and into the next morning, Flad closed the last arch at 7:40 on the morning of the eighteenth.

Carnegie and associates were well pleased that the deadline had been met and that real progress was now evident. Once-faded visions of the financial rewards to come after so many long years of effort began to rematerialize. By January 31, 1874, all of the towers and cables had been removed, and construction of the remainder of the superstructure, including the roadway, pedestrian walkways, and rail deck, was not expected to cause much further delay.

Whatever the status of other aspects of the project, the bridge had materialized from dream to reality.

17

The Consummation So Devoutly Wished For

I am truly rejoiced that a ray of sunshine is likely to gleam at last through our long troubles & will indeed be truly glad to see the "consummation so devoutly wished for."

—Walter Katté to Andrew Carnegie, May 6, 1874

By the beginning of 1874, the two greatest challenges of building the first bridge across the Mississippi River at St. Louis had been met and conquered. Foundations rested securely on the bedrock of the river, ensuring permanence of the bridge's substructure. Steel arches connected the piers and abutments, providing support for the nearly complete wagon and rail decks, which were the means by which traffic, and revenues, would flow. The project seemed, therefore, finally headed toward a successful conclusion.

Carnegie, after a week in New York settling all claims against the bridge company, wrote to Junius Morgan on February 9 to express his sense of optimism. He expected Morgan to rejoice in learning that Carnegie was "personally bound" to lose $1,000 per day for each day after June 1 that the bridge was not ready for traffic and stood to gain the same amount for every day prior to June 1 that it was ready. "I expect to take at least $1,000 out of that bargain," he bragged to the bridge's financier. He also stated that everyone who had examined the enterprise was excited about the great revenues that would soon accrue from operation of the bridge. "Allowing one year to enable the railway companies to get their business fully changed from ferry to bridge, the expectations of the most sanguine will be realized."[1]

With work on the bridge proceeding well, the attention of the company could now turn to completion of the tunnel and approaches, and to the anticipated connection of the bridge tracks with those of the railroads contracted to use the bridge.

Construction of the tunnel had increasingly become a source of irritation to the residents of St. Louis owing to damage caused to businesses, either because of weakening of building foundations or difficulty of access, or to the ever-present mud, filth, and general chaos associated with the work. One enterprising merchant located at Eighth and Washington, a druggist named Crawford, had attempted to make the best of the situation by having a "tunnel sale" from December 5 until Christmas in an effort to encourage shoppers to brave the difficulties of crossing over the excavation.[2] Mayor Brown, having somewhat less patience, ordered that if conditions at Eighth and Chestnut did not improve he would have the contractors arrested.[3] For the most part, however, tunnel construction was merely a nuisance until January 20.

At about six o'clock that morning, a 150-foot-long portion of the north wall of the tunnel on Washington Avenue between Sixth and Seventh Streets collapsed. No one was injured, but the foundations of the newly constructed Lindell Hotel were threatened and about $40,000 worth of damage was done. Heavy rains in the days following made repair of the wall particularly difficult.[4]

Even the sympathetic *St. Louis Republican* had to admit the following month that a walk down Eighth Street along the line of the tunnel "is suggestive of rather unpleasant reflections. Here are lines of buildings that are deserted on account of their insecurity and inaccessibility. They were once the homes of prosperous citizens, but will probably have to be taken down and rebuilt before they can be of any use."[5]

At least the tunnel was under construction. Nothing, on the other hand, had been done by the railroads contracted to use the bridge regarding establishment of new freight facilities or construction of connecting tracks. Both actions were necessary for the transfer of business envisioned by Carnegie to take place.

On March 7 the bridge company executive committee met with William Clement and William D. Griswold of Cincinnati, Ohio.[6] Griswold, a former resident of St. Louis, was current president of one of the most important eastern companies slated to use the bridge, the Ohio and Mississippi Railroad.[7] The two men suggested formation of a corporation for purposes of transshipment of freight and passenger cars from East St. Louis to St. Louis via the bridge and tunnel.

Although a contract for use of the bridge had been before the Ohio and Mississippi Railroad board of directors since 1871, it wasn't until February 18, 1874, that the executed contract was delivered to the bridge company. Apparently, it was Griswold who soon thereafter figured out that formation of a transfer company, by persons other than those involved in the bridge and tunnel companies, was necessary in order for the bridge use contract to have any validity. The lawyers for the bridge and tunnel company confirmed that their charters gave them no right to operate a railroad in Illinois, and having no funds to organize a transfer company they decided to go along with the proposal.[8]

On March 28 the bridge company executive committee approved a contract that allowed the incorporators of the proposed transfer company to pay 10 percent of their stock subscription out of revenue, with all purchases of real estate, rails, locomotives, and the like being subject to approval by the directors of the bridge company.[9] The Union Railway and Transit Company of St. Louis and the Union Railway and Transit Company of East St. Louis were thereby organized with the intention of transporting freight and passengers across the bridge and through the tunnel to Mill Creek Valley, as well as for the purpose of constructing additional tracks and terminal facilities on both sides of the river for the interchange of cars between the various railroads contracted to use the bridge.

With the superstructure and tunnel rapidly nearing completion and an organization effected for construction of connecting tracks and transfer of rail cars, the only task remaining was reactivation and formal organization of the long-dormant Union Depot Company of St. Louis. Articles of Association were signed April 10, 1874, and the capital stock was set at $1 million. Both Griswold and Clement were incorporators. Taussig and Samuel Gaty were the only representatives from St. Louis, all others being from Ohio.

The inability of the bridge company to handle the additional financial burdens of a transfer company and a depot company is not surprising considering that the organization was, once again, virtually out of money. On February 4, a stockholders meeting had been held in New York at which President Allen announced that approximately $1,250,000 would be required to complete the bridge and tunnel, pay all obligations, and pay interest due in April and July on the first and second mortgage bridge bonds and the first mortgage bonds of the tunnel company. In response to this financial crisis, the stockholders decided on the following day to authorize an issue of $3 million in third mortgage, 7 percent gold bonds, two-thirds of which would be offered to stockholders pro rata at the rate of 60 percent. The remaining $1 million would be held by the company as an investment.[10] The St. Louis stockholders met and ratified this action on February 18.[11]

In this moment of financial crisis, it was becoming increasingly apparent to Taussig, if not to anyone else, that the national financial crisis had begun to erode Scott's commitment to the enterprise. Taussig sent a personal letter to Carnegie at the end of February stating that Scott was not answering his letters, and complaining "of the careless and torpid manner in which the Penn. interest attends to its affairs."[12] Taussig could little realize how bad things were about to get.

At the annual stockholders meeting of the Pennsylvania Railroad Company on March 10, 1874, the usual cash dividend of 5 percent was paid, but Thomson announced that the semiannual dividend to be disbursed in November would be paid in scrip equivalent to a 5 percent dividend, redeemable in cash in fifteen months with interest at 6 percent. This announcement caused considerable anxiety in the minds of many stockholders who were concerned about the large increases in the company's capitalization required to support the expansion program of Thomson and Scott. As a result a resolution was passed at the meeting of March 10 requesting appointment of a seven-member committee to review Thomson's annual report and examine the condition of the corporation. This committee was also empowered to appraise the value of the company's assets; examine its liabilities and obligations, including all of its guarantees for other lines; and analyze its contracts and relations with other companies and parties of every kind.[13] The investigating committee, composed of gentlemen identified with large financial, commercial, and manufacturing interests in Philadelphia, but not connected with the management or operation of the company, would spend just over six months preparing its report.

Thomson's poor health, no doubt aggravated by formation of the committee and by the breakdown of his relationship with Scott, was progressively becoming worse. Generally more principled than his young protégé, Thomson was the bridge company's last hope for seeing the Pennsylvania group adhere to its commitment to arrange bridge use contracts and enforce their use. But early in April 1874 Thomson had a heart attack that severely reduced his ability to manage the Pennsylvania Railroad Company and to protect the integrity of the various bridge use agreements so laboriously worked out in previous years. He chaired his last meeting of the Pennsylvania Railroad Company's board of directors on April 22. For several weeks he tried to continue work from his home, but he was finally forced to turn over virtually all responsibility for operation of the company to others.[14]

On April 13, shortly after Thomson's heart attack, a meeting was held in St. Louis of both eastern and western railroad managers. These men reached an agreement for construction of a temporary depot on Poplar Street, between Ninth and Tenth Streets, at which the eastern railroads might deliver some or all of their passengers to St. Louis until a permanent union depot could be constructed. The Atlantic and Pacific Railroad via its lease agreement with the Missouri Pacific Railroad, the property owner of record, provided most of the land for the site of the temporary depot.[15]

Immediately following the meeting of the thirteenth, all tenants occupying the property on which the temporary depot was to sit were ordered by the railroad to vacate, and the work of demolishing buildings to make room for new improvements commenced. The newly revitalized union depot association also began acquiring, either through purchase or condemnation, land not owned by the railroad located between Twelfth and Fourteenth Streets, and from the north line of Randolph Street about 200 feet deep to a line within 120 feet of Poplar Street.

Within a month of the site selection, the depot association received a guarantee of a certain percentage of income from all of the eastern railroads expected to use the facilities except for those controlled by the Pennsylvania Railroad.[16] Apparently, Thomson's illness allowed the increasingly conservative management of the company to renege on its earlier commitments to the overall scheme of improved transportation facilities at St. Louis. And Thomson's presumed successor, Thomas Scott, wasn't in a position to prevent abrogation of those obligations.

On April 15, just two days after Eads returned to St. Louis from a trip to Washington, the annual meeting of the stockholders of the St. Louis, Kansas City and Northern Railroad (the renamed North Missouri Railroad) was held in the directors' room of the *Republican* building. Five of the men elected to the board of directors that night—Solon Humphreys, Joseph A. Jameson, James Eads, James Britton, and Thomas Scott—presumably had an interest in seeing that the railroad connect its tracks to those emerging from the tunnel. But reelected directors who might be less inclined to aid the Eads faction in its endeavors were joined by new directors James H. Winslow and R. P. Tansey.

The election came at a time when Scott had to direct all his attention to an attempt to save the Texas and Pacific Railroad, thus making it difficult for him to prevent the new leadership of the St. Louis, Kansas City and Northern Railroad from nullifying a certain agreement between that company, the Kansas Pacific

Railroad, the Chicago and Alton Railroad, and the Pennsylvania Railroad that had been in place since the reorganization of the North Missouri Railroad. Under the terms of that agreement, which was secret at the time it was made in May 1872, each company was bound to deliver to its associates all the traffic, both freight and passenger, that came to it from whatever source. Moreover, the railroad was prohibited from accepting traffic from railroads not part of the agreement. This restraint of trade was good for the Pennsylvania Railroad since it tied the St. Louis, Kansas City and Northern Railroad to the St. Louis, Vandalia and Terre Haute Railroad, a line controlled by the Pennsylvania Railroad. But it worked to the disadvantage of the St. Louis, Kansas City and Northern because that company was cut off from serving the interest of any railroad not part of the agreement. Therefore, two weeks after the new board of directors and officers of the company were elected, they canceled the trust by which the common stock of the railroad was held as an indemnity or guarantee for the performance of its part of the agreement.[17]

Eads, who might have been expected to assume a leadership role in protection of the agreement, was not much help either. Since the beginning of the year, with the majority of his duties as chief bridge engineer behind him, he had increasingly diverted his attention from the activities in St. Louis to the task of building a levee system at the mouth of the Mississippi. In February 1874 he made a formal proposal to Congress to create and maintain a twenty-eight-foot-deep channel between the so-called Southwest Pass and the Gulf of Mexico for $10 million. The proposal immediately met strong opposition, but with characteristic faith in the infallibility of his own ideas Eads began to orchestrate the involvement of his bridge company associates in the new venture. They would all, he assured them, profit handsomely from participation in the levee construction company that he planned to form, if they invested at the beginning. And the levee construction company was just one part of a greater plan.

Eads joined with some friends and a few old adversaries, including Charles P. Chouteau, Joseph Brown, Gerald Allen, and Henry Blow, in formation of a company to manufacture ocean-going iron steamboats at Carondelet.[18] Additional plans were made for creation of a separate organization that would initiate direct trade between St. Louis and Brazil using boats purchased from the first company. Direct trade with Europe was contemplated as well. After Eads opened the mouth of the Mississippi River, it was assumed, the commerce of the world could flow up the river to St. Louis. It would no longer matter if the bridge was an obstruction to navigation, because that portion of the levee located south of the bridge would become cluttered with the products of southern states and foreign lands.

One of the partners in this plan from New Orleans, Samuel C. Reed, delivered an address to the St. Louis Board of Trade on April 10, 1874, in which he challenged the businessmen of the city to support the scheme. "Will you do it?" he asked. "Will you take this step, that shall make you the founders of another bridge, adding to your commercial greatness and prosperity—aye, another great marine bridge, that shall connect the two great American continents together, and unite the Mississippi and the Amazon?"[19]

It was about at this point, toward the end of April, that Carnegie began to turn on his St. Louis associates. Earlier in the month, on the morning of April 6, Katté and Taussig had a discussion concerning the agreement signed between Keystone and the bridge company on February 7 regarding the bonus to be paid Carnegie and associates upon early completion of the bridge. It was clear to both men that there was a difference of opinion regarding what constituted "completion."

Katté held that the spirit and intent of the clause regarding completion would be met when the highway deck was sufficiently finished to allow traffic to pass over the main portion of the bridge in safety, even though there was still a sixty-foot drop from the east abutment to the ground below. Since the contract for the east approach bridge had been given to a competing firm, Katté held that its completion had no bearing on Keystone's obligations. He dispatched a letter to Taussig that afternoon which stated his opinion. No mention was made of the rail deck.[20]

Taussig fired back a curt letter the following day in which he stated that it was up to Eads, as chief engineer, to determine when both decks were ready to receive traffic. He further gave notice that instead of receiving a bonus, Carnegie and associates might have to pay a penalty. "You will receive shortly from the Chief Engineer," he wrote Katté, "his directions as to what will be considered necessary to entitle Mr. Carnegie to the bonus or this Company to the penalty under the agreement of February 7th 1874."[21]

As soon as Carnegie received notice of Taussig's letter he made arrangements to travel to St. Louis with John Piper and Keystone's attorney, a man named Schoyer, to determine for himself the status of the bridge. He was not present, however, at a meeting of the bridge company executive committee held on Saturday, April 18, at which an agreement regarding the resolution of differences between the two firms was signed by Schoyer. After signing, Schoyer informed the bridge company that it could open the bridge for pedestrian traffic on the following day.[22] Following the meeting, Taussig ordered announcements for publication in all morning editions of the St. Louis newspapers and then went home.[23] It was assumed at this point that a large crowd would show up on Sunday and pay a small toll for the privilege of crossing the river on foot, even though the rail and wagon deck would not be completely finished until the end of May.

Later that evening, however, Carnegie received additional legal advice recommending that Keystone not allow the bridge to be open for any revenue-generating traffic until all money due the company was paid. Carnegie therefore directed that sections of the planking at both ends of the bridge be torn up, and armed guards were posted to keep people off the upper deck. About midnight Taussig was awakened and handed a note from Keystone rescinding the agreement approved by Schoyer. Three hours later a very heavy downpour began that lasted for two days, thus discouraging anyone from attempting to pass over the bridge and sparing the company some measure of embarrassment.

A contingent of St. Louis police, assigned to control the nonexistent crowd and ignorant of the seizure, arrived at dawn to execute their duty. The Keystone employees, thinking that the police had been called to evict them, responded by tearing up more of the deck. A standoff ensued that was to last for weeks, even as work continued on the superstructure and decks.

Carnegie wrote Eads a personal letter on Monday morning, April 20, in which he cloaked his displeasure in the most solicitous language. Referring to his nemesis as "My Dear Captain," Carnegie made it plain that he blamed Eads's absence above all other factors for the regrettable conflict. "I do not think any personal consideration (except sickness and death) should have taken you away before it was settled."[24] But Eads would never again directly involve himself in financial issues regarding the bridge, the tunnel, or the proposed union depot if there was any way to avoid doing so. New projects demanded his attention, and it would increasingly fall to Taussig and the bridge company's lawyers to resolve lingering issues.

After about a month of negotiation, and despite a failure to fully resolve the bonus issue, Keystone surrendered the structure on Saturday, May 23, allowing about twenty-five thousand visitors to pay a dime for the unique pleasure of promenading across the first bridge between St. Louis and southern Illinois. They were unable to cross into Illinois, however, because the eastern approach was still not complete. And little progress had been made at this point to connect the tracks extending over the bridge and across the approaches to the tracks of the railroads.

The difficulties caused by lack of foresight became acutely apparent toward the middle of May when W. H. Clement, president of the Union Railway and Transit Company, informed Taussig that several of the railroads contracted to use the bridge, and whose endorsement to the contract between the bridge and transit company was required under provisions of the contract, had not yet endorsed it and would not do so until their representatives visited St. Louis to determine the status of the city's transportation network. Subsequently, the transit company had been unable to complete the purchase of locomotives and associated equipment or to make arrangements for connection of the tracks of the bridge and tunnel with those of the railroads.[25]

The ability of the transit company to make useful rail connections partly depended on a larger effort to create a connecting railway that would unite the tracks of all railroads entering the city with the tracks of the Union Depot Company and with those emerging from the tunnel. For years the city had been inconvenienced by the tracks of the Missouri Pacific, which ran down Poplar Street nearly dividing the city in two. And for years people had been talking about the eventual necessity of lowering the grade of the tracks, erecting bridges over the resulting cut, and constructing tunnels where needed.

Early in February 1873, a thirteen-member "citizens' executive committee," an ad hoc group of St. Louis businessmen wishing to create a unified rail system as soon as possible, appointed Henry Flad to meet with other engineers and determine a solution to the problem.[26] Shortly thereafter, the Atlantic and Pacific Railroad, on behalf of the Missouri Pacific, agreed to the establishment of a board of engineers consisting of Flad, C. Shaler Smith, and J. Blickersdoerfer, the latter representing the two railroads. The board was expected to make a full and complete plan for proposed changes, including an estimate of costs, which would be submitted to the city council for approval.[27]

The matter was complicated by a suit filed by the city against the Missouri Pacific due to the alleged nuisance created by its Poplar Street tracks. The case was first brought before United States Circuit Court No. 4 on July 2, 1873. After hearing initial arguments the court adjourned without making a decision, and the next day the city requested a dismissal. Apparently, the city's attorneys decided that since the city had already proposed an ordinance on July 1 declaring the tracks a nuisance, it had authority to order their removal without an action by the court. If the railroad objected, it had the option of suing the city.[28] The burden of proof would then be on the railroad, not the city. On July 11, the city council passed ordinance number 8,433, giving the railroad thirty days to take up its tracks.

On August 11, while Mayor Joseph Brown was out of the city, Acting Mayor Elon G. Smith issued orders to the city engineer, J. B. Moulton, to tear up those portions of the Missouri Pacific track at street crossings; he further stated that "the remainder of the track can be removed by the railroad company if they desire, and if they decline to do so, after a reasonable time, you can remove same."[29] Under protection of a squad of police, Moulton executed the order the next day. As expected, the railroad company responded by suing Mayor Brown and Moulton in United States Circuit Court on August 14, claiming $100,000 in damages.[30] The court issued a temporary injunction against any further action by the city, and the railroad threatened to re-lay the tracks. The city responded by stating that the police would not protect the railroad crews from mob violence if such were to break out.[31]

While all of this was going on, a meeting of the Atlantic and Pacific Railroad stockholders was held in New York in July 1873, at which Scott was elected president of the company and Thomson was reelected to the board of directors.[32] But if these men had any power thereafter to resolve the dispute between the railroad and the city—a suit clearly not in the interest of the community, the railroad, or the bridge company—that power was not exercised. It appears that Andrew Pierce Jr., the vice president and general manager, actually wielded more influence over the affairs of the company at this time than did Scott, and Pierce was not a supporter of the bridge.

No solution to the problem presented itself until the following January, when several prominent members of the Merchants Exchange, including Pierce, Thomas Allen, William Taussig, John Mitchell, and E. O. Stannard, petitioned the city council to authorize formation of the St. Louis Connecting Railroad and Warehouse Company. This company was organized to buy the right-of-way extending from Seventh Street to the levee and to lay tracks along that right-of-way in a sunken roadway; to connect the tracks of the Missouri Pacific Railroad and the tracks emerging from the tunnel with those of any railroad terminating in St. Louis; and to construct warehouses on the levee for temporary storage of freight. As the *St. Louis Republican,* noted, "the importance of this enterprise to the city is second only to that of the bridge and tunnel, to which, indeed, it is a necessary addition."[33]

The plan proposed by backers of the connecting railway was so complex, and involved so many conflicting interests among the businessmen of St. Louis, that action on the matter was continually delayed by the city council. The situation became more acute on April 27, 1874, when a ruling of the U.S. Circuit Court rendered permanent the temporary injunction restraining the city from tearing up the tracks of the Missouri Pacific Railroad. The court ruled that the railroad company had a right to lay the tracks where they were and to use them as they had been used in the past. The city decided to appeal the case to the U.S. Supreme Court.[34]

On May 11, the city council considered an amended ordinance authorizing operations of the St. Louis Connecting Railway and Warehouse Company. The amendments included provision for connection of the city's railway system to all the lumberyards, grain elevators, stockyards, cotton compresses, warehouses, and other large mercantile establishments then in existence. Connection to the proposed St. Clair and Carondelet Bridge was also included in order to "give the city another and cheaper connection with the great coal fields of Illinois."[35] Shortly thereafter, on June 1, the engineer board created by the citizen's committee released its report.[36]

The report basically stated what was probably obvious to all. The growing city had one railroad (the Missouri Pacific) with a line down Mill Creek Valley that divided the city to its detriment; two other railroads pursuing their own plans with no thought to unity of purpose; and a grand bridge, connected to a tunnel that connected to nothing. The solution the engineer board presented should have been just as obvious: the city needed to develop unified transportation facilities that took into account the needs of rail, river, and highway transportation.[37]

No sooner was the report made public, and an amended ordinance referred to the city council committee on streets and alleys, than a petition against the ordinance began to circulate. Persons owning property along the wharf were opposed because the company would be allowed to purchase or condemn a one-hundred-foot swathe through their property without purchasing the remainder, thus leaving it subject to taxation but of dubious commercial value. The steamboat interests also opposed the plan due to problems that might be caused in unloading and handling freight along the levee.

The committee on streets and alleys decided to study the matter in concert with a proposal to construct a grand union passenger depot, in replacement of the temporary depot already being planned.[38] The proposals had to be considered together since the switching yards and tracks of the depot had to be laid at essentially the same grade level as the tracks of the connecting railroad.

The inability of the community to resolve the issue of a connecting railroad was not the only thing causing problems for the bridge-tunnel-depot scheme that spring. Early in March, the Wiggins Ferry Company sued the Chicago and Alton Railroad Company to restrain the latter from transferring its passengers and freight to and from East St. Louis, via Venice, Illinois, on its own transfer boats. The ferry company claimed that its contract with the railroad required that all freight and passengers of the railroad had to be carried across the river by the ferry company. The railroad responded by saying that the contract had no reference to bulk freight or passengers carried over the river in railroad cars, but only to passengers and freight in separate packages, that is, not contained in railroad cars. If the ferry company won the suit, a stinging blow to the fortunes of the bridge and tunnel companies would be dealt because all the railroads then having contracts with the ferry company would be forced to continue transferring freight and passengers via that company.

As an indication of the ever-shifting alignment of interest among participants in the drama of St. Louis transportation improvement, John Noble represented the ferry company in its suit. He had been the attorney representing the interest of the bridge company before the army board of engineers the previous year. The Chicago and Alton Railroad, on the other hand, was represented by Corydon Beckwith, Lucius Boomer's partner in the organization of the first Illinois and St. Louis Bridge Company in 1867.[39] If Noble won the case, his former employer would suffer. If Beckwith successfully defended the railroad, the people who drove him and Boomer from St. Louis would win.

Despite lack of progress toward establishment of a coherent rail system for St. Louis, the eastern approach to the bridge was completed on June 2, thus allowing one event of promise for bridge backers to occur at half past five o'clock on the morning of June 4, 1874. A driver for the Gartside Coal Company, having paid a toll of ten cents for his highly decorated (but empty) wagon and one cent for each of his four horses, claimed the honor of being the first customer to cross the bridge. Even though there was scant public notification of the opening, more than seven hundred wagons completed the journey from one state to another on the first day.[40] Each evening thereafter found the wagon deck and pedestrian walkway jammed solid with wagons, horses, and people as each fought the other for space on the upper deck. The lower deck, however, remained unused.

It wasn't until the end of the first week of June that agents for the St. Louis, Vandalia and Terre Haute Railroad organized an unofficial test of the rail deck. At first, it was intended only that a locomotive be run across the bridge to test the straightness of the track. Soon, however, a decision was made to attach two passenger coaches and invite certain members of the press, some employees of the railroad, a few local politicians, and sundry other individuals to ride across. Taussig and George Knapp were the only bridge company directors present. It took several trips by omnibus to transport everyone across the wagon deck and into the East St. Louis yard of the railroad. As the group of men stood around watching workmen make a few final connections, someone induced Gen. William T. Sherman to pick up a hammer and drive the last spike that linked the tracks of the railroad to those of the bridge. At half past four in the afternoon Sherman finished the task and looked up with an expression that said "there it is."[41]

News that a train was about to cross the bridge had spread rapidly, and soon the banks of the river on both sides were packed with people. A great hurrah went up as the locomotive puffed across the rail deck, its whistle shrieking, and disappeared into the tunnel. Smoke from the engine nearly asphyxiated the passengers before the train could be stopped at about Seventh Street and slowly backed out of the tunnel. Some of those present, glad to be in the fresh air once again, departed the coaches at the little station located under the western arcade. Most, however, stayed aboard as the train backed to the center of the bridge and came to a stop. Champagne was produced and several toasts were made in honor of James Eads and the officers of the bridge company. Taussig and several others made short speeches, the engine driver was toasted, and then the train completed the journey back to the Vandalia depot in East St. Louis.

Some of the men taking the short ride across the bridge that day determined that a proper, formal celebration should be organized, and soon thereafter they formed a committee for that purpose. Sylvester Laflin, Eads's successor as president of the Western River Improvement and Wrecking Company, led the group. It was Laflin, more than any other, who saw the event as an opportunity to draw the attention of the nation to the expanding commercial potential of St. Louis. By common consent it was agreed that the ceremony would be held on the Fourth of July. There would be just enough time to plan a celebration worthy of the occasion.

In the meantime, the bridge company engineers conducted tests of progressing severity. Single locomotives were run across the rail deck and measurements taken on June 29 and 30 and on July 1. The wagon deck was tested on July 2 by means of leading an elephant across. It was widely believed that elephants had canny instincts and wouldn't cross an unsafe structure. The huge beast lumbered over to the Illinois side without hesitation as the crowd along the levee roared.

By July 2 the bridge was ready for its first real, full-scale public trial. The standard method of testing railroad bridges in that era was to burden them far beyond their usual operating load and then measure the deflection of the structural members. The bridge company engineers borrowed fourteen locomotives from seven of the railroads terminating in East St. Louis to conduct the test. For five hours these engines, their fully loaded tenders weighing more than 550 tons, went back and forth to the entertainment of thousands of spectators as the engineers took their measurements. Calvin Woodward was riding in one of the locomotives when the engineer turned to him and asked, "Do you think she will hold us?" Woodward responded that in his opinion "she" certainly would, and it did. The deflections were all within acceptable allowances and the engineers, both civil and locomotive, were finally satisfied that the bridge was as safe and solid a structure as modern technology could provide.

While tests of the bridge took place, plans for the official opening ceremony expanded far beyond anyone's initial expectation. The event was to be more than just a celebration of completion or of a national holiday; it would serve as a statement about the character of the community. As an editorial comment in the *St. Louis Republican* put it, "Our bridge was built by private enterprise and by funds from London; but however this may be, it is representative of the mind and commercial importance of this city." The true spirit of the celebration, the editor continued, was "a realizing sense that the Laclede settlement has become the metropolis of the great valley, and that its destiny holds even a greater development."[42]

The city council finally took appropriate steps toward making that vision a reality on July 3, just one day before the official opening of the bridge, by passing an ordinance authorizing the Union Depot Company to construct a depot and switching yards. Those council members on the losing end of the vote made some nasty accusations concerning the possibility that the bridge company had bribed certain members of the council, but no proof of this was offered. The ordinance authorizing the connecting railroad was also brought up for discussion at this meeting but quickly tabled for consideration at a later date.

Plans for terminal facilities and connecting tracks, negotiations among bridge company and railroad officials for use of the bridge and tunnel, and all other conundrums yet to be solved would have to wait. It was time to honor the accomplished fact.

18

Stately Pomp and Ceremony

In classic times the building of a bridge was a sacred undertaking.
The beginning of the work was consecrated with pontifical rites and
liturgies, and the completion was solemnized with stately pomp and
ceremony.

—Sylvester Waterhouse, Professor of Greek, Washington University,
1870

At last, the long-anticipated moment had arrived. Saturday, July 4, 1874, was to be the greatest day of celebration in the history of St. Louis. Not only would the city honor the birth of the Great Republic, it would also commemorate the official birth of the Illinois and St. Louis Bridge. For seven long years the citizens of the city had followed the slow progress of construction, but their wait now seemed more than justified. It was truly a unique structure; no other in the world was quite like it.

The upper deck, for wagon, pedestrian, and streetcar traffic, provided an unobstructed view for those passing between Missouri and Illinois. The lower deck had a double set of rails to accommodate the differing gauges of eastern and western railroads. The two river piers and the eastern abutment were founded on bedrock utilizing pneumatic caissons of an unprecedented size, sunk to an unprecedented depth. The three river spans were each composed of arched steel ribs, the most extensive use of that metal for any structure of any type. No other bridge had ever been designed so that a portion of its major structural components could easily be removed for repair or replacement without the use of supporting cables or falsework. In fact, no falsework was needed at all during superstructure erection because it was the first bridge built entirely by a new, patent method of cantilever construction.

The main channel span, 520 feet from pier to pier, was flanked by two spans of 502 feet. Each was longer than any other arch span in existence. The two river piers together added approximately 108 feet to the total length, making the distance from the western abutment to the eastern abutment about 1,630 feet. This length alone made it a very long bridge, but when the entire distance from the end of the eastern approach to the end of the western approach was included it measured a truly impressive 4,414 feet in length.

Finished more than three years after the date initially projected for completion, at a cost approximately six million dollars more than anticipated, the bridge had been every bit as difficult a task of construction as its detractors assumed when the project was announced in 1867. But despite all the many problems it had been built, which was more than some had thought possible. Now, with the magnificent structure before them, the citizens of St. Louis seemed ready to forgive the delays and forget the controversies of the past. As a reporter for the *Chicago Times* acerbically summed up the mood of the day, "The child is born: procreation was painful, the period of gestation was fearfully long, and the pangs of parturition most acute. Delivery, however, has been safely accomplished, and the miniature world of St. Louis breathes easier."[1]

Before dawn the streets of the city, littered with the remnants of firecrackers exploded during the pre-Fourth celebration of the previous evening, were filled with visitors who had spent a restless night as chair-sleepers in offices, billiard halls, barrooms, and reading rooms. The number of hotel rooms in the city was inadequate to accommodate the hundreds of thousands of out-of-town guests. Some visitors had slept in chairs on the sidewalk in groups, while the more fortunate found places in parlors that had been transformed into stag bedrooms with, as the *St. Louis Republican* noted, "15 cots in a room, $1 a wink, with bugs thrown in."[2]

At daylight, those who were not already up and about were awakened by a thunderous thirteen-cannon salute fired from the western levee near the bridge, with one cannon for each of the original states in the union. The report was matched by a simultaneous salute fired from the federal arsenal down river.

As early as seven o'clock the crowd, continuing to swell as more visitors entered the city, began to drift down to the riverfront to observe the day's activities. Many spectators had already selected choice spots on rooftops or in windows that gave them a good view of the area where the dedication ceremony would take place, located near the bridge entrance at Washington Avenue and Third Street. Soon there would not be a decent vantage point left unoccupied, and the streets would be so congested that all streetcar traffic came to a halt.

It was already hot and muggy at this early hour, and sellers of iced drinks had been doing a brisk business since first light. By some accounts, there were as many as 200,000 people in the central portion of the city by midday, when the temperature reached well over 100 degrees in the shade. As one reporter for the *Indianapolis Journal* described the scene, "the streets were packed with one vast crowd of perspiring idiots from home and abroad."[3]

Exactly how many of these people were permanent residents and how many visitors is hard to say, since no one knew how many people actually lived in the city at the time. The federal census of 1870 showed that St. Louis still had a slight advantage over Chicago in terms of metropolitan status: St. Louis County reported a population of 351,189 in that year, while Chicago's Cook County reported 349,966.[4] But it was later revealed that certain St. Louis citizens, in their neurotic need to demonstrate their superiority over their rivals on Lake Michigan, had falsified the figures.[5]

At nine o'clock one hundred cannons, fifty on each side of the river, proceeded to exchange salutes as the first event of the official program began. Three locomotives provided by the Illinois Central Railroad and the St. Louis, Vandalia and Terre Haute Railroad, still the only railroad with tracks actually connected to those of the bridge, began to pull a fifteen-car trainload of distinguished guests from the Vandalia depot in East St. Louis. The train was scheduled to move across the bridge and through the tunnel to Mill Creek Valley, the site of the proposed Union Passenger Terminal. Each engine was highly polished and the tenders were gaily decorated with flags at every possible point. The richly adorned palace cars held slightly more than five hundred passengers, although the official events committee had freely distributed over a thousand tickets for the crossing.

The *St. Louis Republican* reported that passage of this inaugural train was witness to the consummation of the great design of the bridge, which gave "unbroken, and hence undelayed, transit of railway trains from the Northwest and Southwest to the Atlantic Seaboard, and from the East and the South to this side of the

Mississippi."[6] The claim was premature but accurately reflected expectations of what the bridge would soon accomplish.

For those on board, the ride across the bridge was full of excitement, but the plunge into the tunnel was not so agreeable. As the darkness closed in, relieved only by an occasional flickering gaslight, and the air became close and unpleasant, the large company on the train became silent. The heat in the cars near the engine was simply intolerable, and several of the passengers became sick and faint.[7]

A brief respite from the stifling conditions in the tunnel was provided when the train reached the opening at Mill Creek Valley, but on the return trip something caused the train to stop. Some of the dignitaries began to feel that they would suffocate. As they started to cough and gasp for breath, someone expressed the fear that the occurrence might "get into the Chicago papers." It did.

A reporter for the *Chicago Times* wrote that "it was an inauspicious beginning of the day." He questioned Eads about the incident and was told that "the unfortunate occurrence" resulted from the fact that the bridge company had not yet secured the "smoke-consuming engines" they planned to use on the bridge and in the tunnel for the transfer of freight and passenger cars.[8]

These engines were to be provided by the Baldwin Locomotive Works of Philadelphia, a company created by Matthius Baldwin, a sometime-member of the Philadelphia group. The Baldwin company had successfully responded to customer needs in the past by constructing locomotives designed to meet specific requirements, and it had long been a supplier of engines for the Pennsylvania Railroad. But no one with an interest in the bridge and tunnel had taken the initiative of ordering the special smoke-consuming (coke-burning) engines far enough in advance for them to be available by July 4.

Moreover, despite claims to the contrary, the tunnel was not fully complete. The tunnel actually consisted of two tunnels, each having its own track so that traffic could move in both directions without the need of switching. But on the day of opening, only one tunnel was available for use and there were inadequate outlets for tunnel ventilation. As the *St. Louis Republican* observed, "it is quite evident some improvement in the ventilation of the tunnel must be made before regular passenger traffic can be commenced through it."[9]

More important than the problems of ventilation, however, was a fact unacknowledged by any newspaper reporter, including the otherwise critical writers for the Chicago papers. Termination of the tunnel tracks at Mill Creek Valley left the bridge connected with nothing. Taussig described the valley on the day of dedication as "a depression of filth and nastiness . . . occupied only by old shanties, slaughter-houses and pig-styes, shunned by everybody."[10]

Nor was much notice taken of the fact that the ornamental towers and gigantic statues planned for the bridge, which were prominently illustrated on the official invitations to the ceremony and on almost every rendering of the bridge made public since 1867, were not in place. As the *St. Louis Republican* claimed in its account of the day's events, the beauty of the bridge was not harmed by lack of "those artistic embellishments which the designs of the projector contemplate adding at some future day."[11] The bridge seemed grand enough without them.

Immediately following the inaugural train excursion, a christening ceremony was held at the western end of the bridge. An elevated platform about fifty feet long and twenty-five feet wide, capable of seating six hundred persons, was erected on an open area at the corner of Washington Avenue and Third Street, near the entrance to the upper wagon deck of the bridge. To the south of this main grandstand was a street-level area where an additional four hundred people were to be seated, including a band and several singing societies. The floor of the main platform was covered with an elegant Brussels carpet, and the entire stand was sheltered from the sun by a tent, the ceiling of which was decorated with lace curtains. The outside of the stand was wreathed in evergreens and festooned with red, white, and blue bunting. Here various United States senators, state governors, generals, city officials, and families of the bridge company directors and officers "gazed in luxurious comfort from cushioned seats at the less fortunate many, sweltering and weary at their feet."[12]

Immediately above the pavilion an entablature decorated with two large symbolic figures representing Missouri and Illinois gazed down upon the crowd, and above that, starred and striped banners hung from six large flagstaffs. Between these banners a gigantic portrait of Eads soared seventy feet into the air. A man passing below on the following day looked up at the visage and was heard to remark that Eads was a big man, but not quite that big.

Behind the pavilion and portrait, next to the tollhouse located at the entrance of the bridge, James Lyon sat at a table selling photographs of the grand structure. Once subforeman of a work crew in the pneumatic caisson that now formed the base foundation of the east pier, Lyon was permanently disabled by caisson disease. Stricken in April 1870, he had been very sick for three months. He still suffered partial paralysis and had little control over his anal sphincter or his bladder. Although this humiliating condition would gradually improve, his joints remained sensitive to changes in temperature and barometric pressure for the rest of his life.

On this hot Independence Day, however, he considered himself fortunate. Many of his fellow workers had experienced greater suffering, or death, as a result of their labor in the caisson.

After completing the inaugural train ride, dignitaries began ascending the grand-stand steps about 10:00 A.M. They were just in time to view the leading elements of a great parade, the magnitude of which the city had never experienced. Although the procession had actually begun moving from its starting point at Washington Avenue and Jefferson Street about 9:30 A.M., it took almost a half-hour to reach the area of the grandstand. When the head of the column reached this point, a curtain made from various national flags was drawn aside revealing the platform.

At the front of the stand sat the bridge company directors and their families. Gerald B. Allen, the third and current president, introduced Josephine Walsh, wife of Julius S. Walsh and daughter of Charles K. Dickson, first president of the bridge company. It was Mrs. Walsh's duty to christen the bridge by pouring onto it the commingled waters of the Pacific and Atlantic Oceans, the Great Lakes, the Gulf of Mexico, and the Mississippi River. The act was meant to symbolize "the arrival of the river town to the dignity of being the controlling inland metropolis of the Western world."[13] After the baptism was performed with an invocation to the Al-mighty, the parade continued its noisy progress across the bridge while speeches commenced on the grandstand.

The procession was not just a celebration of the bridge and the nation's inde-pendence, it was also a grand triumphal display of the business features of St. Louis. The entire country was invited to bear witness to the commercial strength of the city, in hopes that business people from other areas would be encouraged to in-vest their capital in the city's future. A reporter for the *Chicago Post and Mail* was so struck by the amount of advertising displayed that he estimated four-fifths of the procession was made up of bulletin boards and displays showing that every dealer in St. Louis was bent on "tooting his horn."

Winding some fourteen to fifteen miles through the city streets, the parade included virtually every civic and social group, military organization, and com-mercial interest of St. Louis, and a few from East St. Louis as well. Such was its in-clusiveness that it took five hours to pass one point.

At the head of the procession was a squad of Metropolitan police, followed by the grand marshal and his aides, twenty-two of whom were boys mounted on ponies and wearing uniforms consisting of a black jacket, white pants, and a red sash. Following immediately behind were blue-clad companies of United States Cavalry, the National Guards of both states, German Uhlans, two hundred Knights of Pythias, five hundred of the Ancient Order of Hibernians, five hundred Knights of Father Matthew (with fife band), three hundred Druids, five hundred Sons of Hermann, two hundred United Brethren of Friendship, twenty members of the Bohemian Gymnastic Club, and hundreds of other members of various organizations, large and small. After the passage of the societies no particular attention was paid to order.

There were wagons and floats representing the Merchants Exchange, the fire department, several federal agencies, brewers, pork packers, leaf tobacco dealers, grain elevator operators, wool and fur traders, stove manufacturers, boat builders, furniture makers, dry-goods merchants, sewing machine manufacturers, medicine and tonic makers, lumber companies, glassware manufacturers, framers and moulders, painters and plumbers, carpenters and bakers, stationers and printers, tinners, stair builders, jute bagging makers, artisans of all types, farm machinery wholesalers, safe manufacturers, potters, distillers, and railroad equipment suppliers. There were so many different types of civic, social, and commercial activity represented that the Sunday edition of the *St. Louis Republican* could not list all the participants in thirteen columns of small type. On the following Monday another two and one-half columns were devoted to mention of those who "got left."

The wagon of the St. Louis Life Insurance Company, which Eads served as president, featured a facsimile of the company's building at Sixth and Locust Streets. The six-story structure was the tallest in town when constructed in 1869, and it featured the first hydraulic passenger lift in St. Louis. Anyone paying twenty-five cents could ride to the top of the building, stand next to the numerous twelve-foot-tall sandstone statues of Greek divinities that ringed the roof, and enjoy an unobstructed view in every direction.

The model of the building displayed on the day of celebration was constructed of pasteboard by the Italian decorator Minnegerodi. It was thirteen feet across the front, over fourteen feet deep, nine feet high, and was mounted on a platform transfer wagon pulled by six richly decorated horses. It was well detailed and had small tin reflectors arranged inside to simulate plate glass windows. The flag of the United States streamed from the top of the model, and the horses pulling the wagon were also decorated with flags.

Some of the other wagons in the procession displayed one-of-a-kind exhibits such as that in the insurance company wagon. Dr. J. H. McLean, for example, had a small wagon containing a "pyramidal load of his white, crystal-coated universal pills," as the *St. Louis Republican* put it dryly, "enough to physic the whole procession." On top of the pyramid was a pillbox eight feet long, and following behind was a larger wagon with a representation of McLean's laboratory. Inside the lab were a number of boys and girls preparing medicines for shipment. There was also a printing press in this wagon, and freshly printed copies of "The Star Spangled Banner" were freely distributed to the crowd as the procession moved along.

The contribution of Leggat, Hudson and Butler, St. Louis Tobacco Works, consisted of one very large wagon drawn by four bay horses. At the front of the wagon was a seven-foot-high mound of cut tobacco, topped by a plume of leaves, and a sign bearing the firm's name and the words "Gilt-edge" in letters representing different nationalities. A display of the company's principal brands occupied the center of the wagon, and on the back was a miniature tobacco field showing the plants in different stages of growth. The Reverend Haalington Dedman, described by the *St. Louis Republican* as "a happy, cheery old darkey," pretended to hoe and cultivate the crops. Above Dedman a banner announced: "Tobacco—Missouri's staple; it supports government and comforts all."

A majority of the wagons featured elaborate displays of manufacturing processes. The firm of E. Anheuser and Company, which conducted an extensive business in South America, sponsored three wagons designed to exhibit a miniature brewing establishment. In the first wagon was a supply of hops, barley, and brewers' utensils, along with a number of healthy beer drinkers who exhibited the advantageous effects of using malt liquors. The second wagon contained a small model of a bottling room, including the necessary machinery for corking the product.

This firm was just one of many in a long line of brewers, each of whom conspicuously displayed the business sign and trademark of the proprietor. Most wagons also displayed mottoes in English or German that questioned the wisdom of temperance while extolling the virtues of beer, such as the sign on the back of the Excelsior brewery wagon that read,

Oh, thou royal lager beer,
The fountain of health and comfort;
In spite of fanatical sneer,
Blessed is thy civilizing purport.

At the head of the line of brewer's wagons "Jolly Old King Gambrinus" downed foaming goblets of lager "in a manner that sent pangs of envy to the parched throats of thousands" who no doubt desired a free sample. Instead they received free cigars rolled out en route by the cigar makers; copies of the Declaration of Independence and other items printed at the back of Levison and Blythe's large platform wagon, which also sailed a model of Franklin's famous kite; two thousand tin cups manufactured by a team of nine journeymen and three boys working out of A. Geisel and Company's handsomely decorated four-horse wagon; pictures of the bridge, fourteen by thirteen inches in size, inscribed by the Excelsior Manufacturing Company motto: "Our Mammoth Hotel Charter Oak [stove] will cook a square meal for a regiment"; and chairs made by craftsmen in the second four-horse wagon of the St. Louis Chair Factory.

The first wagon of this last firm had a lathe in complete running order manned by men turning pieces that were passed to the craftsmen in the second wagon. Thus, everyone along the line of march could see the product actually being manufactured. Less believable, no doubt, was the mechanism set up in the first of two wagons sponsored by the rival Missouri Chair Factory. This large and well-decorated float featured a huge machine, supposedly containing apparatus for manufacturing chairs entirely by automation. Rough cordwood was inserted into a hopper at one end, and a perfect chair came out the other. Some, according to the *St. Louis Republican,* may have thought "there was a little humbug about this." But in the second wagon there was a "whopping big rocking chair" in which was seated the St. Louis baby of the day, a blessed infant sixteen feet high, and oddly enough, according to the newspaper, "there was no humbug about that baby."[14]

If there was any humbug to be noted during the celebration, perhaps it could be found on the grandstand, where the dignitaries of the day were engaged in oratory even as the procession wound its way past them over the bridge to Illinois and back again through the streets of St. Louis. The christening performed by Mrs. Walsh was followed by a prayer, which was followed in turn by the remarks of the Honorable Barton Able, one of the principal organizers of the event and the chairman of the committee of arrangements. Able, though claiming not to be boastful concerning his city, went on record as saying that the time was not far off when St. Louis would be not only the commercial and financial center of the country, but the national capital as well.

Able echoed a long-expressed notion concerning the future possibilities of St. Louis that picked up considerable support following the Civil War. A convention hosted by the Merchants Exchange was held in October 1869 at the Mercantile Library, during which governors and delegates from twenty-one states and territories discussed the feasibility of moving the capital from Washington to St. Louis. The convention urged Congress to take such action and created a committee to promote the cause. The secretary of that committee, Logan U. Reavis, wrote a widely read book the following year in which the argument for capital relocation was logically laid out. Reavis dedicated the first edition of *Saint Louis: The Future Great City of the World* (1870) to James Eads.

Able's speech was followed by that of Joseph Brown, mayor of St. Louis. Brown mentioned the difficulties of the bridge's creation, which included the fact that those opposed to it "threw every obstacle in the way." Acknowledging his initial opposition to the location of the bridge, he claimed that upon seeing the first pier rearing its head out of the water he had said to himself, "I will not only not oppose the bridge [on account of location], but I will do everything in my power to hasten its completion."[15] What Brown did not say was that he was then actively leading an effort to boycott the bridge.

After Brown concluded his remarks, the singing societies in attendance sang "Spanning the Mississippi," and then Governors Beveridge of Illinois and Woodson of Missouri made their obligatory and long-winded speeches. Following some more singing, the featured orator of the day stepped to the front of the podium. The Honorable B. Gratz Brown, ex-governor of Missouri and former United States senator, provided a stirring speech that included a short history of his involvement in the bridge's federal legislation.

At the conclusion of his speech, Brown revealed that in the last conversation he had with Eads, on the day the central span was being joined, the chief engineer had stated with a sigh of regret, "If this were merely my own enterprise, and if my own fortune alone were at stake, I would have bridged yonder river with a single arch fifteen hundred feet in length."[16]

As Eads strolled to the front of the stand following a spirited rendition of "The Star-Spangled Banner," there were probably many investors on the platform who wished it had been only Eads's fortune at stake. As Taussig later admitted, "while orators held dedicatory speeches in presence of all the dignitaries of City and State, the hearts of those of the bridge directors who knew, and especially that of myself, as the responsible manager, were heavy with the forebodings of impending bankruptcy."[17]

Perhaps it was knowledge of the financial condition of the bridge that led Eads to skip any mention of the commercial possibilities of the structure during his speech. Instead he devoted his remarks to three main themes: the debt he owed others who assisted in financing and construction; the safety and permanence of the bridge; and his sorrow at the passing of those who died while the bridge was under construction.

The first theme was most certainly a genuine expression of Eads's gratitude for the considerable aid offered by the other men involved in the project. He, more than anyone else, knew that the bridge and tunnel would never have been built without the expertise of his engineering staff, nor without the organizational and financial assistance offered by the officers and directors of the bridge company. With this knowledge, Eads humbly stated, "It is itself a high privilege to feel that I stand before you as the representative of a community of earnest men, whose combined labor, brains and wealth, have built up this monument of usefulness for their fellow men."[18] But except for brief mention of Walter Katté, Eads made no acknowledgment of the role played by the Keystone Bridge Company or his associates from Pennsylvania.

The second theme of Eads's address was the most telling of the three in terms of revealing what he believed to be the most important reality of the bridge—that it would "endure as long as it is useful to man." Other great bridges might fall, but Eads's bridge would not. It was the bridge's permanence, more than its commercial worth, that justified excessive delays and cost. Eads boasted that "everything which prudence, judgment and the present state of science could suggest to me and my assistants, has been carefully observed, in its design and construction."

Toward the end of his speech, Eads also noted that "a great work is rarely erected without the sacrifice of human life, and our bridge is no exception to the rule." Moreover, he claimed that if the loss of life had been particularly great in this instance, it was due not to negligence of the part of Eads or his staff, but only to the greatness of the endeavor. As an example, Eads offered that "the loss of life in the caisson of the east pier resulted from the fact that no such depth had been obtained before, and experience of others could not be had to guide our operations in it with safety."

The *St. Louis Republican* had demonstrated a similar fatalistic determinism regarding these deaths in the previous day's edition. Some lives were lost, the paper acknowledged, but "Human lives are always sacrificed in discovering new paths to great public benefit. They appear to be given freely, and the work never stops till the end is gained."[19]

With a few additional comments concerning his debt of gratitude to the two deceased former presidents of the bridge company, William McPherson and Charles Dickson, Eads concluded the last scheduled oration of the day. The crowd, however, demanded to hear from Governor Hendricks of Indiana, who was mercifully brief, and Senator Thomas Ferry of Michigan.

Ferry elicited more laughter than any other speaker with his gentle jabs at the city of Chicago, and he won applause for identifying the bridge as a matchless factor in the provision of cheap transportation. He also stated his belief that the monopoly of railroad transportation was on that day breaking the monopoly of river navigation, and they were both breaking each other, "by inviting the public to the privileges of each."

More laughter came forth when Ferry mentioned newspaper pronouncements that said the bridge had broken the monopoly of the ferry. In fact, the *St. Louis Republican* would claim on the following day that railroad stations in eastern cities were already placarded: "No ferry crossing at St. Louis." And enthusiastic applause followed when Ferry stated, "Your Wiggins Ferry has no longer any vitality in it." Soon, the citizens of St. Louis would realize just how accurate the senator's remarks were about the two forms of transportation breaking each other, and just how wrong he was about the immediate demise of the ferry company.

With the speeches, singing, band playing, marching, and associated activities completed, one climactic event remained. For weeks the citizens of St. Louis and East St. Louis had been promised the greatest and most extravagant fireworks show ever to be seen on the American continent. No less than $10,000 worth of pyrotechnic illuminations, enough material to fill four railroad cars, were to be brought to the city from the factory of the Excelsior Fireworks Company in New Jersey.

Approximately fifty boats and barges filled the river between Illinois and Missouri, in a double rainbow that allowed the smaller craft to be nearest the bridge. Hundreds of people, including Eads and guests of the bridge company, were thus afforded a close-up view of the pyrotechnics, such as they were.

It would later be determined that only $4,500 had actually been allocated for fireworks, and perhaps less than that had been spent. The overall impression left by the St. Louis papers was that the event was a disgraceful failure, but there were some high spots.

Several "grand Temple pieces" had been set off, including one of the bridge itself surmounted by allegorical figures representing Missouri and Illinois, clasping hands, and another of Eads in the Temple of Honor, flanked by a locomotive and a steamboat, being crowned by Genius. This accolade to the chief engineer was one of the more popular portions of the show.

The biggest disappointment of the evening was caused by the nonappearance of the most anticipated of all the scheduled displays. A "Phantom Train" with illuminated engine and cars was supposed to run the entire length of the bridge as a finale. But like the "smoke-consuming" engines to be used in the tunnel, and like the revenue-generating trains anticipated to cross the bridge, the phantom train failed to arrive. One wag was heard to remark that perhaps the man in charge of the fireworks had run the phantom train through the tunnel instead of over the bridge.

With the last official event completed, the boats began to disperse, and most of the weary revelers drifted home or back to their hotels. Many, however, wishing to escape the lingering heat of the city, strolled out on the bridge to the middle of the river. There the cool breeze encouraged some to linger through the last few minutes of the day. Perhaps, in leaning over the rail, they took note, along with a reporter for the *New York World,* as "one of the superseded ferry boats, coughing regularly like an asthmatic mule, trailed a broken wing of sparks and smoke across the glittering stream."[20]

The Elements of a Great City

St. Louis is fast losing its identity as a semi-southern city. It is taking on the manners and customs and vigor and breeziness that
characterize the wide-awake Western towns. New life has been
infused into it within the past five or six years. The St. Louis of today
has the elements of a great city, with prospects of a near future that
will make it . . . the great metropolis of the Southwest.

—*Harpers Weekly,* 1888

Completion of the St. Louis Bridge was the catalytic
event in a series of occurrences that marked the
progress of railroad facility development in St.
Louis during the latter part of the nineteenth century. It forced the city to grapple with the difficult tasks of
creating suitable terminal facilities and establishing a system of connecting tracks to serve those facilities.[1] This development was an integral part of the larger process whereby St. Louis realized much of its potential as a center of trade
during the heyday of rail transportation in America.

The long duration of this process is a reflection of the
fractional nature of the city's leadership, of the regional
divisions that separated the interests of eastern and western railroad corporations, and of the business practices

that characterized the world of big business during the era of railroad development.

In order for the common welfare of the St. Louis community to be realized, new leadership that encompassed both managerial competency and entrepreneurial vision had to emerge. The men originally behind creation of the bridge and tunnel were not up to the task.

J. Edgar Thomson, the one man from outside the community perhaps most capable of bringing about a resolution of conflicting interests, did not live to see the bridge completed. He died on May 27, 1874. As expected, the board of directors of the Pennsylvania Railroad elected Thomas Scott as Thomson's successor on June 3, one day before the bridge officially opened.

At that time, most of the findings and pending recommendations of the Pennsylvania Railroad stockholders' investigating committee were already known. Those findings would force adoption of new, more restrictive policies that severely curtailed Scott's highly speculative and expansionist business practices. The aggressiveness he had displayed in the past would no longer be acceptable to the company's stockholders, its board of directors, or its financial backers.

The full report of the investigating committee was officially released in a voluminous document circulated at a special stockholders' meeting on October 3, 1874. It was the product of one of the most exhaustive and revealing investigations ever conducted into the status and operations of a large nineteenth-century railroad corporation. In the words of one official company history, it was not only a monument to the career of J. Edgar Thomson, but also "a monument to an economic epoch, the period of postwar prosperity and expansion."[2] Yet anyone reading the report could plainly see that it was also a thinly veiled indictment of past railroad management practices.

As part of an entire chapter devoted to uncovering the sources of the "existing distrust in the value of railway stocks and securities," the report found that the problem was rooted in the "tendency in the leading officials of railroad companies to act as if the property they manage is their own." The report also expressed fears that "the property of the company may be used by officials and favored employees for their own personal benefit."[3]

As a result of the report the management of the company was made more accountable to its board and stockholders and forced to restrict its financial interests and curtail its commitments, particularly those commitments west of the Mississippi River.[4] This included all those obligations necessary for the St. Louis Bridge and tunnel to succeed.

Prior knowledge of the committee's findings, combined with Scott's election to a newly weakened presidency, probably had some influence on the actions of a group of eastern railroad executives who met at the Southern Hotel in St. Louis on the evening of July 9, 1874. These gentlemen, most connected to the Pennsylvania Railroad in some way, agreed that none of their companies would run trains across the bridge until the union passenger depot was completed. Furthermore, it was agreed that no railroad terminating in East St. Louis would use the bridge until all such railroads agreed to do so.[5] This agreement by the railroads stemmed, in part, from a disagreement concerning tolls to be charged for use of the structure.

Under the existing system the eastern railroads delivered all their freight to the terminals in East St. Louis (or in Alton). In 1869 the Madison County Ferry Company had installed a double set of tracks on some of its boats, thus accommodating the different gauges of eastern and western railroads. The company then began transferring railroad cars loaded with freight across the river between Alton and St. Louis. The Wiggins Ferry Company soon met its competition by putting its own car ferries into service. Moreover, it still owned the land on which the terminals of eastern railroads sat, and it owned extensive warehouse and switching facilities as well. The company was therefore able to preserve its dominant position as freight hauler across the river.

The introduction of car ferries meant that it was no longer necessary to break bulk at the river's edge when dealing with certain commodities like coal or grain. Other types of freight would still be broken into wagon loads and transported down to the river by the East St. Louis Transfer Company. The ferry's charge began at water's edge on one side and ended at the water's edge on the other side. The boats could land at any point along the levee for the convenience of the transfer companies that actually performed the delivering and receiving.[6]

On the Missouri side the St. Louis Transfer Company (which absorbed the East St. Louis Transfer Company in 1869) took over and delivered through westbound freight to the terminals of the western railroads, either in whole cars or in wagons. Goods destined for St. Louis merchants were delivered right to the door, to warehouses, or were piled on the levee or streets for later delivery. When freight was stacked or stored, the merchant had to pay an additional charge for "drayage."

The cost of this service was added to the rates charged by the railroads to deliver freight or passengers to either St. Louis or East St. Louis. The total charge therefore essentially equaled what it would have cost if a landlocked St. Louis had been located hundreds of miles east or west of the point at which the railroads terminated. This was the "tax" that the city engineer, Truman J. Homer, had railed against in 1865.

The bridge was supposed to eliminate this flexible but very expensive system. But there were several obstacles to elimination with which the Illinois and St. Louis Bridge Company had to deal. The first problem was that several of the railroad officials involved had a personal financial interest in preservation of the status quo. As Taussig would later claim, the St. Louis Transfer Company was "mainly owned and controlled by railroad officers. This is an interesting fact in so far as it shows how different the ethics of official propriety on the part of railroad officers were then from what they are now."[7]

These gentlemen were not likely to take action that removed money from their own pockets, even if it was in the interest of the railroads that employed them. But elimination of the old system was not necessarily in the interest of either the railroads or the merchants of St. Louis.

When the bridge opened it offered an immediate 50 percent reduction in the cost of transport over the river. But the Wiggins Ferry Company and the St. Louis Transfer Company reduced their rates to match those of the bridge company, thus offsetting the price differential.

Moreover, freight moving over the bridge had to go through the tunnel, but there was no place for it to go at that point because the bridge and tunnel companies had no terminal facilities. The same was essentially true for passengers. Without a union depot they could either disembark at the very small station under the west arcade of the bridge or they would be left in the middle of nowhere when they reached the end of the tunnel.

The existing system had a certain familiarity and functional usefulness despite its flaws. The merchants of St. Louis found that it was easier to continue doing things the way they had always been done in the past rather than switch. And the ferry company was very competitive; it usually found a way to counter the moves of the bridge company. For example, whereas the bridge company began offering free ice water to thirsty teamsters in an attempt to win their patronage, the ferry company offered free whiskey.[8] The Wiggins company also installed clean accommodations and began treating customers better.[9]

It was no surprise, therefore, that the railroad officials voted to boycott the bridge at their meeting of July 9. While officers of the depot company worked to change the railroad officials' collective mind, only a very limited amount of traffic moved across the rail deck of the bridge.

On July 16, a locomotive pulling nine cars loaded with stone for the new post

office and custom house crossed over, followed two weeks later by a four-car shipment of coal for Evans and Howard's fire-clay works. But that was about it as far as
freight was concerned.

A temporary passenger depot was completed on September 18, 1874, one year
and a day after closure of the first arch of the bridge. As the *St. Louis Republican*
noted, "it is not a very imposing structure."[10] But at least it was complete. The railroads, however, continued to boycott the bridge and tunnel while negotiations
lagged for creation of a permanent union passenger depot and for construction of
associated connecting tracks.

With little business yet available from the railroads to offset operating expenses
and floating debt, the bridge company resorted in October to running Sunday
"excursion" trains through the tunnel and over the bridge as a means of providing some small bit of revenue. The trains left the temporary depot at Eleventh and
Poplar Streets five times a day, passed through the tunnel, stopped at the center
arch of the bridge long enough for everyone aboard to enjoy the partially obstructed view, and then chugged on into East St. Louis.[11]

The bridge company also installed a double set of tracks for a horse-car line,
which began operations shortly after the bridge opened. It was not immediately
profitable, but at least it was self-sustaining.

Rumors regarding the potential demise of the Illinois and St. Louis Bridge Company increased after October 16, when a large contingent of railroad executives and
investors, including J. S. Morgan, J. P. Morgan, and Thomas Scott, met at the Lindell Hotel. The reasons for lack of progress on construction of a permanent union
passenger depot were discussed, along with many other issues relating to railroad
traffic through St. Louis.

The following month, on November 24, a meeting was held in East St. Louis at
which Scott and J. S. Morgan proposed to the officers of the Cairo and St. Louis
Narrow-gauge Railroad the construction of a union depot and transfer tracks at
Cairo, Illinois. In exchange for making these improvements and providing a loan
to the railroad, Scott and Morgan wanted a half interest in certain tracts of land
owned by the railroad around Cairo. They also wanted control of all freight destined for the East from the line of the Cairo and St. Louis Railroad to the line of
the Pennsylvania Railroad.[12]

A few days later, Scott, Morgan, and several other railroad officials, including
Thomas Allen, president of the St. Louis, Iron Mountain and Southern Railroad,
took an excursion over the lines of that company down to Cairo. It was here that
Scott wished to make a connection between the Pennsylvania Central and the

Texas and Pacific Railroads via the Cairo and Vincennes Railroad, and the St. Louis, Iron Mountain and Southern Railroad.

Morgan was president of the Cairo and Vincennes Railroad Company, and like several of the directors of that company he had a small investment in the St. Louis Bridge. But his and the other directors' allegiance to the bridge company was second to that for their overall plan. Morgan had simply determined that in order to connect the Penn Central with the Texas and Pacific it would be necessary to cross land owned by the Cairo and St. Louis Railroad. This is what motivated his offer to the latter railroad for assistance in constructing a union depot.

Since the St. Louis, Iron Mountain and Southern was already shipping Texas cattle and cotton into St. Louis without use of the St. Louis Bridge, the larger purposes behind Scott, Morgan, and Allen's excursion were the subject of gossip in St. Louis. It was alleged that the railroads terminating in East St. Louis had threatened to build a union depot on that side of the river, and many people wondered if a plan was underway to abandon the bridge and tunnel. In essence, it was.

All of this should have been of great concern to Eads, the man most responsible for bringing about the existence of the bridge and tunnel, but he had already moved on to other projects. On July 28, 1874, he had submitted his resignation as chief engineer to the bridge company board of directors. He also submitted a letter stating that he owed the company about $100,000 on stock subscriptions and he asked that his debt be extended to August 1, 1876, with interest payable at 6 percent, and that his stock be retained by the company as security for payment of the debt.

Eads justified his request on the grounds that he had performed services for the company in regard to negotiations for loans and had never been paid for those services. Eads claimed that circumstances of his stock deficit would surely justify the company's canceling the subscription, which would be fine with him, but the arrangement he suggested would allow the company to use his indebtedness as collateral. Eads also asked that his son-in-law, John A. Ubsdell of New York, be allowed to extend payments on his stock subscription.[13]

The executive committee approved Eads's request and directed the auditor and treasurer of the company to exchange Eads's existing notes for new notes drawn under the conditions expressed in his letter.[14] It was a sweet deal for Eads because he would lose little if the bridge company went bankrupt, but if at any point in the future the company started making money he could pay for the stock at that point and reap the rewards.

On October 7 it was revealed that since September 17 the bridge company had been overdrawn by a considerable sum on its account with the National Bank of Missouri. In order to cover this debt President Allen agreed to sell the bank the remaining fifty-nine third mortgage bonds held by the bridge company at 60 percent of face value plus interest. He also agreed to execute a $50,000 note of the company, secured by several hundred shares of stock in the Union Railway and Transit Company and in the bridge company. To cover a loan from J. S. Morgan and Company, Allen asked the bank to resell the fifty-nine third mortgage bonds as collateral.

In order to secure the bank for the amount of bonds resold to Morgan for payment of the daily maturing liabilities of the bridge company, and also for funds advanced by the bank to pay September interest on third mortgage bonds, Allen agreed to offer the bank certain assets of the bridge company. Among those assets were bills receivable on stock subscriptions, but the outstanding debts of Eads and Ubsdell were specifically eliminated from the list of assets pledged. Thus, Eads and his son-in-law were given additional protection from at least some of the financial liability of the bridge corporation.

After these arrangements were made, Eads left for Europe to do a little consulting work and look at some water control projects. Although he would be in town again on March 23, 1875, as guest of honor at a banquet, he would have little to do with transportation facilities in St. Louis in the future.

William Taussig, not Eads, Thomson, Scott, or Carnegie, was the man chiefly responsible for negotiating a new agreement between the bridge company and the railroads for use of the bridge, tunnel, and depot. But at a meeting of the railroad managers, the bridge company, and the depot company held at the Lindell Hotel on November 24, 1874, Taussig was informed that the railroads considered the recently completed temporary depot and associated transfer facilities inadequate to handle any of their traffic. After all, the men behind the bridge, tunnel, depot, and bridge-related transfer companies were attempting to do with approximately twenty acres of terminal faculties in St. Louis what was currently being done on about 660 acres in East St. Louis.

In an attempt to put the best face on this turn of events the *St. Louis Republican* stated, "The trouble with St. Louis is that there are so many railroads centering here that, to provide room for them all, requires an immense area of ground and a compactness of system in handling them, which it takes large capital and a good deal of time to prepare. Ours is an *embarras de riches* as regards railroads; we have so many we don't know what to do with them."[15]

Although the problems faced by St. Louis were somewhat more complex than indicated by the newspaper, it was certainly correct to state that it takes a great deal of capital and time to create a compact system of terminals and rails in the heart of a major metropolis. Such creation also takes leadership and commitment on the part of those who intend to use the system.

Taussig, though competent as a manager, occupied no position of power or authority with the railroads in question. With no strong general entrepreneur present to provide that leadership, the project in St. Louis foundered.

Due to the continued boycott, the Illinois and St. Louis Bridge Company defaulted in payment of interest on its first, second, and third mortgage bonds on April 19, 1875, and no funds were available for the payment of interest on the bonds of the St. Louis Tunnel Company. Therefore, both companies had to declare bankruptcy and were given over to the hands of two receivers: J. Pierpont Morgan and Solon Humphreys.

Less than two months later, on June 11, 1875, after more delay than anyone could have anticipated, the first permanent union passenger depot in St. Louis opened with a capacity of fourteen trains a day. Two days later the first regularly scheduled revenue-generating passenger train passed over the bridge and through the tunnel.

Completion of the depot served as leverage to entice R. P. Tansey, president of the St. Louis Transfer Company after its absorption of the East St. Louis Transfer Company in 1869, to make a deal with Taussig whereby the transfer company broke its contract with the ferry company and allied itself with the bridge and tunnel companies. This arrangement went into effect in October 1875 and the ferry company soon responded by organizing a transfer company of its own, the appropriately named Wiggins Ferry Transfer Company. More than a year of bitter competition between the bridge and ferry companies (and their associated organizations) would follow before a compromise was reached.

Bridge receivers Morgan and Humphreys proposed an agreement between the ferry and the bridge company that would keep both of them in business. The agreement recognized that both companies had contracted with certain railroads, and that each had facilities that made it superior to the other in certain respects. The bridge and tunnel would therefore take 75 percent and the ferry company 25 percent of their combined net earnings up to $400,000. As income rose, the bridge's share would increase to 95 percent of the net above $1 million a year.[16]

An Illinois court invalidated the agreement in 1881, but it continued as an unofficial arrangement until outlawed by passage of the Interstate Commerce Act in 1887.[17] Yet it did not eliminate all competition between the bridge and the ferry companies. Agents for each began offering kickbacks to railroad agents and merchants to use the facilities of one company or the other, and creative accounting was not uncommon.

Shortly after the terms of this agreement were worked out an event occurred that revealed how a bit of creative accounting on the part of bridge company officials had temporarily kept the bridge and tunnel companies in business.

In June 1877, the National Bank of the State of Missouri closed its doors. It was the largest bank failure in the nation's history. When the bank failed, several of the bridge company investors, including Eads, Bates, and Britton, each owed the bank about $250,000. As would later be revealed, funds of the bank that were not lent to individual members of the syndicate that owned the bank were loaned to the bridge company, the tunnel company, the railroads in which syndicate members were involved, and the Mississippi River Jetty Works (later named the South Pass Jetty Company), which Eads had set up in 1874.

On June 26, 1877, Eads wrote to James Andrews, former contractor for the bridge and tunnel and now Eads's partner in the jetty company, to say that suspension of the bank had greatly increased the difficulty of raising money for the jetty project. He explained his difficulties in regard to the bank by stating, "My connection with it and large indebtedness to it have been published all over the country and naturally make those hesitate who would before have looked upon my name on a note as adding additional strength to it. For sometime past there were rumors about the bank in which my name was connected as one of its largest borrowers which fact had got out by a leaky U.S. Examiner."[18]

On January 15, 1879, Eads again wrote to Andrews concerning the bank failure, reporting that the grand jury had met that day. "I suppose they will be through in a day or two and that I can leave for Washington Friday or Saturday," Eads wrote. "They will indict no one, but I shall not leave until the case of my friends Bates & Britton is settled."[19]

Eads was wrong. The grand jury found sufficient cause to return an indictment against Britton, the bank president; Bates, the vice president; and E. P. Curtis, the cashier. The indictments were for declaring unearned dividends, unlawfully purchasing the bank's capital stock, the making of false reports by the cashier concerning the amount of bad debts held by the bank, and for other sundry offenses. Since Eads was not an officer of the bank at that time, he was not indicted. Shortly after the charges against his friends were handed down he again left town.

There were many in the community who agreed with an editorial in one of the local newspapers that claimed, "There is no sane or unprejudiced person in the city of St. Louis who would not . . . regard the conviction of Mr. Barton Bates as an unmitigated outrage, as long as Mr. Eads, who was the real spirit of the bank, is free and unindicted."[20] But Eads was too smart to get caught.

Those individuals who held the most responsibility for prosecuting the guilty parties each avoided taking aggressive action in pursuit of Eads. When public outrage forced them to defend their behavior, they each claimed it was the other's responsibility to press the case.

Certain papers, such as bank notes for large sums of money that Eads made out to himself or others, which needed to be presented to the grand jury for prosecution of those indicted or likely to be indicted (Eads), were surrendered by the comptroller to Eads in March 1879. This was done upon the advice of the receiver's attorney, who also happened to be attorney for the defense. In exchange for turning over the incriminating documents the comptroller accepted from Eads a certain sum of money in full satisfaction of his indebtedness to the bank. Although evidence of Eads's indebtedness could still be proven by examination of the books of the bank, as Bliss later pointed out, "there are indorsements [sic] upon the notes which are material, and which cannot be shown except by the notes themselves. The notes have been, I am informed, destroyed."[21] Eventually, all charges were dropped.[22]

An interesting summary of the whole affair was provided by C. Shaler Smith in a letter to Barton Bates's son Onward, who worked for Smith on the St. Charles Bridge project. Smith wrote, "You have probably heard that the grand jury here have indicted Col. Britton—Judge Bates and poor old Curtis in connection with the State Bank failure. . . . The result was curious—Eads—smartest of the smart slipped out from under and the technical net caught men it was not intended to catch and the arch beguiler went his way rejoicing."[23]

Eads had plenty of reason to rejoice in 1879. On July 8 of that year the United States inspecting officer at the jetties reported that the depth and width of the channel created by Eads had met the terms of his contract and he soon thereafter received a multi-million-dollar payment from the federal government. After years of opposition from army engineers, Eads had won again.

Another project immediately grabbed his attention. Following publication of the proceedings of the Inter-Oceanic Canal Congress held in Paris in 1879, Eads proposed a ship railway across the Tehuantepec Isthmus in Mexico as an alternative to the sea-level canal proposed by Ferdinand de Lesseps, builder of the Suez Canal from 1859 to 1869. This plan, which certainly was no less feasible than the disastrous attempt by de Lesseps to dig a sea-level canal through Panama, was the greatest challenge of Eads's life. The project immediately received support in Congress due to Eads's growing reputation as an engineering genius.

That reputation also led to a number of lucrative consulting contracts, and in 1884 Eads further divorced himself from events in St. Louis by opening up a private engineering office in New York. Requests for his services poured in from around the world while he continued to work on his ambitious ship railway scheme. The only thing that stopped him was death. On March 8, 1887, just when it seemed that his ship railway scheme was about to take off, his health failed him for the last time.

As Eads went his way through the 1870s and 1880s, others were left behind to figure out a way of making the bridge and tunnel work as part of St. Louis's rail system, and how to make the bridge, tunnel, and transfer companies work as corporations.

Under terms of a reorganization agreement signed August 28, 1878, by the first, second, and third mortgage bondholders, two new corporations were organized in 1878. These were the St. Louis Bridge Company and the Tunnel Railroad of St. Louis. The assets of the Illinois and St. Louis Bridge Company, which were mainly the $10 million bridge, were sold for $2 million on December 17 at public auction. The buyer was a representative of the bond holders, who turned these assets over to the new bridge company. No provision was made in the reorganization agreement for the stockholders of the previously existing companies, and most of these persons lost their investments.[24]

Two additional companies were formed in 1880 in the interest of the new St. Louis Bridge Company: the Terminal Railroad of St. Louis and the Terminal Railroad Association of East St. Louis. These companies, created like their defunct predecessors for the purpose of constructing tracks and terminal facilities in St. Louis and East St. Louis, leased all their properties to the St. Louis Bridge Company and the Tunnel Railroad of St. Louis under a joint lease agreement.

On July 1, 1881, the bridge and tunnel companies leased the bridge and tunnel to the Missouri Pacific Railroad (a western railroad) and to the Wabash, St. Louis and Pacific Railway Company (an eastern railroad) as joint lessees. Both of these railroads had recently come under the control of Jay Gould, who had been closely watching events in St. Louis for decades.

Gould also leased the Missouri, Kansas and Texas Railroad in 1880 and took over the St. Louis, Iron Mountain and Southern Railroad in 1881. In addition he gained control of Scott's Texas and Pacific Railroad at about the same time, which he then extended to New Orleans.

In 1889 Gould and Taussig cooperated in forming the Terminal Railroad Association of St. Louis (TRRA). This company combined the Union Railway Transit Companies of St. Louis and East St. Louis, the Terminal Railroads of St. Louis and East St. Louis, and the Union Depot Company of St. Louis into one organization. This reorganization of terminals grew out of an agreement between Gould and the seven railroads he then controlled, which terminated in one or the other city.

Although Gould died in 1892, the plans he had put in place before his death were successfully carried out. In 1893 an agreement was also entered into between the St. Louis Merchants Bridge Terminal Railway Company and the Terminal Railroad Association of St. Louis whereby the association acquired stock in the former company and received the right to use the bridge and facilities owned by that company. Businessmen opposed to the St. Louis Bridge had built the Merchants Bridge, completed in 1890 at a point slightly up river from the site suggested in 1867 for construction of the St. Louis and Madison County Bridge.

In 1894 the TRRA completed construction of a new and much larger union passenger station north of the first union passenger depot completed in 1875. Completion of the new station gave St. Louis one of the largest such facilities in the United States and the largest terminal system in the country.

Gould, therefore, with help from Taussig, had done what no one else before had been able to do. He united the railroads operating on either side of the Mississippi River at St. Louis under a cooperative plan of transportation improvements that included two bridges, a tunnel, several freight depots, and a union passenger depot of adequate capacity to meet the city's needs well into the future. Despite a reputation as the most predacious of all Gilded Age capitalists, Gould had become the leading force for development of St. Louis as a great rail center. By the end of the century, the "St. Louis Plan" of unified railway facilities had become the model for cities across the country, including Chicago.

The crowning moment of the process that had begun with completion of the St. Louis Bridge occurred on September 1, 1894, when Union Station opened for business. The entire project covered approximately forty-two acres, and the main building was 606 feet long and 80 feet wide, stretching from Eighteenth to Twentieth on Market Street, with a ten-acre train shed to the south along Eighteenth Street. The station had taken about fourteen months to build and cost approximately $6.5 million.[25]

One of the most prominent features of the building was the large stained glass window over the main entrance, which depicted three seated women representing the three great rail cities of America: New York on the right, San Francisco on the left, and St. Louis in the center. The window symbolized, better than anything else ever could, the importance of the station as the last link in a transcontinental chain forged by a number of managerial and general entrepreneurs over a period of nearly forty years. Although St. Louis had lost its once commanding position as central city of the Great West, it had become a great metropolis. And as far as its citizens were concerned, on the day the station opened, St. Louis had finally become the center of the world.

Epilogue

The idea of an epoch always finds its appropriate form.

—Georg Wilhelm Friedrich Hegel

D r. Denton J. Snider, one of the nineteenth-century Hegelians who constituted that group of philosophers known as the St. Louis Movement of Speculative Philosophy, once said of the St. Louis Bridge, "For me it was the solidest, purest, truest fact of the time." Every Sunday, and sometimes more often, week after week, he went down to the banks of the river to gaze at the bridge and "contemplate it in a sort of adoration and with a soul-renewing wonder and sympathy." It was also, for him, the "chief reality of that other-wise phantasmal epoch."[1]

In the century and a quarter of the structure's existence, countless others have stood on the banks of the river and gazed upon it with similar appreciation. Just five years after its completion, Walt Whitman wrote, "I have haunted the river every night lately, where I could get a look at the bridge by moonlight. It is indeed a structure of perfection and beauty unsurpassable, and I never tire of it."[2]

Over the course of years, however, the St. Louis Bridge became known less for its beauty than for its status as an unprecedented achievement of American engineering. For many years now it has been designated officially as the "Eads Bridge," in deference to the engineer who built it.

The Eads Bridge certainly suffers in comparison with its more visually stunning contemporary, the Brooklyn Bridge, which opened in 1883. Whereas the bridge linking Brooklyn and New York seems to soar above the East River, the Eads Bridge, without towers or statues to enhance its "verticality," seems to squat on the Mississippi.

Modifications have diminished the bridge's beauty throughout the years. After a tornado ripped away approximately three hundred feet of upper roadway and stone atop the east arcade in 1896, the damage was repaired with masonry of a noticeably lighter color. The west arcade also suffered in 1920 when some of its openings were bricked up in a most unsightly manner. The original hand railing and lights along the pedestrian walkway were removed long ago, as was the Third Street entrance.

Perhaps the most damaging alterations to its appearance were made in response to the needs of the railroads. Steel plate girders have been installed in lieu of the original rail deck floor beams and stringers to accommodate heavier loads at cross streets on the west approach, and one of the arched openings was rebuilt with a steel beam to provide greater clearance for north-south traffic. The impressive wrought-iron Phoenix columns of the east approach, a fairly substantial bridge in and of itself, were replaced with steel supports well before the fiftieth anniversary of the bridge's dedication. Other additions and subtractions, too numerous to mention, have further harmed its appearance.[3]

These changes, coupled with our exposure to grander, more modern structures, prevent us from appreciating the bridge in quite the same way Walt Whitman did in 1879. But if we cannot agree with Whitman regarding the bridge's beauty, perhaps we may grasp the inherent rightness of its functionalism, the way that Louis Sullivan did during its construction.

The form of the bridge, so different from that of the other bridges authorized by Congress in 1866, is suited to its purpose. It was built to link permanently the East with the trans-Mississippi West, and it has done so with a timeless simplicity unmatched by its long forgotten contemporaries.

It seems appropriate that in 1898 the United States Postal Service issued 56,200 copies of a two-cent stamp depicting the bridge as one in a set of stamps commemorating the Trans-Mississippi Exposition held in Omaha, Nebraska. Along with images depicting an American Indian hunting buffalo, Frémont standing on the

Rocky Mountains, a prospector seeking wealth, immigrants facing hardships, and other tableaus of the frontier, it harked back to a closed chapter in the history of the country.

Neither lack of ornament nor the ravages of time and heavy-handed modification lessen the boldness with which the bridge spans the river. It is understandable that Sullivan, who built his first tall office building near the western opening of the St. Louis tunnel in 1890, found inspiration in the bridge's metal arches and masonry. They remain essentially as they were when he viewed them.

Unfortunately, however, the manner in which the bridge actually functioned through the years as part of a transportation system has never quite matched its reputed contribution to American engineering. In economic terms, it never really worked very well as either a highway bridge or a railroad bridge.

Although purchase of the rail-only Merchants Bridge by the Terminal Railroad Association offset some of the competition presented by that structure, each subsequent bridge erected in the St. Louis area managed to siphon off a share of the traffic that otherwise would have crossed the St. Louis Bridge.

The Municipal Bridge, built by the City of St. Louis and opened in 1912, initially had both a road and a rail deck. It offered a toll-free crossing of the river just when Henry Ford's mass-produced Model Ts began to flood the nation's highways. Now known as the MacArthur Bridge, it no longer carries automobile traffic. But its rail deck is still the most important St. Louis railroad crossing.

The McKinley Bridge (1910), Chain of Rocks Bridge (1929), Jefferson Barracks Bridge (1944), Veterans Bridge (1951), Poplar Street Bridge (1967), and other additions to the area's transportation infrastructure further weakened the financial viability of the first St. Louis bridge. After better-connected structures began to carry increasing amounts of traffic, proportional revenues began to decline.

The trolleys stopped running across the Eads Bridge in 1935, and the tracks were taken up in 1942. The Veterans Bridge (now known as the Martin Luther King Jr. Memorial Bridge), built by the City of East St. Louis as a highway toll bridge just about one block north of the Eads Bridge, was particularly damaging because it opened with tolls much lower than those of its neighbor.

Forced to reduce its toll structure at a time when the costs of operating, repairing, and maintaining the oldest bridge on the river were steadily increasing, the Terminal Railway Association had a hard time keeping the road deck open at all. But even as late as 1955 the bridge still carried an outstanding mortgage indebtedness of approximately $5 million.[4]

The caption attached to a newspaper photograph of one of its tollbooths, published in 1978, indicates what little vehicular traffic remained by that time. "The toll taker's job on the Eads Bridge is a lonely occupation. Most of the traffic crossing the Mississippi River uses the toll-free Poplar Street Bridge leaving the Eads Bridge empty except for use by Bi-State business, Terminal Railroad employees (who cross the bridge for free) and others who find it more convenient."[5]

By the early 1990s, use of the road deck had been restricted to one lane of automobile traffic (no trucks or busses), reversed from westbound flow during the morning peak to eastbound flow during the evening peak, due to severe structural weakness in the eastern approach.[6] Eventually it had to be completely closed.

After carrying its highest railroad traffic load around the time of the Second World War, the Eads Bridge, like Union Station, fell out of favor as travelers switched from trains to planes. The last revenue-generating locomotive crossed over in 1974, and the tracks were taken up. But it was obsolete as a railroad bridge long before that.

The structure survived, however, because it was built so solidly that it would be prohibitively expensive to remove it from the river. As part of a difficult-to-explain dual ownership agreement, the Bi-State Regional Transportation Authority became owner of the reconstructed rail deck and currently runs commuter trains through the tunnel and over the river to East St. Louis. The City of St. Louis became owner of the road deck, which was removed in 1997. A replacement deck is in the works as this history is being written (2001).

Some day in the near future, the bridge will reopen with both decks in operation. There will be no pomp, no ceremony to match that of July 4, 1874. Times have changed and people have changed. Americans celebrate neither the opening of bridges nor the birth of their country with the same enthusiasm as did their ancestors. But well into the twenty-first century there will be individuals who wander down to the banks of the Mississippi River, as Sullivan, Snider, and Whitman did before them, to gaze upon a great national landmark and learn of what it has to teach.

Notes

Chapter 1: A Creature of Hope

1. Quoted in the *St. Louis Republican,* July 5, 1874.

2. Ellet was not the first engineer to propose a bridge at St. Louis. F. C. Lowthorp, who patented several cast-iron bridge designs in the 1850s and 1860s, traveled to St. Louis in the late 1830s, examined the situation, and drew up plans for a bridge. He received no support, however, and abandoned the effort. See *St. Louis Republican,* July 5, 1874. Although the newspaper spelled Lowthorp's last name wrong, he certainly was the engineer referred to.

3. C. M. Woodward, *A History of the St. Louis Bridge* (St. Louis: G. I. Jones, 1881), 9.

4. Two of the incorporators, John O'Fallon and James Lucas, had earlier (about 1851 or 1852) formed the St. Louis and Illinois Wire Suspension Bridge Company, but they were unable to secure funding. See Floyd Calvin Shoemaker, *Missouri and Missourians: Land of Contrasts and People of Achievements,* vol. 1 (Chicago: Lewis, 1943), 662.

5. *Rock Island Weekly Argus,* April 23, 1856.

6. Timothy R. Mahoney, *River Towns in the Great West: The Structure of Provincial Urbanization in the American West, 1820–1870* (Cambridge: Cambridge University Press, 1990), 248.

7. *Chicago Tribune,* May 9, 1856.

8. *Rock Island Weekly Argus,* May 14, 1856.

9. *Chicago Daily Press,* September 26, 1857.

10. *Rock Island Weekly Argus,* December 24, 1856.

11. *Rock Island Daily Advertiser,* December 27, 1856, as quoted in Benedict K. Zorbist, "Steamboat Men versus Railroad Men: The First Bridging of the Mississippi River," *Missouri Historical Review* 59 (January 1956): 167.

12. *Chicago Daily Press,* September 25, 1857.

13. J. Thomas Scharf, *History of St. Louis City and County, from the Earliest Period to the Present Day,* vol. 2 (Philadelphia: Louis H. Everts, 1883), 638–41; L. U. Reavis, *Saint Louis: The Future Great City of the World,* 2d ed. (St. Louis: Missouri Democrat Printing House, 1870), 261–69; Robert E. Riegal, *The Story of the Western Railroads* (New York: Macmillan, 1926), 49.

14. *Acts of Incorporation of the St. Louis and Illinois Bridge Company* (St. Louis: George Knapp, 1867), 1–7.

15. *Reports of the City Engineer and Special Committee to the Board of Common Council of the City of St. Louis, in Relation to a Bridge Across the Mississippi River, at St. Louis* (St. Louis: McKee, Fishback, 1865), 3.

16. Ibid., 5.

17. James Neal Primm, *Lion of the Valley: St. Louis, Missouri, 1764–1980,* 3d ed. (St. Louis: Missouri Historical Society Press, 1998), 278.

18. Agnes Wallace, "The Wiggins Ferry Monopoly," *Missouri Historical Review* 42, no. 1 (October 1947): 1–19; Scharf, *History of St. Louis City and County,* 1068–73.

19. Wallace, "Wiggins Ferry Monopoly," 8.

20. Quoted in Primm, *Lion of the Valley,* 278.

21. Wallace, "Wiggins Ferry Monopoly," 6.

22. *Reports of the City Engineer and Special Committee,* 18.

23. Ibid., 22.

24. Ibid.

25. *Acts of Incorporation of the St. Louis and Illinois Bridge Company,* 10.

26. Woodward, *History of the St. Louis Bridge,* 12.

Chapter 2: Destined to Become

1. Most of the biographical information about Eads in this chapter may be found in a book written by Eads's grandson, Louis How, or in a biographical sketch written by his son-in-law, Estill McHenry. See Louis How, *James B. Eads,* Riverside Biographical Series, no. 2 (Boston: Houghton, Mifflin, 1900); and Estill McHenry, *Addresses and Papers of James B. Eads, Together with a Biographical Sketch* (St. Louis: Slawson, 1884), vii–xv.

2. Primm, *Lion of the Valley,* 167.

3. Martha Eads died in 1852.

4. *Missouri Republican,* April 19, 1866.

5. *St. Louis Republican,* July 5, 1874.

6. Woodward, *History of the St. Louis Bridge,* 13; see also Dorothy R. Adler, *British Investment in American Railways, 1834–1898* (Charlottesville: University Press of Virginia, 1970), 72–93.

7. Woodward, *History of the St. Louis Bridge,* 14.

8. *Missouri Republican,* January 18, 1867.

9. This was to be Homer's last involvement in the bridge project. He died October 8, 1867.

10. *Illinois and St. Louis Bridge Company: Laws of Illinois and Missouri, and Acts of Congress Authorizing the Construction of a Bridge over the Mississippi River Opposite the City of St. Louis, Together with Articles of Association, and the Organization of Both the Illinois and Missouri Corporations in Their Respective States* (St. Louis: George Knapp, 1867), 3.

11. Ibid., 6.

12. Ibid.

13. Woodward, *History of the St. Louis Bridge,* 14, 15.

14. William Taussig, "Origin and Development of St. Louis Terminals," a paper prepared to be read at a meeting of the St. Louis Railway Club in 1912, but never delivered; William Taussig Papers, Missouri Historical Society, St. Louis (hereafter MHS), 2.

15. See John A. Kouwenhoven, "James Buchanan Eads: The Engineer as Entrepreneur," in *Technology in America: A History of Individuals and Ideas,* ed. Carroll W. Pursell Jr. (Cambridge, Mass.: MIT Press, 1981), 80–91.

16. E. W. Gould, *Fifty Years on the Mississippi; or Gould's History of River Navigation* (St. Louis: Nixon-Jones, 1889), 486.

17. Ibid.

18. W. Milnor Roberts to Capt. James B. Eads, Chief Eng., Ill. and St. Louis Bridge, May 5, 1869, letter, James Buchanan Eads Papers, MHS.

19. Robert Moore, Joseph P. Davis, and J. A. Ockerson, "Memoir of Henry Flad," *Transactions of the American Society of Civil Engineers* 42 (December 1899): 561–66; Scharf, *History of St. Louis City and County,* 1075.

20. William Hyde and Howard L. Conrad, eds. *Encyclopedia of the History of St. Louis,* 4 vols. (New York: Southern History Company, 1899), 1:561; McCune Gill, *The St. Louis Story,* vol. 1 (St. Louis: Historical Record Associates, 1952), 188; John A. Kouwenhoven, "Downtown St. Louis as James B. Eads Knew It When the Bridge Was Opened a Century Ago," *Bulletin of the Missouri Historical Society* 30 (April 1974): 185; Gould, *Fifty Years on the Mississippi,* 484.

21. Scharf, *History of St. Louis City and County,* 1377; Thomas P. Kane, *The Romance and Tragedy of Banking: Problems and Incidents of Governmental Supervision of National Banks* (New York: Bankers Publishing Company, 1923), 92.

22. *Bill Providing for Sale of Bank Stock to James B. Eads, with His Protest to the Governor* (St. Louis: Missouri Democrat Book and Job Printing House, 1871), 3, 4.

23. Kane, *Romance and Tragedy of Banking,* 92.

24. Jas. B. Eads to Charles H. Russell, June 15, 1868, letter, Eads Papers, MHS.

25. Several of these notes are in the Eads Papers, MHS.

26. H. Craig Miner, *The St. Louis–San Francisco Transcontinental Railroad: The Thirty-fifth Parallel Project, 1853–1890* (Lawrence: University Press of Kansas, 1972), 36.

Chapter 3: Other People's Money

1. James A. Ward, *J. Edgar Thomson: Master of the Pennsylvania* (Westport, Conn.: Greenwood Press, 1980).

2. James A. Ward, "Thomas A. Scott," in *Railroads in the Nineteenth Century,* ed. Robert L. Frey, Encyclopedia of American Business History and Biography, series ed. William H. Becker (New York: Bruccoli Clark Layman and Facts on File, 1988), 358–62.

3. Harold C. Livesay, *Andrew Carnegie and the Rise of Big Business* (Boston: Little, Brown, 1975), 46.

4. George Diggs, ed., *Corporate History, Mortgages, Principal Leases, Agreements, Deeds and Papers, of the Pittsburgh, Cincinnati and St. Louis Railroad Company, and the Various Corporations Whose Lines of Railroads Are Operated by It. In Force October 14th, 1876,* vol. 1 (Pittsburgh: Stevenson and Foster, 1876), 33–39.

5. Joseph Frazier Wall, *Andrew Carnegie* (New York: Oxford University Press, 1970), 188–89, 228–29; Ward, *J. Edgar Thomson,* 177.

6. The foundations of a bridge, the piers and abutments, are usually referred to as the substructure. Everything else, including the arches or trusses, and the deck or roadway, is referred to as the superstructure.

7. Woodward, *History of the St. Louis Bridge,* 15.

8. Vincent P. Carosso, *The Morgans: Private International Bankers, 1854–1913* (Cambridge, Mass.: Harvard University Press, 1987), 73, 154.

9. Kouwenhoven, "Downtown St. Louis," 188.

10. Woodward, *History of the St. Louis Bridge,* 15.

11. Kouwenhoven, "Downtown St. Louis," 192.

12. Scharf, *History of St. Louis City and County,* 915; Reavis, *Saint Louis,* 705–6; Hyde and Conrad, *Encyclopedia of the History of St. Louis,* 2:1183–86.

13. Illinois and St. Louis Bridge Company Executive Committee Minute Book, May 27, 1869, Terminal Railroad Association of St. Louis Records (hereafter TRRA Records), MHS.

14. Jas. B. Eads to Col. John Knapp, May 31, 1883, letter in Newspaper Envelope, MHS.

15. Scharf, *History of St. Louis City and County,* 1161, 1207, 1490; Kouwenhoven, "Downtown St. Louis," 188.

Chapter 4: Mongrel Structures

1. *Alton and St. Charles County and the St. Louis and Madison County Bridge Companies Consolidated,* undated pamphlet, Special Collections, St. Louis Public Library, 6–8.

2. Ibid., 8, 9; Henry V. Poor, *Manual of the Railroads of the United States, for 1868–69, Showing Their Mileage, Stocks, Bonds, Cost, Earnings, Expenses, and Organizations; With a Sketch of Their Rise, Progress, Influence, & c.* (New York: H. V. and H. W. Poor, 1868), 389.

3. Primm, *Lion of the Valley,* 214.

4. Ibid.

5. Scharf, *History of St. Louis City and County,* 1195; Poor, *Manual of the Railroads, for 1868–69,* 173.

6. Wallace, "Wiggins Ferry Monopoly," 10, 11.

7. Poor, *Manual of the Railroads, for 1868–69,* 100.

8. Reavis, *Saint Louis,* 401, 402.

9. *Missouri Republican,* April 11, 1867.

10. John A. Kouwenhoven, "The Designing of the Eads Bridge," *Technology and Culture* 32 (October 1982): 551.

11. *Alton and St. Charles County and the St. Louis and Madison County Bridge Companies Consolidated,* 17.

12. Charles C. Schneider, "The Evolution of the Practice of American Bridge Building," *Transactions of the American Society of Civil Engineers* 54 (1905): 217; Theodore Cooper, "American Railroad Bridges, with Discussion," *Transactions of the American Society of Civil Engineers* 21 (July–December 1889): 16.

13. Eric DeLony, "The Golden Age of the Iron Bridge," *American Heritage of Invention and Technology* (Fall 1994): 16; Keystone Bridge Company, *Descriptive Catalogue of Wrought-Iron Bridges* (Philadelphia: Allen, Lane and Scott, 1975), 12.

14. Andrew Carnegie, *Autobiography of Andrew Carnegie* (Cambridge, Mass.: Riverside Press, 1920), 115.

15. Ibid.

16. Woodward, *History of the St. Louis Bridge,* 16.

17. Carnegie, *Autobiography,* 115.

18. Kouwenhoven, "Designing of the Eads Bridge," 551.

19. Woodward, *History of the St. Louis Bridge,* 16.

20. In "The Designing of the Eads Bridge," Kouwenhoven cites this article as evidence that Eads had displayed large drawings of his bridge at the Merchants Exchange by the end of July. But the article makes no mention of this. In fact, in an article published September 30, 1867, the *Republican* states that the plan of the bridge had been placed in the exchange only "during the past few days."

21. See *Chicago Tribune,* July 23, 1867, which quoted the *Democrat's* article at length.

22. J. A. L. Waddell, *Bridge Engineering* (New York: John Wiley, 1916), 617.

23. Kouwenhoven, "Designing of the Eads Bridge," 552.

24. Waddell, *Bridge Engineering,* 27, 617.

25. Ibid., 17; David Plowden, *Bridges: The Spans of North America* (New York: W. W. Norton, 1974), 125.

26. Kouwenhoven, "Designing of the Eads Bridge," 547–48.

27. Cooper, "American Railroad Bridges," 277–78.

28. Carnegie, *Autobiography,* 120.

29. *Missouri Republican,* August 5, 1867.

30. Apparently, the plans of the Alton and St. Charles Bridge Company were of little public concern at this point because there was virtually no mention of this company in the St. Louis papers.

31. Kouwenhoven, "Designing of the Eads Bridge," 553, 554; Kouwenhoven, "Downtown St. Louis," 190; Howard S. Miller and Quinta Scott, *The Eads Bridge,* 2d ed. (Columbia: University of Missouri Press, 1999), 76, 84.

32. *Proceedings and Report of the Board of Civil Engineers Convened At St. Louis, in August, 1867, To Consider the Subject of the Construction of a Rail and Highway Bridge Across the Mississippi River At St. Louis* (St. Louis: George Knapp, 1867), 5.

33. Ibid., 79.

34. Ibid., 35.

35. U.S. House, *Annual Report of the Chief of Engineers to the Secretary of War for the Year 1878,* 45th Cong., 3d sess., 1878, Ex. Doc. 1, pt. 2, vol. 2, 1069.

36. Ibid., 1076.

37. Ibid.

38. *St. Louis Democrat,* July 21, 1867.

39. McHenry, *Addresses and Papers of James B. Eads,* 497.

40. Ibid., 498.

41. Primm, *Lion of the Valley,* 285.

42. *Proceedings and Report of the Board of Civil Engineers Convened At St. Louis, in August, 1867,* 16.

43. *Missouri Republican,* November 18, 1867.

Chapter 5: Fighting for It Still

1. *Missouri Republican,* September 30, 1867.

2. McHenry, *Addresses and Papers of James B. Eads,* 552, 553.

3. Ibid., 553.

4. *Missouri Republican,* November 21, 1867.

5. Andrew Carnegie to James B. Eads, October 29, 1867, letter in Carnegie Papers, United States Steel Corporation archives, Boyer, Pennsylvania (hereafter, USSC). At the time I did my research, USSC was in the process of turning over this collection to the Western Pennsylvania Historical Society in Pittsburgh.

6. Woodward, *History of the St. Louis Bridge,* 23.

7. Primm, *Lion of the Valley,* 214.

8. Miner, *St. Louis–San Francisco Transcontinental Railroad,* 49, 50.

9. Ibid., 67.

10. *St. Louis Democrat,* January 30, 1868.

11. Woodward, *History of the St. Louis Bridge,* 29; S. H. Church, *Corporate History of the Pennsylvania Lines West of Pittsburgh, Comprising Charters, Mortgages, Decrees, Deeds, Leases, Agree-*

ments, Ordinances, and Other Papers, with Descriptive Text, vol. 10 (Philadelphia: Pennsylvania Railroad Company, 1905), 31.

12. Woodward, *History of the St. Louis Bridge,* 30.

13. McHenry, *Addresses and Papers of James B. Eads,* 486, 487.

14. Ibid., 485.

15. *Reports of the City Engineer and Special Committee,* 17.

16. McHenry, *Addresses and Papers of James B. Eads,* 531–35.

17. Jas. B. Eads, St. Louis, to Hon. Gideon Wells, Washington, June 29, 1868, letter, Gideon Wells Papers, Library of Congress.

18. Gene D. Lewis, *Charles Ellet, Jr.: The Engineer as Individualist, 1810–1862* (Urbana: University of Illinois Press, 1968), 147, 148; George H. Burgess and Miles C. Kennedy, *Centennial History of the Pennsylvania Railroad Company: 1846–1946* (Philadelphia: Pennsylvania Railroad Company, 1949), 124.

19. Woodward, *History of the St. Louis Bridge,* 55.

20. Ibid.

Chapter 6: The Center of the World

1. The Winona and Saint Peter's Railway Company built the bridge at Winona between 1869 and 1870. Except for the 360-foot-long draw span, the trusses for this bridge were made of wood. The bridge authorized by Congress in 1866 at Prairie du Chien was never built. Separate congressional legislation was passed in 1874, authorizing construction of a pontoon bridge. This bridge was opened for railway traffic in April 1874.

2. Carnegie, *Autobiography,* 123–25.

3. Wall, *Andrew Carnegie,* 269.

4. The quotes in this and the next paragraph come from Carnegie, *Autobiography,* 124.

5. My description of Smith is borrowed from Leland L. Sage, "Platt Smith," in *Railroads in the Nineteenth Century,* ed. Robert L. Frey, Encyclopedia of American Business History and Biography, series ed. William H. Becker (New York: Bruccoli Clark Layman and Facts on File, 1988), 367.

6. Andrew Carnegie, Pittsburgh, to the President and Directors of the Keystone Bridge Co., January 25, 1868, Union Iron Mills Letterbook, 1866–69, USSC. Wall incorrectly cites this letter as being written on January 20, 1868, and presents paraphrased material from the letter in the form of a quotation. See Wall, *Andrew Carnegie,* 271 n. 6.

7. Ibid.

8. George W. Kittredge, "Memoir of Walter Katté," *Transactions of the American Society of Civil Engineers* 81 (1917): 1728; *Bailey and Edwards Chicago Directory for 1869-70* (Chicago: Bailey and Edwards, 1870), 1049.

9. A. C., Pittsburgh to J. H. Linville, Pittsburgh, October 1, 1868, Union Iron Mills Letterbook, 1866–69, USSC.

10. A. Carnegie, Pittsburgh, to Brig. Genl. Rodman, Rock Island, October 26, 1868, Union Iron Mills Letterbook, 1866–69, USSC. The long-delayed bridge at Cincinnati, featuring a truss span of 517 feet, was the longest of its type when completed in 1877.

11. Andrew Carnegie, Pittsburgh, to J. Edgar Thomson, October 29, 1868, Union Iron Mills Letterbook, 1866–69, USSC.

12. Carnegie, *Autobiography,* 125.

13. Andrew Carnegie and Associates, Philadelphia, to Genl. H. T. Reid, Pres. Keokuk Bridge Co., December 10, 1868, Carnegie Papers, USSC.

14. Ward, *J. Edgar Thomson*, 181; A. C. to Hon. W. B. Allison, December 17, 1868, Union Iron Mills Letterbook, USSC.

15. Draft Agreement in Carnegie's handwriting, n.d., USSC; A. C. to Hon. W. B. Allison, Pres., Dunleith and Dubuque Bridge Company, December 17, 1868, Union Iron Mills Letterbook, 1866–69, USSC.

16. Woodward, *History of the St. Louis Bridge,* 56.

17. L. B. Boomer, to Messrs. Chouteau, Harrison, and Valle, St. Louis, copy of letter in USSC Collection.

18. See *Pittsburgh &c. Railway vs. Keokuk and Hamilton Bridge, Pennsylvania Railroad vs. Same,* Nos. 11 and 13, October Term, 1888, Supreme Court of the United States.

19. Agreement, with amendments, November 25, 1871, USSC Collection.

20. "Prospectus of the Keokuk and Hamilton Bridge Company," n.d., document in the USSC Collection.

21. Wm. M. McPherson, St. Louis, to James B. Eads, January 12, 1869, letter, Eads Papers, MHS.

22. Woodward, *History of the St. Louis Bridge,* 56, 57.

23. "St. Louis Bridge Memoranda," n.d., USSC. Although this memorandum is unsigned and undated, there can be little doubt that it was written by Carnegie soon after the Illinois and St. Louis Bridge Company board of directors finalized its new plans for financing the project early in 1869.

24. Ibid.

25. Wm. M. McPherson, St. Louis, to James B. Eads, New York, January 12, 1869, letter, Eads Papers, MHS.

Chapter 7: The Great Bugbear

1. Woodward, *History of the St. Louis Bridge,* 58, 59.

2. David McCullough, *The Great Bridge* (New York: Simon and Schuster, 1972), 173, 174.

3. *Proceedings and Report of the Board of Civil Engineers Convened At St. Louis, in August, 1867,* 20, 31.

4. Woodward, *History of the St. Louis Bridge,* 59.

5. For information on the city directrix, see Scharf, *History of St. Louis City and County,* 128; Hyde and Conrad, *Encyclopedia of the History of St. Louis,* 1:382; and *Missouri Republican,* July 24, 1873. In *Designing of the Eads Bridge,* 542 n. 20, Kouwenhoven incorrectly states that the city directrix was marked by the high water of 1828.

6. Edward Noyes, "A Letter of James B. Eads, In Which He Discusses Plans for the Great Bridge at St. Louis with Rear Admiral J. A. Dahlgren," *Bulletin of the Missouri Historical Society* 26, no. 2 (January 1970): 113–18. Most of the information Eads supplied to Dahlgren is repeated in greater detail in "Report to the President and Directors of the Illinois and St. Louis Bridge Company, September 1, 1869." See McHenry, *Addresses and Papers of James B. Eads,* 539.

7. Andrew Carnegie to Thomas Carnegie, April 27, 1869, Union Iron Mills Letterbook, March 2 to June 26, 1869, USSC.

8. A. Carnegie to Capt. J. B. Eads, June 18, 1869, Union Iron Mills Letterbook, March 2 to June 28, 1869, USSC.

9. Carnegie to Linville, June 19, 1869, Union Iron Mills Letterbook, March 2 to June 28, 1869, USSC.

10. Carnegie to Piper and Shiffler, July 11, 1869, Union Iron Mills Letterbook, July 1 to December 11, 1869, USSC.

11. Unsigned typescript from Estill McHenry, St. Louis, to Mr. John S. Worley, Curator, Transportation Library, University of Michigan, August 5, 1937, Eads Collection, MHS.

12. Illinois and St. Louis Bridge Company Construction Committee Minute Book, May 17, 1869, TRRA Records, MHS.

13. Scharf, *History of St. Louis City and County,* 540. *Missouri Republican,* October 26, 1869.

14. Captain James B. Eads, "Recollections of Foote and the Gun-Boats," in *Battles and Leaders of the Civil War,* vol. 3, ed. Robert U. Johnson and Clarence C. Buel (New York: Century Company, 1884–89; reprint, New York: Thomas Yoseloff, 1956), 343.

15. U.S. War Department, *Official Records of the Union and Confederate Navies in the War of the Rebellion,* ser. 1, vol. 22 (Washington, D.C.: Government Printing Office, 1908), 67, 70, 71.

16. *Missouri Republican,* October 18, 1869.

17. In addition to the information Eads acquired in his conversations with European engineers, he probably had access to Octave Chanute's series of reports on seventeen European bridges founded with the aid of pneumatic tubes or caissons, published in the summer of 1868, which covered both the Koblenz and Kehl bridges. See Octave Chanute, "Pneumatic Caissons," *Journal of the Franklin Institute* 56 (July 1868): 17–29 and (August 1868), 89–99.

18. Woodward, *History of the St. Louis Bridge,* 201, 206; James B. Eads, "Letter to the Editor," *Engineering,* May 16, 1873.

19. Woodward, *History of the St. Louis Bridge,* 61.

20. *Missouri Republican,* October 26, 1869.

21. Information concerning the design and operation of the air locks and conditions within the air chamber is taken from Woodward, *History of the St. Louis Bridge,* unless otherwise noted.

Chapter 8: The Grecian Bend

1. *Sport Diver Manual,* 3d ed. (Denver: Jepperson Sanderson, 1978), 2-44, 2-45.

2. Woodward, *History of the St. Louis Bridge,* 218.

3. On page 62 *(History of the St. Louis Bridge)* Woodward states that filling began on March 1, but on page 219 he says that it began on March 7.

4. *Missouri Republican,* March 25, 1870.

5. Woodward, *History of the St. Louis Bridge,* 247.

6. Ibid., 249.

7. Ibid., 256.

8. *Missouri Republican,* March 25, 1870.

9. Ibid.

10. *Missouri Republican,* March 30, 1870.

11. *Missouri Republican,* April 1, 1870; Woodward, *History of the St. Louis Bridge,* 249.

12. Woodward devotes all of chapter 22, "Special Subject No. 5—The Physiological Effects of Compressed Air," to a discussion of the problem caused by decompression sickness and Jaminet's attempts to solve it. Much of the information in that chapter was derived from Jaminet's publication, *Physical Effects of Compressed Air, and of the Causes of Pathological Symp-*

toms Produced on Man, by Increased Atmospheric Pressure Employed for the Sinking of Piers, in the Construction of the Illinois and St. Louis Bridge Over the Mississippi River at St. Louis (St. Louis: R. and T. A. Ennis, 1871).

13. *Missouri Republican,* April 3, 1870; Woodward, *History of the St. Louis Bridge,* 220, 251.

14. Roebling credited "F. E. Sickles" for providing information on the use of air locks in construction of the Omaha Bridge. See *Engineering,* June 17, 1873. The patent on the process used at Omaha belonged to Boomer's newly organized American Bridge Company.

15. Woodward, *History of the St. Louis Bridge,* 256.

16. *Missouri Republican,* March 25, 1871.

17. Illinois and St. Louis Bridge Company Executive Committee Minute Book, October 4, 1871, TRRA Records, MHS.

18. Ibid.

19. Ibid., April 18, 1871, August 28, 1872.

20. *Missouri Republican,* April 13, 1870.

21. *Missouri Republican,* April 18, 1870; McHenry, *Addresses and Papers of James B. Eads,* 573.

Chapter 9: Golden Eggs

1. Augustus J. Veenendaal, Jr., *Slow Train to Paradise: How Dutch Investment Helped Build American Railroads* (Stanford, Calif.: Stanford University Press, 1996), 50, 51; Livesay, *Andrew Carnegie,* 47.

2. Livesay, *Andrew Carnegie,* 45, 46.

3. Adler, *British Investment in American Railways,* 71–75, 90; stock proposal headed "No. 238 South Third Street, Philadelphia," n.d., Carnegie Papers, USSC.

4. Wm. M. McPherson, St. Louis, to Andrew Carnegie, New York, December 2, 1869, USSC.

5. Illinois and St. Louis Bridge Company Executive Committee Minute Book, December 18, 1869, TRRA Records, MHS; copies of the memoranda in Carnegie Papers, USSC.

6. Andrew Carnegie and Associates, New York, to Messers E. W. Clarke and Co. [*sic*], December 18, 1869, Carnegie Papers, USSC.

7. Andrew Carnegie and Associates, New York, to Messers E. W. Clarke and Co., December 29, 1870, Carnegie Papers, USSC.

8. Kouwenhoven, "Designing of the Eads Bridge," 560. Kouwenhoven mentions two letters from Carnegie to Eads, one dated February 25, 1870, and the other, October 18, 1870, as confirmation of his claim that Sellers had a connection with both the banking house and the steel company. The two letters in question do confirm Sellers's controlling interest in the Butcher Steel Works, as do many others in the Carnegie Papers of U.S. Steel Corporation. See also Andrew Carnegie to Wm. Butcher, September 15, 1870, Union Iron Mills Letterbook, February 26, 1870, to October 31, 1870, USSC.

9. Henry V. Poor, *Manual of the Railroads of the United States, for 1870–71, Showing Their Mileage, Stocks, Bonds, Cost, Earnings, Expenses, and Organizations; With a Sketch of Their Rise, Progress, Influence, & c.* (New York: H. V. and H. W. Poor, 1870), advertisement opposite index.

10. DeLony, "Golden Age of the Iron Bridge," 16; Llewellyn Nathaniel Edwards, *A Record of History and Evolution of Early American Bridges* (Orono, Me.: University Press, 1959), 107.

11. Andrew Carnegie and Associates, Philadelphia, to Genl. H. T. Reid, Prest., Keokuk Bridge Co., December 10, 1868, Carnegie Papers, USSC.

12. Memoranda of Agreement between Andrew Carnegie and Associates and the Ills. and St. Louis Bridge Co., February 3, 1870, Handwritten document in Carnegie Papers, USSC. See also Illinois and St. Louis Bridge Company Executive Committee Minute Book, vol. 4, pp. 13, 14, TRRA Records, MHS; Memorandum from Executive Committee to Andrew Carnegie and Associates, February 5, 1870, Carnegie Papers, USSC.

13. Eads states, in his third report to the president and directors of the bridge company, dated October 1, 1870, that the contract was signed February 26, 1870. See McHenry, *Addresses and Papers of James B. Eads,* 576. But the minute book of the bridge company construction committee shows that the contract was dated February 7, 1870. See Illinois and St. Louis Bridge Company Construction Committee Minute Book, June 18, 1870, TRRA Records, MHS, which refers to the contract.

14. When the *Missouri Republican* reported the signing of the contract on April 3, 1870, the price was given as $1,560,000.

15. Andrew Carnegie to Capt. Jas. B. Eads, February 25, 1870, Book No. 1869–70, Carnegie Papers, USSC.

16. Woodward, *History of the St. Louis Bridge,* 122–56; Kouwenhoven, "Designing of the Eads Bridge," 560.

17. Andrew Carnegie to George B. Roberts, February 28, 1870, Book No. 1869–70, Carnegie Papers, USSC; Andrew Carnegie to W. M. McPherson, February 16, 1870, Book No. 1869–70, Carnegie Papers, USSC.

18. Burgess and Kennedy, *Centennial History of the Pennsylvania Railroad Company,* 199, 205.

19. Wall, *Andrew Carnegie,* 213–18.

20. "The Saint Louis Bridge," n.d., handwritten document in the Carnegie Papers, USSC. Certain portions of this document, particularly a section titled "Present Condition of the Work," narrow the date of the document's origination to the early months of 1870.

21. See "Prospectus, Illinois and St. Louis Bridge Company," printed by Metchim and Son, March 1870, Carnegie Papers, USSC Collection.

22. Andrew Carnegie and Associates to Messrs. J. S. Morgan and Co., London, March 28, 1870, Carnegie Papers, USSC.

23. J. S. Morgan and Co. to Andrew Carnegie and Associates, March 31, 1870, Carnegie Papers, USSC.

24. A. Carnegie to William McPherson, St. Louis, cablegram, April 1, 1870, Carnegie Papers, USSC.

25. Thomson to Andrew Carnegie, Charing Cross Hotel, cablegram, April 2, 1870, Carnegie Papers, USSC.

26. Carnegie, *Autobiography,* 157.

27. Andrew Carnegie, London, to J. Edgar Thomson, April 6, 1870, Carnegie Papers, USSC.

28. Wm. Taussig to "Dear Friend," April 16, 1870, William Taussig Letterbook, typescript of translation in Taussig Papers, MHS.

29. Andrew Carnegie and Associates to Messrs. McPherson, Taussig, and Britton, June 2, 1870, Union Iron Mills Letterbook, February 26, 1870, to October 31, 1870, USSC.

30. A. Carnegie to "Dear Harry," June 3, 1870, Union Iron Mills Letterbook, February 26, 1870, to October 31, 1870, USSC.

31. Livesay, *Andrew Carnegie,* 69.

32. Undated note in Andrew Carnegie's handwriting, Carnegie Papers, USSC.

Chapter 10: Untried Methods

1. Woodward, *History of the St. Louis Bridge,* 67; Jas. B. Eads, Saint Louis, to Andrew Carnegie, January 9, 1871, Carnegie Papers, USSC.

2. *Missouri Republican,* March 27, 1870.

3. *Missouri Republican,* April 18, 1870.

4. Andrew Carnegie to J. H. Linville, June 1, 1870, and Andrew Carnegie to Messrs. J. S. Morgan and Co., July 18, 1870, both in Union Iron Mills Letterbook, February 26, 1870, to October 31, 1870, USSC.

5. McHenry, *Addresses and Papers of James B. Eads,* 577.

6. Andrew Carnegie to Wm. Butcher, September 15, 1870, Union Iron Mills Letterbook, February 26, 1870, to October 31, 1870, USSC. In this letter, Carnegie incorrectly refers to Samuel Huston as "Houston."

7. Andrew Carnegie to Jas. B. Eads, September 16, 1870, Union Iron Mills Letterbook, February 26, 1870, to October 31, 1870, USSC.

8. Andrew Carnegie to Jas. B. Eads, October 4, 1870, Union Iron Mills Letterbook, February 26, 1870, to October 31, 1870, USSC.

9. Ibid.

10. Andrew Carnegie to W. M. McPherson, October 5, 1870, Union Iron Mills Letterbook, February 26, 1870, to October 31, 1870, USSC.

11. Andrew Carnegie to James B. Eads, October 18, 1870, Union Iron Mills Letterbook, February 26, 1870, to October 31, 1870, USSC.

12. There had been some use of steel in bridges prior to construction of the St. Louis Bridge, but its high cost limited its application, and few engineers considered it a suitable replacement for iron in the fabrication of major structural members.

13. A. Carnegie to Walter Katté October 18, 1870, Union Iron Mills Letterbook, February 26, 1870, to October 31, 1870, USSC. Carnegie sent a similar letter to Linville on the same day.

14. A. Carnegie to Wm. Taussig, December 30, 1870, Union Iron Mills Letterbook, November 1, 1870, to March 14, 1871, USSC.

15. Ibid.

16. Woodward, in *History of the St. Louis Bridge,* states that there were 112 anchor bolts in all, but he miscounted.

17. Andrew Carnegie to Wm. Taussig Esq., December 30, 1870, Union Iron Mills Letterbook, November 1, 1870, to March 14, 1871, USSC.

18. Kouwenhoven, "Downtown St. Louis," 190.

19. Woodward, *History of the St. Louis Bridge,* 116.

20. A. Carnegie to Thos. A. Scott, March 8, 1869, Union Iron Mills Letterbook, March 2 to June 28, 1869, USSC.

21. Andrew Carnegie to R. D. Barclay, March 29, 1869, Union Iron Mills Letterbook, March 2 to June 28, 1869, USSC.

22. McHenry, *Addresses and Papers of James B. Eads,* 593.

23. Illinois and St. Louis Bridge Company Minute Book, May 12, 1869, TRRA Records, MHS.

24. Woodward, *History of the St. Louis Bridge,* 85.

25. *Missouri Republican,* March 9, 1871.

Chapter 11: Proper Facilities

1. Andrew Carnegie to W. M. McPherson, June 29, 1870, Union Iron Mills Letterbook, February 26, 1870, to October 31, 1870, USSC.

2. Wm. Taussig, Saint Louis, to A. Carnegie, October 6, 1870, Carnegie Papers, USSC.

3. Ibid.

4. William Taussig, *Development of St. Louis Terminals* (St. Louis: Woodward and Tiernan, 1894), 26.

5. Ibid., 27.

6. See *Description and Plans of the Proposed Grand Union Passenger Depot in Saint Louis* (St. Louis: Missouri Democrat Book and Job Printing House, 1870).

7. This figure did not include costs that would be borne by the tunnel company. See Carnegie's letter to Taussig, March 22, 1871, as cited in note 11.

8. Wm. Taussig, Saint Louis, to A. Carnegie, March 1, 1871, Carnegie Papers, USSC.

9. Wm. Taussig, City of Jefferson, to A. Carnegie, March 18, 1870, Carnegie Papers, USSC.

10. Ibid.

11. A. Carnegie to Wm. Taussig, March 22, 1871, Carnegie Papers, USSC.

12. There are several uncataloged draft proposals in Carnegie's handwriting, Carnegie Papers, USSC.

13. Taussig, *Development of St. Louis Terminals,* 28.

14. Wm. Taussig, Saint Louis, to A. Carnegie, March 29, 1871, Carnegie Papers, USSC.

15. Taussig, *Development of St. Louis Terminals,* 29n, 30n.

16. Wm. Taussig, Saint Louis, to A. Carnegie, April 10, 1871, Carnegie Papers, USSC.

17. Wm. Taussig, Saint Louis, to A. Carnegie, April 20, 1871, Carnegie Papers, USSC.

18. Wm. Taussig, Saint Louis, to A. Carnegie, May 1, 1871, Carnegie Papers, USSC.

19. Wm. Taussig, Saint Louis, to A. Carnegie, May 19, 1871, Carnegie Papers, USSC.

20. Ibid.

21. Illinois and St. Louis Bridge Company Executive Committee Minute Book, June 9, 1871, and Illinois and St. Louis Bridge Company Construction Committee Minute Book, February 18, 1874, both in TRRA Records, MHS. Torrance signed the contract on July 1, 1871.

22. Wm. Taussig, Saint Louis, to A. Carnegie, June 20, 1871, Carnegie Papers, USSC.

23. Andrew Carnegie, New York, to Wm. Taussig, December 30, 1870, Union Iron Mills Letterbook, November 1, 1870, to March 14, 1871, USSC.

24. Andrew Carnegie to Thomas A. Scott, June 25, 1871, Book No. 1871–72, Carnegie Papers, USSC.

25. W. T., Saint Louis to A. C., August 7, 1871, Carnegie Papers, USSC.

26. Andrew Carnegie to Wm. Taussig, August 14, 1871, Book No. 1871–72, Carnegie Papers, USSC.

27. Henry V. Poor, *Manual of the Railroads of the United States, for 1872–73, Showing Their Mileage, Stocks, Bonds, Cost, Earnings, Expenses, and Organizations; With a Sketch of Their Rise, Progress, Influence, & c.* (New York: H. V. and H. W. Poor, 1872), 569; Wm. Taussig, Saint Louis, to A. Carnegie, November 6, 1871, Carnegie Papers, USSC.

28. Andrew Carnegie to "My Dear Doctor" [Taussig], December 8, 1871, Book No. 1871–72, Carnegie Papers, USSC.

29. Andrew Carnegie to J. Edgar Thomson, November 27, 1871, Book No. 1871–72, Carnegie Papers, USSC.

30. Ibid.

31. A. Carnegie to Thomas Scott, December 14, 1871, Book No. 1871–72, Carnegie Papers, USSC.

32. "In the Circuit Court of the United Sates for the Eastern District of Pennsylvania. Third Circuit," uncataloged document, Carnegie Papers, USSC.

33. Henry V. Poor, *Manual of the Railroads of the United States, for 1871–72, Showing Their Mileage, Stocks, Bonds, Cost, Earnings, Expenses, and Organizations; With a Sketch of Their Rise, Progress, Influence, & c.* (New York: H. V. and H. W. Poor, 1871), 526.

Chapter 12: A Little Mixture of Conciliation

1. Livesay, *Andrew Carnegie,* 41.

2. Woodward, *History of the St. Louis Bridge,* 106.

3. A. Carnegie to Geo. B. Rogers, January 15, 1872, Book No. 1871–72, Carnegie Papers, USSC.

4. Quoted in A. Carnegie to J. Edgar Thomson, January 26, 1872, and in A. Carnegie to Thomas A. Scott, January 27, 1872, both in Book No. 1871–72, Carnegie Papers, USSC.

5. Woodward, *History of the St. Louis Bridge,* 106–21.

6. Ibid., 124.

7. A Cooper-designed bridge being erected over the St. Lawrence River at Quebec collapsed on August 29, 1907, and about seventy-five men were killed. Many engineers, including Washington Roebling, blamed Cooper for not having personally supervised the work. Cooper retired the same year and never fully recovered from the tragedy.

8. Woodward, *History of the St. Louis Bridge,* 125.

9. A. Carnegie to J. S. Morgan and Co., September 24, 1872, Book No. 1872–73, Carnegie Papers, USSC.

10. Woodward, *History of the St. Louis Bridge,* 130; J. H. Linville, Philadelphia, to A. Carnegie, November 13, 1872, Carnegie Papers, USSC.

11. The Midvale Steel Company is perhaps best known as the company where Frederick Winslow Taylor developed his theories of "scientific management" following his promotion to chief engineer of the plant in the 1880s.

12. Andrew Carnegie, to J. S. Morgan and Co., December 19, 1872, Book No. 1872–73, Carnegie Papers, USSC.

13. *Missouri Republican,* May 8, 1873.

14. Ibid.

15. McHenry, *Addresses and Papers of James B. Eads,* 568.

16. Andrew Carnegie to J. H. Linville, January 29, 1873, Book No. 1872–73, Carnegie Papers, USSC.

17. The Baltimore Bridge Company was formed by Benjamin Henry Latrobe II and C. Shaler Smith in 1869, not long after it became apparent that their plans for a bridge to be built by the consolidated Alton and St. Charles County and St. Louis and Madison County Bridge Companies would never be realized. When the contract with the Baltimore Bridge Company was finally signed on August 8, the price was lowered to $367,000. A copy of the contract may be found in the TRRA Records, MHS.

18. J. S. Morgan and Co., London, to Andrew Carnegie, New York, May 8, 1873, Carnegie Papers, USSC.

Chapter 13: The Elements of Commercial Supremacy

1. *Missouri Republican,* August 29, 1872; Illinois and St. Louis Bridge Company Executive Committee Minute Book, August 28, 1872, TRRA Records, MHS.

2. *Missouri Republican,* August 31, 1872.

3. Church, *Corporate History of the Pennsylvania Lines West of Pittsburgh,* 534.

4. Scharf, *History of St. Louis City and County,* 723.

5. *Missouri Republican,* July 9, 1872.

6. F. W. Taussig, "My Father's Business Career," *Harvard Business Review* (Winter 1941): 180, 181.

7. Scharf, *History of St. Louis City and County,* 706.

8. Elliot C. Bennett, *Index: St. Louis City Ordinances from Incorporation in 1822 to 1903* (St. Louis: Wm. H. O'Brien, 1904), 7785A; Church, *Corporate History of the Pennsylvania Lines West of Pittsburgh,* 56, 560.

9. Adler, *British Investment in American Railways,* 208; Church, *Corporate History of the Pennsylvania Lines West of Pittsburgh,* 535–44.

10. *Missouri Republican,* March 9, 1873.

11. Illinois and St. Louis Bridge Company Executive Committee Minute Book, April 10, 1873, TRRA Records, MHS.

12. *Missouri Republican,* June 22, 1873.

13. Ibid.

14. *Missouri Republican,* July 13, 1873.

15. *Missouri Republican,* June 1, 1873.

16. Ibid.

17. *Missouri Republican,* February 5, 1872.

18. Andrew Hurley, "On the Waterfront: Railroads and Real Estate in Antebellum St. Louis," *Gateway Heritage* (Spring 1993): 4–17.

19. Carnegie, *Autobiography,* 183.

20. *Missouri Republican,* February 5, 1872.

21. *Missouri Republican,* February 12, 1872, and March 13, 1872.

22. *Missouri Republican,* March 29, 1872.

23. *Missouri Republican,* April 19, 1872.

24. *Missouri Republican,* May 7, 1872.

25. *Missouri Republican,* May 16, 1872.

26. *Missouri Republican,* November 8, 1872; Poor, *Manual of the Railroads of the United States for 1872–73,* 565.

27. James J. Goodwin, New York, to James B. Eads, St. Louis, June 26, 1872, Carnegie Papers, USSC.

28. L. B. Boomer, Chicago, to Walter Katté, February 27, 1871, Carnegie Papers, USSC.

29. James B. Eads and Walter Katté, St. Louis, to James J. Goodwin, July 12, 1872, uncataloged Report, Carnegie Papers, USSC.

30. *Missouri Republican,* February 5, 1873.

31. *St. Louis Republican,* January 29, 1875.

Chapter 14: The Texas Trade

1. *Missouri Republican,* April 20, 1873.

2. *Boston Globe,* May 2, 1873, as printed in *Missouri Republican,* May 7, 1873.

3. Ibid.

4. *Missouri Republican,* August 10, 1873.

5. V. V. Masterson, *The Katy Railroad and the Last Frontier* (Norman: University of Oklahoma Press, 1952), 93.

6. Ibid., 150, 151.

7. Scharf, *History of St. Louis City and County,* 1169.

8. *Missouri Republican,* November 4, 1872.

9. Henry V. Poor, *Manual of the Railroads of the United States, for 1873–74, Showing Their Mileage, Stocks, Bonds, Cost, Earnings, Expenses, and Organizations; With a Sketch of Their Rise, Progress, Influence, & c.* (New York: H. V. and H. W. Poor, 1873), 641.

10. *Missouri Republican,* March 12, 1873.

11. *Missouri Republican,* April 14, 1873.

12. Edward King, *The Great South: A Record of Journeys* (Hartford, Conn.: American Publishing Company, 1875), 220–21.

13. The quotations in this and the next paragraph come from the *Missouri Republican,* May 29, 1873.

14. The quotations from the *Cincinnati Commercial* in this and the next several paragraphs are drawn from an account reprinted in the *Missouri Republican,* May 31, 1873.

15. Livesay, *Andrew Carnegie,* 68.

16. Woodward, *History of the St. Louis Bridge,* 162.

17. Jas. B. Eads to Mr. Andrew Carnegie, August 11, 1873, USSC.

18. Woodward, *History of the St. Louis Bridge,* 165.

19. Ibid.

20. Ibid., 167.

21. Jas. B. Eads to Mr. Carnegie, August 11, 1873, Carnegie Papers, USSC.

Chapter 15: Honor at the Stake

1. *Missouri Republican,* July 24, 1873.

2. *St. Louis Republican,* November 23, 1873.

3. *Missouri Republican,* July 31, 1873.

4. *St. Louis Republican,* November 19, 1873; U.S. House, *Annual Report of the Chief of Engineers,* 1077.

5. Woodward, *History of the St. Louis Bridge,* 265.

6. *St. Louis Republican,* November 23, 1873.

7. *St. Louis Republican,* December 15, 1873.

8. *St. Louis Republican,* November 19, 1873.

9. Ibid.

10. Ibid.

11. *St. Louis Republican,* November 30, 1873.

12. *St. Louis Republican,* December 6, 1873.

13. *St. Louis Republican,* November 23, 1873.

14. Andrew Carnegie to J. S. Morgan and Co., December 5, 1873, Book No. 1873–74, Carnegie Papers, USSC.

15. U.S. House, 43d Cong., 1st sess., 1874, Ex. Doc. 194, 7.

16. Ibid., 28.

17. Ibid., 18.

18. *St. Louis Republican,* December 5, 1873.

19. U.S. House, *Annual Report of the Chief of Engineers,* 1055.

20. Woodward, *History of the St. Louis Bridge,* 282.

21. Washington Roebling to Colonel Smith, New York, July 5, 1913, Roebling letters typescript, Roebling Collection, Rutgers University Libraries, as quoted in McCullough, *The Great Bridge,* 161. Essentially the same quote, with slightly different wording, is provided by Harry W. Pranz, *Gettysburg: The Second Day* (Chapel Hill: University of North Carolina Press, 1987), 201.

22. Johnson and Buel, *Battles and Leaders of the Civil War,* vol. 3, 307. Warren's account is contained in a letter he wrote to a former Union officer named Farley, dated July 13, 1872.

23. Ibid., 461. Warren was finally exonerated.

24. McHenry, *Addresses and Papers of James B. Eads,* 599.

25. William Taussig, "Personal Recollections of General Grant," *Missouri Historical Society Publications* 2 (1903): 10–12.

26. U.S. Army Corps of Engineers, "An Act to authorize the Construction of certain Bridges, and to establish them as Post Roads," *Laws of the United States Relating to Construction of Bridges over Navigable Waters of the United States: From March 2, 1805, to March 3, 1887* (Washington, D.C.: Government Printing Office, 1887), 42–43.

Chapter 16: Capital and Influence

1. Walter Katté, "A Description of the Proposed Plan for Erecting the Superstructure of the Illinois and St. Louis Bridge," *Transactions of the American Society of Civil Engineers* 2 (1873): 143.

2. Theodore Cooper, "The Erection of the Illinois and St. Louis Bridge," *Transactions of the American Society of Civil Engineers* 3 (1875): 247.

3. Woodward, *History of the St. Louis Bridge,* 178.

4. Ward, *J. Edgar Thomson,* 199.

5. Julius Grodinsky, *Transcontinental Railway Strategy, 1869–1893: A Study of Businessmen* (Philadelphia: University of Pennsylvania Press, 1962), 15, 16.

6. Ibid., 16; James A. Ward, "Pennsylvania Railroad," in *Railroads in the Nineteenth Century,* ed. Robert L. Frey, Encyclopedia of American Business History and Biography, series ed. William H. Becker (New York: Bruccoli Clark Layman and Facts on File, 1988), 314.

7. Ward, *J. Edgar Thomson,* 206.

8. Wall, *Andrew Carnegie,* 310.

9. Illinois and St. Louis Bridge Company Executive Committee Minute Book, October 7, 1873, TRRA Records, MHS.

10. Illinois and St. Louis Bridge Company Executive Committee Minute Book, October 18, 1873, TRRA Records, MHS.

11. Andrew Carnegie to J. S. Morgan and Co., December 5, 1873, Book No. 1873–74, Carnegie Papers, USSC.

12. Illinois and St. Louis Bridge Company Executive Committee Minute Book, December 5, 1873, TRRA Records, MHS.

Chapter 17: The Consummation So Devoutly Wished For

1. Andrew Carnegie to J. S. Morgan and Co., February 9, 1874, Book No. 1873–74, Carnegie Papers, USSC.

2. *St. Louis Republican,* December 5, 1873.

3. *St. Louis Republican,* December 24, 1873.

4. *St. Louis Republican,* January 21, 1874.

5. *St. Louis Republican,* February 27, 1874.

6. Illinois and St. Louis Bridge Company Executive Committee Minute Book, March 7, 1874, TRRA Records, MHS.

7. Reavis, *Saint Louis,* 403, 404; Poor, *Manual of the Railroads of the United States, for 1871–72,* 322.

8. Taussig, "Origin and Development of St. Louis Terminals," 9, 10.

9. Illinois and St. Louis Bridge Company Executive Committee Minute Book, March 28, 1874, TRRA Records, MHS; Taussig, "Origin and Development of St. Louis Terminals," 10.

10. *St. Louis Republican,* February 17, 1874.

11. *St. Louis Republican,* February 19, 1874.

12. W. T., St. Louis, to A. Carnegie, February 21, 1874, Carnegie Papers, USSC.

13. Burgess and Kennedy, *Centennial History of the Pennsylvania Railroad Company,* 314, 315.

14. Ward, *J. Edgar Thomson,* 216.

15. *St. Louis Republican,* April 14, 1874.

16. *St. Louis Republican,* May 13, 1874.

17. *St. Louis Republican,* May 2, 1874.

18. In May 1869, Eads had recommended to the New Orleans Chamber of Commerce that a fleet of iron boats and barges be built as a means of lowering the cost of shipping grain between St. Louis and New Orleans. His duties as chief engineer had prevented him from acting on the idea at the time. In the years since, he had expanded the concept.

19. *St. Louis Republican,* April 13, 1874.

20. Walter Katté, Engr. Keys. Br. Co., to Wm. Taussig Esq., Chrm. Exc. Com. Ills. & St. L. Br. Co., April 6, 1874, letter, Carnegie Papers, USSC.

21. Wm. Taussig, Chm. Exec. Com., to Walter Katté Esq., Engr. Keystone Bridge Co., April 8, 1874, letter, Carnegie Papers, USSC.

22. Illinois and St. Louis Bridge Company Executive Committee Minute Book, April 19, 1874, TRRA Records, MHS.

23. Woodward, *History of the St. Louis Bridge,* 196.

24. Andrew Carnegie to "My Dear Captain," April 20, 1874, letter marked "Private," Carnegie Papers, USSC.

25. Illinois and St. Louis Bridge Company Executive Committee Minute Book, May 18, 1874, TRRA Records, MHS.

26. *Missouri Republican,* February 2, 1873.

27. *Missouri Republican,* February 7, 1873.

28. *Missouri Republican,* July 6, 1873.

29. *Missouri Republican,* August 12, 1873.

30. *Missouri Republican,* August 15, 1873.

31. *Missouri Republican,* August 20, 1873.

32. Henry V. Poor, *Manual of the Railroads of the United States, for 1874–75, Showing Their Mileage, Stocks, Bonds, Cost, Earnings, Expenses, and Organizations; With a Sketch of Their Rise, Progress, Influence, & c.* (New York: H. V. and H. W. Poor, 1874), 680.

33. *St. Louis Republican,* January 3, 1874.

34. *St. Louis Republican,* March 27, 1874.

35. *St. Louis Republican,* May 12, 1874.

36. See *Report of the Engineer Board to Citizen's Committee, On Lowering the Tracks of the Pacific Railroad, and Connecting All Commercial Outlets of St. Louis, June 1, 1874* (St. Louis: Times Printing House, 1874), a document contained in Special Collections, St. Louis Public Library.

37. *St. Louis Republican,* May 28, 1874.

38. *St. Louis Republican,* June 6, 1874.

39. *St. Louis Republican,* March 14, 1874.

40. *St. Louis Republican,* June 5, 1874.

41. *St. Louis Republican,* June 10, 1874.

42. *St. Louis Republican,* June 28, 1874.

Chapter 18: Stately Pomp and Ceremony

1. *Chicago Times,* July 5, 1874. My account of the day's activities is taken mainly from contemporary reports in the *St. Louis Republican* and the *Chicago Times,* including plans for the day published weeks in advance, and from *The Central Magazine* 6 (August 1874). The *St. Louis Republican,* July 8, 1874, also contained reprints from accounts published in the *Chicago Post and Mail, Indianapolis Journal,* and *New York World.* Additional information was obtained from John Kouwenhoven, "Eads Bridge: The Celebration," *Bulletin of the Missouri Historical Society* 30 (April 1974): 159–80. Kouwenhoven basically relied on the same sources but also utilized a translation of the St. Louis *Westliche Post,* July 9, 1874, and various undocumented sources compiled during his many decades of research.

2. *St. Louis Republican,* July 5, 1874.

3. As quoted in the *St. Louis Republican,* July 8, 1874.

4. William Cronon, *Nature's Metropolis: Chicago and the Great West* (New York: W. W. Norton, 1991), 301.

5. Primm, *Lion of the Valley,* 272.

6. *St. Louis Republican,* July 5, 1874.

7. Ibid.

8. As quoted in the *St. Louis Republican,* July 8, 1874.

9. *St. Louis Republican,* July 5, 1874.

10. Taussig, *Development of St. Louis Terminals,* 25.

11. *St. Louis Republican,* July 5, 1874.

12. Ibid.

13. *St. Louis Republican,* July 4, 1874.

14. *St. Louis Republican,* July 5, 1874.

15. Ibid.

16. Ibid.

17. Taussig, "Origin and Development of St. Louis Terminals," 7.

18. Unless noted otherwise, the quotations from Eads and other speakers in this and the remaining paragraphs of this chapter come from the *St. Louis Republican,* July 5, 1874. Eads's speech was printed in its entirety by the newspapers the following day, and it may also be found in McHenry, *Addresses and Papers of James B. Eads,* 42–45.

19. *St. Louis Republican,* July 4, 1874.

20. As quoted in the *St. Louis Republican,* July 8, 1874.

Chapter 19: The Elements of a Great City

1. See Carl Abbott, "The Location of Railroad Passenger Depots in Chicago and St. Louis," *Bulletin of the Railway and Locomotive Historical Society* 120 (April 1969): 31–47. Abbott correctly notes the role played by the bridge in altering the relationships among railroads within the city, but he overestimates the speed with which that alteration took place.

2. Burgess and Kennedy, *Centennial History of the Pennsylvania Railroad Company,* 315.

3. Ibid., 331.

4. Grodinsky, *Transcontinental Railway Strategy,* 46.

5. *St. Louis Republican,* July 10, 1874.

6. Hyde and Conrad, *Encyclopedia of the History of St. Louis,* 4:2290–91.

7. Taussig, *Development of St. Louis Terminals,* 8.

8. Ibid., 11.

9. Primm, *Lion of the Valley,* 291.

10. *St. Louis Republican,* September 19, 1874.

11. *St. Louis Republican,* October 11, 1874.

12. *St. Louis Republican,* October 26, 1874.

13. Jas. B. Eads to Wm. Taussig, July 28, 1874, letter contained in the Illinois and St. Louis Bridge Company Executive Committee Minute Book, TRRA Records, MHS.

14. Illinois and St. Louis Bridge Company Executive Committee Minute Book, July 28, 1874, TRRA Records, MHS.

15. *St. Louis Republican,* November 11, 1874.

16. Primm, *Lion of the Valley,* 292.

17. Ibid., 293.

18. Jas. B. Eads, St. Louis to "My dear Col.," June 26, 1877, letter, James Andrews Papers, MHS.

19. J. B. E., St. Louis, to Col. James Andrews, January 15, 1879, letter, James Andrews Papers, MHS.

20. Unattributed and undated clipping, vertical files, MHS.

21. *St. Louis Post-Dispatch,* October 24, 1879.

22. Miner claims that Eads went before a grand jury on a charge of "wholesale robbery," but he provides no documentation for this claim. I cannot find any evidence that Eads was ever brought before the grand jury. Miner may be closer to the mark, however, when he describes Eads as "a low thief and a great engineering genius—both despicable and magnificent." See Miner, *St. Louis–San Francisco Transcontinental Railroad,* 64.

23. C. Shaler Smith to Onward Bates, February 7, 1879, Bates Papers, MHS.

24. Church, *Corporate History of the Pennsylvania Lines West of Pittsburgh,* 33–39, 483, 484, 550, 551. Carnegie, who had been smart enough to sell out any interest in the bridge that represented cash investment, lost little. Still, he felt robbed of bonus payments that he felt were due him. He therefore sued Britton, who had foolishly guaranteed some payments on Eads's urging. Britton had no money, however, and Carnegie never got what he thought he deserved.

25. Primm, *Lion of the Valley,* 294.

Epilogue

1. Denton J. Snider, *The St. Louis Movement in Philosophy, Literature, Education, and Psychology, with Chapters of Autobiography* (St. Louis: Sigma Publishing, 1920). See section VI, 107–16.

2. Walt Whitman, *The Complete Writings of Walt Whitman,* ed. Richard M. Bucke et al., vol. 4, *The Complete Prose Works of Walt Whitman* (New York: G. P. Putnam's Sons, 1902), 282–83.

3. Charles E. Smith, "Fiftieth Anniversary of the Eads Bridge," *Railway Review* 18 (November 1, 1924): 653; U.S. Department of the Interior, Historic American Engineering Record [HAER], No. MO-12, "Eads Bridge," 1991, Prints and Photographs Division, Library of Congress, Washington, D.C., 16, 17.

4. Warner Fuller, vice president and general counsel, Terminal Railroad Association of St. Louis, to Colonel George E. White Jr., Corps of Engineers, U.S. Army, St. Louis, November 4, 1955, letter, TRRA Records, MHS.

5. *St. Louis Globe-Democrat,* April 30, 1978.

6. HAER Report, 1.

Bibliography

Manuscript Collections

Library of Congress, Washington, D.C.
    Andrew Carnegie Papers
    Gideon Welles Papers
    Octave Chanute Papers
Missouri Historical Society, St. Louis
    Banking and Currency Papers
    Barton Bates Papers
    James Andrews Papers
    James Buchanan Eads Papers
    Julius S. Walsh Collection
    Terminal Railroad Association of St. Louis Records
    William Taussig Papers
St. Louis Public Library, St. Louis
    Special Collections
United States Steel Corporation Archives, Boyer, Pennsylvania
    Carnegie Papers
Washington University Libraries, St. Louis
    Terminal Railroad Association Collection

Newspapers

Chicago Daily Press
Chicago Tribune
Missouri Republican
Rock Island Weekly Argus
St. Louis Democrat
St. Louis Post-Dispatch
St. Louis Republican

Books, Journals, Magazines, and Pamphlets

Abbott, Carl. "The Location of Railroad Passenger Depots in Chicago and St. Louis." *Bulletin of the Railway and Locomotive Historical Society* 120 (April 1969): 31–47.
Acts of Incorporation of the St. Louis and Illinois Bridge Company. St. Louis: George Knapp, 1867.

Adler, Dorothy R. *British Investment in American Railways, 1834–1898*. Charlottesville: University Press of Virginia, 1970.

Alton and St. Charles County and the St. Louis and Madison County Bridge Companies Consolidated. Undated pamphlet. Special Collections, St. Louis Public Library.

Bailey and Edwards Chicago Directory for 1869–70. Chicago: Bailey and Edwards, 1870.

Bennett, Elliot C. *Index: St. Louis City Ordinances from Incorporation in 1822 to 1903*. St. Louis: Wm. H. O'Brien, 1904.

Bill Providing for Sale of Bank Stock to James B. Eads, with His Protest to the Governor. St. Louis: Missouri Democrat Book and Job Printing House, 1871.

Burgess, George H., and Miles C. Kennedy. *Centennial History of the Pennsylvania Railroad Company: 1846–1946*. Philadelphia: Pennsylvania Railroad Company, 1949.

Carnegie, Andrew. *Autobiography of Andrew Carnegie*. Cambridge, Mass.: Riverside Press, 1920.

Carosso, Vincent P. *The Morgans: Private International Bankers, 1854–1913*. Cambridge, Mass.: Harvard University Press, 1987.

Central Magazine 6 (August 1874).

Chanute, Octave. "Pneumatic Caissons." *Journal of the Franklin Institute* 56 (July 1868): 17–29 and (August 1868): 89–99.

Church, S. H. *Corporate History of the Pennsylvania Lines West of Pittsburgh, Comprising Charters, Mortgages, Decrees, Deeds, Leases, Agreements, Ordinances, and Other Papers, with Descriptive Text*. Vol. 10. Philadelphia: Pennsylvania Railroad Company, 1905.

Cooper, Theodore. "American Railroad Bridges, with Discussion." *Transactions of the American Society of Civil Engineers* 21 (July–December 1889): 1–58, 566–607.

———. "The Erection of the Illinois and St. Louis Bridge." *Transactions of the American Society of Civil Engineers* 3 (1875): 239–54.

Cronon, William. *Nature's Metropolis: Chicago and the Great West*. New York: W. W. Norton, 1991.

DeLony, Eric. "The Golden Age of the Iron Bridge." *American Heritage of Invention and Technology* (Fall 1994): 8–22.

Description and Plans of the Proposed Grand Union Passenger Depot in Saint Louis. St. Louis: Missouri Democrat Book and Job Printing House, 1870.

Diggs, George, ed. *Corporate History, Mortgages, Principal Leases, Agreements, Deeds and Papers, of the Pittsburgh, Cincinnati and St. Louis Railroad Company, and the Various Corporations Whose Lines of Railroads Are Operated by It. In Force October 14th, 1876*. Vol. 1. Pittsburgh: Stevenson and Foster, 1876.

Eads, James B. "Letter to the Editor." *Engineering*, May 16, 1873.

Edwards, Llewellyn Nathaniel. *A Record of History and Evolution of Early American Bridges*. Orono, Me.: University Press, 1959.

Gill, McCune. *The St. Louis Story*. Vol. 1. St. Louis: Historical Record Associates, 1952.

Gould, E. W. *Fifty Years on the Mississippi; or Gould's History of River Navigation*. St. Louis: Nixon-Jones, 1889.

Grodinsky, Julius. *Transcontinental Railway Strategy, 1869–1893: A Study of Businessmen*. Philadelphia: University of Pennsylvania Press, 1962.

How, Louis. *James B. Eads*. Riverside Biographical Series, no. 2. Boston: Houghton, Mifflin, 1900.

Hurley, Andrew. "On the Waterfront: Railroads and Real Estate in Antebellum St. Louis." *Gateway Heritage* (Spring 1993): 4–17.

Hyde, William, and Howard L. Conrad, eds. *Encyclopedia of the History of St. Louis*. 4 vols. New York: Southern History Company, 1899.

Illinois and St. Louis Bridge Company: Laws of Illinois and Missouri, and Acts of Congress Authorizing the Construction of a Bridge over the Mississippi River Opposite the City of St. Louis, Together with Articles of Association, and the Organization of Both the Illinois and Missouri Corporations in Their Respective States. St. Louis: George Knapp, 1867.

Johnson, Robert U., and Clarence C. Buel, eds. *Battles and Leaders of the Civil War*. Vol. 3. New York: Century Company, 1884–89. Reprint, New York: Thomas Yoseloff, 1956.

Kane, Thomas P. *The Romance and Tragedy of Banking: Problems and Incidents of Governmental Supervision of National Banks*. New York: Bankers Publishing Company, 1923.

Katté, Walter. "A Description of the Proposed Plan for Erecting the Superstructure of the Illinois and St. Louis Bridge." *Transactions of the American Society of Civil Engineers* 2 (1873): 135–44.

Keystone Bridge Company. *Descriptive Catalogue of Wrought-Iron Bridges*. Philadelphia: Allen, Lane and Scott, 1975.

King, Edward. *The Great South: A Record of Journeys*. Hartford, Conn.: American Publishing Company, 1875.

Kittredge, George W. "Memoir of Walter Katté." *Transactions of the American Society of Civil Engineers* 81 (1917): 1727–32.

Kouwenhoven, John A. "The Designing of the Eads Bridge." *Technology and Culture* 32 (October 1982): 535–68.

———. "Downtown St. Louis as James B. Eads Knew It When the Bridge Was Opened a Century Ago." *Bulletin of the Missouri Historical Society* 30 (April 1974): 181–95.

———. "Eads Bridge: The Celebration." *Bulletin of the Missouri Historical Society* 30 (April 1974): 159–80.

———. "James Buchanan Eads: The Engineer as Entrepreneur." In *Technology in America: A History of Individuals and Ideas,* ed. Carroll W. Pursell Jr., 80–91. Cambridge, Mass.: MIT Press, 1981.

Lewis, Gene D. *Charles Ellet, Jr.: The Engineer as Individualist, 1810–1862*. Urbana: University of Illinois Press, 1968.

Livesay, Harold C. *Andrew Carnegie and the Rise of Big Business*. Boston: Little, Brown, 1975.

Mahoney, Timothy R. *River Towns in the Great West: The Structure of Provincial Urbanization in the American West, 1820–1870*. Cambridge: Cambridge University Press, 1990.

Masterson, V. V. *The Katy Railroad and the Last Frontier*. Norman: University of Oklahoma Press, 1952.

McCullough, David. *The Great Bridge*. New York: Simon and Schuster, 1972.

McHenry, Estill. *Addresses and Papers of James B. Eads, Together with a Biographical Sketch*. St. Louis: Slawson, 1884.

Miller, Howard S., and Quinta Scott. *The Eads Bridge*. 2d ed. St. Louis: Missouri Historical Society Press, 1999.

Miner, H. Craig. *The St. Louis–San Francisco Transcontinental Railroad: The Thirty-fifth Parallel Project, 1853–1890*. Lawrence: University Press of Kansas, 1972.

Moore, Robert, Joseph P. Davis, and J. A. Ockerson. "Memoir of Henry Flad." *Transactions of the American Society of Civil Engineers* 42 (December 1899): 561–66.

Noyes, Edward. "A letter of James B. Eads, In Which He Discusses Plans for the Great Bridge at St. Louis with Rear Admiral J. A. Dahlgren." *Bulletin of the Missouri Historical Society* 26, no. 2 (January 1970): 113–18.

Plowden, David. *Bridges: The Spans of North America.* New York: W. W. Norton, 1974.

Poor, Henry V. *Manual of the Railroads of the United States, for 1868–69, Showing Their Mileage, Stocks, Bonds, Cost, Earnings, Expenses, and Organizations; With a Sketch of Their Rise, Progress, Influence, & c.* New York: H. V. and H. W. Poor, 1868.

———. *Manual of the Railroads of the United States, for 1870–71, Showing Their Mileage, Stocks, Bonds, Cost, Earnings, Expenses, and Organizations; With a Sketch of Their Rise, Progress, Influence, & c.* New York: H. V. and H. W. Poor, 1870.

———. *Manual of the Railroads of the United States, for 1871–72, Showing Their Mileage, Stocks, Bonds, Cost, Earnings, Expenses, and Organizations; With a Sketch of Their Rise, Progress, Influence, & c.* New York: H. V. and H. W. Poor, 1871.

———. *Manual of the Railroads of the United States, for 1872–73, Showing Their Mileage, Stocks, Bonds, Cost, Earnings, Expenses, and Organizations; With a Sketch of Their Rise, Progress, Influence, & c.* New York: H. V. and H. W. Poor, 1872.

———. *Manual of the Railroads of the United States, for 1873–74, Showing Their Mileage, Stocks, Bonds, Cost, Earnings, Expenses, and Organizations; With a Sketch of Their Rise, Progress, Influence, & c.* New York: H. V. and H. W. Poor, 1873.

———. *Manual of the Railroads of the United States, for 1874–75, Showing Their Mileage, Stocks, Bonds, Cost, Earnings, Expenses, and Organizations; With a Sketch of Their Rise, Progress, Influence, & c.* New York: H. V. and H. W. Poor, 1874.

Pranz, Harry, W. *Gettysburg: The Second Day.* Chapel Hill: University of North Carolina Press, 1987.

Primm, James Neal. *Lion of the Valley: St. Louis, Missouri, 1764–1980,* 3d ed., St. Louis: Missouri Historical Society Press, 1998.

Proceedings and Report of the Board of Civil Engineers Convened At St. Louis, in August, 1867, To Consider the Subject of the Construction of a Rail and Highway Bridge Across the Mississippi River At St. Louis. St. Louis: George Knapp, 1867.

Reavis, L. U. *Saint Louis: The Future Great City of the World.* 2d ed. St. Louis: Missouri Democrat Printing House, 1870.

Report of the Engineer Board to Citizen's Committee, On Lowering the Tracks of the Pacific Railroad, and Connecting All Commercial Outlets of St. Louis, June 1, 1874. St. Louis: Times Printing House, 1874.

Reports of the City Engineer and Special Committee to the Board of Common Council of the City of St. Louis, in Relation to a Bridge Across the Mississippi River, at St. Louis. St. Louis: McKee, Fishback, 1865.

Riegal, Robert E. *The Story of the Western Railroads.* New York: Macmillan, 1926.

Scharf, J. Thomas. *History of St. Louis City and County, from the Earliest Period to the Present Day.* Vol. 2. Philadelphia: Louis H. Everts, 1883.

Schneider, Charles C. "The Evolution of the Practice of American Bridge Building." *Transactions of the American Society of Civil Engineers* 54 (1905): 213–34.

Shoemaker, Floyd Calvin. *Missouri and Missourians: Land of Contrasts and People of Achievements.* Vol. 1. Chicago: Lewis, 1943.

Smith, Charles E. "Fiftieth Anniversary of the Eads Bridge." *Railway Review* 18 (November 1, 1924): 647–54.

Snider, Denton J. *The St. Louis Movement in Philosophy, Literature, Education, and Psychology, with Chapters of Autobiography.* St. Louis: Sigma Publishing, 1920.

Snyder, Charles E. "The Eads of Argyle." *Iowa Journal of History and Politics* 42, no. 1 (January 1944): 73–90.

Sport Diver Manual. 3d ed. Denver: Jepperson Sanderson, 1978.

Taussig, F. W. "My Father's Business Career." *Harvard Business Review* (Winter 1941): 177–84.

Taussig, William. *Development of St. Louis Terminals.* St. Louis: Woodward and Tiernan, 1894.

———. "Personal Recollections of General Grant." *Missouri Historical Society Publications* 2 (1903): 1–13.

U.S. Army Corps of Engineers. "An Act to authorize the Construction of certain Bridges, and to establish them as Post Roads." *Laws of the United States Relating to Construction of Bridges over Navigable Waters of the United States: From March 2, 1805, to March 3, 1887.* Washington, D.C.: Government Printing Office, 1887.

U.S. House. *Annual Report of the Chief of Engineers to the Secretary of War for the Year 1878.* 45th Cong., 3d sess., 1878. Ex. Doc. 1, pt. 2, vol. 2.

———. 43d Cong., 1st sess., 1874, Ex. Doc. 194.

U.S. War Department. *Official Records of the Union and Confederate Navies in the War of the Rebellion.* Ser. 1, vol. 22. Washington, D.C.: Government Printing Office, 1908.

Veenendaal, Augustus J., Jr. *Slow Train to Paradise: How Dutch Investment Helped Build American Railroads.* Stanford, Calif.: Stanford University Press, 1996.

Waddell, J. A. L. *Bridge Engineering.* New York: John Wiley, 1916.

Wall, Joseph Frazier. *Andrew Carnegie.* New York: Oxford University Press, 1970.

Wallace, Agnes. "The Wiggins Ferry Monopoly." *Missouri Historical Review* 42, no. 1 (October 1947): 1–19.

Ward, James A. *J. Edgar Thomson: Master of the Pennsylvania.* Westport, Conn.: Greenwood Press, 1980.

———. "Pennsylvania Railroad." In *Railroads in the Nineteenth Century,* ed. Robert L. Frey, 314. Encyclopedia of American Business History and Biography, series ed. William H. Becker. New York: Bruccoli Clark Layman and Facts on File, 1988.

———. "Thomas A. Scott." In *Railroads in the Nineteenth Century.* ed. Robert L. Frey, 358–62. The Encyclopedia of American Business History and Biography, series ed. William H. Becker. New York: Bruccoli Clark Layman and Facts on File, 1988.

Whitman, Walt. *The Complete Writings of Walt Whitman.* Edited by Richard M. Bucke et al. Vol. 4, *The Complete Prose Works of Walt Whitman.* New York: G. P. Putnam's Sons, 1902.

Woodward, C. M. *A History of the St. Louis Bridge.* St. Louis: G. I. Jones, 1881.

Zorbist, Benedict K. "Steamboat Men versus Railroad Men: The First Bridging of the Mississippi River." *Missouri Historical Review* 59 (January 1956): 159–72.

Index

Robert W. Jackson is an urban planner and historian. He has documented historic bridges and highways in Texas, Iowa, and Pennsylvania for the National Park Service, Historic American Engineering Record.

Composed in 9.5/15 ITC Stone Serif
with Helvetica Neue Condensed display
by Celia Shapland
for the University of Illinois Press
Designed by Paula Newcomb
Manufactured by Cushing-Malloy, Inc.

University of Illinois Press
1325 South Oak Street
Champaign, IL 61820-6903
www.press.uillinois.edu